Modeling Water Demands

Modeling Water Demands

Edited by

J. Kindler and C. S. Russell

in collaboration with

B. T. Bower, I. Gouevsky, D. R. Maidment,
and W. R. D. Sewell

1984

Academic Press
(Harcourt Brace Jovanovich, Publishers)

London   Orlando   San Diego   San Francisco   New York
Toronto   Montreal   Sydney   Tokyo   São Paulo

ACADEMIC PRESS INC. (LONDON) LTD.
24/28 Oval Road
London NW1

United States Edition published by
ACADEMIC PRESS INC.
(Harcourt Brace Jovanovich, Inc.)
Orlando, Florida 32887

British Library Cataloguing in Publication Data

Modeling water demands.
1. Water resources development—Simulation methods
2. Water resources development—Data processing
I. Kindler, J.   II. Russell, C. S.
333.91′00724   TD353

ISBN 0-12-407380-8
LCCCN 83-72315

Printed in Great Britain at St. Edmundsbury Press

Preface

Important questions about water demand arise whenever water resource investments or water policies are being considered. Typically, these questions are about how much water will be used, where it will be needed, what purposes will be served, and when these demands will occur. The actual demands will depend on such time-related variables as government policies, population levels and distribution, energy use and cost, per capita disposable income, technological development, consumer habits and lifestyles, and the prices of water withdrawals and wastewater disposal. Developing relations between these variables and using them to estimate water demands under various conditions requires analytical approaches. This book describes some of these approaches and shows how they can be used to analyze water demands for industry, agriculture, and urban settlements.

The volume is directed primarily toward analysts responsible for generating information on water demands in relation to planning decisions in water resources management. Because by definition this is an interdisciplinary task, the audience of the book may be expected to consist of persons with diverse professional backgrounds, such as hydrologists, water resources planners, experts in the technology of water use (industrial, agricultural, or municipal), economists, and systems analysts who largely, although not exclusively, are working within water management or regional development agencies. The treatment of the methodological framework and of the models themselves is such that the book is not aimed exclusively at those interested in modeling *per se*. It is recognized throughout the text that any attempt to influence and improve planning methods in water resources systems must pay careful attention to practical issues and take account of the institutional, administrative, legal, and economic constraints under which those systems operate. The alternative approaches to water demand modeling described here should always be interpreted in the light of these case-by-case varying constraints.

Chapter 1 of this volume defines the problem and introduces the relevant terms. Chapter 2 discusses the methodological framework, and lays out water demand modeling as the foundation for the case studies described in the later chapters. Chapters 3–5 discuss modeling water demand relations for individual and aggregated water-use activities in industry, agriculture, and municipalities. These three chapters have similar structures; after discussing briefly a given water-use category, each presents case studies from the cooperative program on water demands of the International Institute for Applied Systems Analysis (IIASA). These studies, initiated in response to needs in the IIASA National Member Organization countries, exemplify the approaches introduced in the first two chapters. The book continues with a discussion of how some of these approaches can be used in addressing water demand issues at the regional level, where water demands and water supply are integrated, this integration being the principal objective of water resources management. Following a discussion of the national perspective in water demand modeling, the volume ends with a summary and some thoughts on the role of water demand modeling, its limitations, and further research needs.

We hope that the approaches in this book, which build on IIASA's water demand work during the years 1976–80, will find direct application in other water resources management studies, and that these approaches will stimulate further refinements and additional research

Although the chapters were written by the authors indicated, the underlying research involved many others, including the participants in two IIASA workshops on water demand modeling in January and December 1977. Thus the product uses inputs from many sources.

We acknowledge with gratitude several sources of support outside IIASA. The work was generously supported by two grants from the Stiftung Volkswagenwerk, Hannover, Federal Republic of Germany; the Rockefeller Foundation of New York supported D. R. Maidment's work at IIASA; and Resources for the Future, Inc., Washington, DC, supported C. S. Russell's work in writing Chapter 6 and co-editing the volume. In addition, the Johns Hopkins University and the Lund Institute of Technology provided partial financial support for the authors of Chapter 5.

This Preface cannot be terminated without reflecting our appreciation for the even-tempered tolerance, patience, and perseverance of Denise Baker-Promper, Vicky Hsiung, and Lis Jaklitsch in typing the manuscript.

J. Kindler
C. S. Russell

Contents

1 *Water Demand**

The management of water resources is becoming an increasingly serious concern throughout the world: in market and centrally planned economies, in developed nations and developing ones. The growth of population and the spread of suburbs and vacation homes; industrialization; the growing virtuosity of organic chemists and the use of new forms of fossil fuel; and the pressure on agriculture at both the extensive and intensive (fertilizers, pesticides, and herbicides) margins are only a few of the major headings under which one could catalog the reasons for the new urgency being felt in this field. A combination of tradition, the nature of the water resources, and the very large size to which water projects often lend themselves, also makes this a field for public, and specifically government concern. This is true in countries of widely differing economic and political philosophies, whatever the level of development.

It also seems to be becoming increasingly felt that "the water problem" can no longer be seen simply as one of new source development or of interbasin transfers, as a matter of creating a new reservoir or digging a new canal. In some areas, such as the Lower Colorado River basin of the United States, new reservoirs will add nothing to the reliable flow of our rivers—indeed, that river may now be over-regulated, with evaporation from reservoirs cancelling gains from storage. In other areas concern over government budget deficits, over special features of the natural or man-made environment, or rising levels of regional chauvinism in water-rich areas may place overwhelming obstacles in the way of water resources "development"; hence the interest in a broader notion of "management" in which both the uses of water and its supply receive attention. The possibility that some of those uses may be less than imperative becomes more attractive as the cost of supply becomes greater.

This book addresses the growing interest in the examination of water uses and does so particularly from the perspective of lessons and techniques developed over the past two decades in engineering, economics, and systems analysis. It necessarily excludes a great deal; just how much can be seen by

* This chapter was written by B. T. Bower, J. Kindler, C. S. Russell, and W. R. D. Sewell.

MODELING WATER DEMANDS
ISBN 0-12-407380-8

Table 1.1. Some functions of water resources management.

Planning	Design	Construction	Operation
Problem definition and delineation of objectives and constraints	Engineering design of individual structures, e.g., dams, dykes, and treatment plants	Construction of facilities and monitoring networks	Operation and maintenance of facilities, e.g., reservoirs, treatment plants, pipelines, irrigation canals
Data collection, short- and long-term research	Design of monitoring networks, e.g., number and type of monitoring stations, frequency of measurement	Acquisition and equipping of mobile laboratories	Monitoring of ambient water quality Monitoring of wastewater discharges Inspection of water-use activities
Forecasting future conditions	Design of random inspection system for monitoring wastewater dischargers	Establishment of inspection system	Issuing flood warnings, evacuating individuals, animals/goods, and resettlement after flooding is over Operation of water-based recreational facilities
Formulation and evaluation of alternative water management strategies			Application of sanctions for failure to comply with standards
Analysis of administrative structures for carrying out the proposed strategies	Establishment of charging system		Evaluation of performance of facilities, e.g., removals achieved by treatment plants in relation to design levels, efficiency of irrigation method (system) in relation to efficiency assumed in planning, comparison of actual water-based recreational behavior with that assumed in planning Feedback of information from evaluation performance into planning

glancing at the summary of water resources management functions in Table 1.1.

The analysis of water uses is important to the first function (planning) where the focus is usually on medium- and long-term forecasts of use, or on medium- and long-term prospects for public policies to change patterns of water use. Analysis keyed to the short term can be important in informing the operation function, although, of course, the options open at that stage depend on decisions made in planning; so that planning appears to be the key market for water-use analysis. Planning can be defined here as the orderly consideration of a water management scheme from the original statement of purpose, through the evaluation of alternatives, to the final decision on a course of action (Linsley and Franzini 1979). It involves the identification of future water use levels, supply sources, and the possibilities for bringing these into balance. Further, it includes the review of the balancing possibilities in terms of criteria that reflect economic, social, environmental, institutional, and political feasibility. This definition includes quite specific decisions about projects, their output targets, and their special features. These decisions leave the design function, then, one largely of the application of engineering techniques to meet desired physical targets. There is, of course, nothing sacred in this breakdown.

Various time horizons may be used in water resources planning, ranging from one to perhaps as many as 30 years. The areal basis of planning also varies; it may be focused upon a small town or the service area of a water utility, or the plan may embrace a large region, such as a metropolis or an entire river basin. In some instances it may cover a country as a whole. The selection of the time horizon and the areal unit have important implications for water-use analysis because the selection determines the nature and the amount of information required. In addition, the extent to which the planning process is systematic (continuous) rather than *ad hoc* will condition the frequency with which data should be gathered and analyzed. In broad terms, there has been a move in many countries towards long-term, comprehensive planning, with provision for periodic revision, in order to incorporate changes in problems, technologies, social values, and government policies.

The operational phase of water management involves the day-to-day, or even hour-to-hour, implementation of the selected courses of action. This embraces such functions as monitoring of water intakes and discharges, the imposition of sanctions for noncompliance with regulations, and the collection of charges for water withdrawal and wastewater discharge. The operational phase should also embrace analysis of performance, aiming to determine the extent to which the goals of a project or policy have been achieved. Thus such analyses might ascertain how much water from an irrigation scheme has actually been used and why, and whether the projected crop production targets have been attained and if not, why not. Such *ex post* evaluations can be very useful in assessing the effectiveness of policy initiatives and may help to avoid future mistakes. Unfortunately, there tends to be a reluctance to examine past experience, perhaps because there may be a fear that goals have not been attained or that unanticipated results have been achieved. While such reluctance is understandable, especially where the analysts might share some of the responsibility for past decisions, the future is better served by a system that creates positive incentives for the pursuit of this kind of feedback in operation.

Specific Problems for Water-use Analysis

While the hydrological, economic, and institutional contexts for water resources management may vary enormously from situation to situation, the sort of problems to be addressed in the analysis of water-use patterns can be conveniently divided under three headings:

- baseline forecasting;
- predicting impacts of direct policy intervention, and indirect impacts of related policies;
- balancing use and supply.

Here, baseline forecasting will be taken to mean the projection of water-use quantities and patterns in the future under the assumption that no conscious attempt will be made to affect that use. Thus, an agency might be interested in obtaining an estimate of how many years it has until the flow available (say with 95 % assurance) from an existing supply reservoir will be fully committed to irrigation, given certain assumptions about population, income, import policies, farming practices, and government farm policies—and given that there will be no attempt to change things. But it will often be the case that the policies intended to change things are exactly what is at stake. Then the question becomes one of predicting the impact of such policies. In the irrigation example, the responsible agency might consider lengthening the "life" of the reservoir by raising the price of water at the farm gate; and it would thus be interested in knowing how much time it could buy with various price increases. In other situations, the problem may be that a public policy not directed at water use explicitly may still be expected (or should be expected) to have some effect on that use. Turning again to irrigation, changing the system of crop price supports will have an effect on cropping patterns and hence, in general, on water use in irrigation, although the motivation for the changes may be to build (or reduce) a butter mountain, to protect the family farm, or to reward a faithful constituency. Finally, and most importantly, analysis of water use may be undertaken in combination with analysis of supply. Some attempt may be made to bring the two into balance by increasing the supply or by introducing use-dampening policies, consistently with some criterion of the social good, for example, maximizing the sum of net benefits "to whomsoever they may accrue", or maximizing net benefits to the citizens of the region, or to users of irrigation water.

In the following chapters, examples will be presented to illustrate most of these applications of water-use analysis. For the moment let us only pause to see just how important these applications can be and, not incidentally, how prone to serious errors have been some of the past analyses. To do so, we can look at a few examples from several different decades and countries:

- The Columbia Basin project, begun in 1936 in the Pacific Northwest of the United States, was intended to irrigate over a million acres. So far, almost 50 years later, only one-half of that total has been irrigated. The South Saskatchewan project in Canada was hailed on its completion in 1958 as a major means of overcoming the problems of monoculture in the Prairie provinces. It was planned to irrigate some 500 000 acres of land but, after 25 years, less than 10 000 acres have actually come under irrigation. In both cases, investment decisions were based on water-use projections that subsequently proved to be incorrect (Sewell 1978).

- The 1965 forecast of total Swedish water withdrawals for the period to year 2000 predicted $6{\cdot}3 \times 10^9 \, m^3/yr$ withdrawals in 1976 and over $8 \times 10^9 \, m^3/yr$ by 2000. The actual figure for 1976 was about $3 \times 10^9 \, m^3/yr$, or less than half of the forecast. The problem here was a failure to anticipate the effects of the environmental legislation of the 1960s. These laws led Swedish industrial users to install new water-recycling equipment to cut the costs of complying with water quality requirements, and with the incidental effect of dramatically reducing water withdrawals (Falkenmark 1977). It should be noted that this reduction of water withdrawals took place in spite of a substantial increase in industrial production over the same period. This experience, shown graphically in Figure 1.1, underlines the importance of understanding the various factors that determine the use of water in different activities, in this case, particularly the introduction of new government policies relating to water quality management and the impact of changes in technology.

- In 1973 it was estimated that water requirements in England and Wales would double in the period 1971–2001, from $14 \times 10^6 \, m^3/day$ to $28 \times 10^6 \, m^3/day$ (Water Resources Board 1973). An elaborate system of barrages, reservoirs, and water transfer schemes was proposed to meet these burgeoning demands, at an estimated cost of over £1500 million (about US$3000 million). A number of projects were begun and detailed designs were prepared for others. Recently, however, there has been a serious questioning of the 1973 forecasts. Demands have continued to

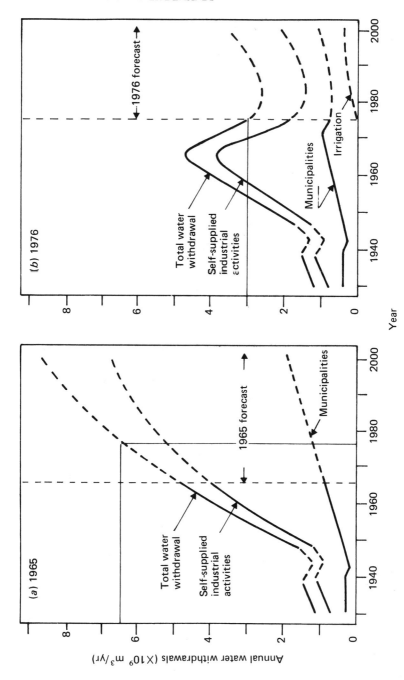

Figure 1.1. Evolution of water withdrawal in Sweden, actual and according to forecasts in 1965 and 1976 (Falkenmark 1977).

expand, but the rate of increase has fallen below the 2 % per annum trend that was used in the forecast. The rate of population growth, on which the water demand estimates were primarily based, has decreased considerably, and the rate of economic expansion has declined from 3·8 % per annum to about 2·5 % per annum. Moreover, the introduction of new charging schemes and the imposition of stricter controls on water quality have apparently had effects on water use that were not considered in the 1973 forecast (National Water Council 1975). The overall result of these events has been to reduce the forecast of overall demands by the end of the century by one-half (National Water Council 1978).

Where public policies or private decisions are based on such faulty predictions, serious misallocation of resources can result. In particular, because there appears to be a bias toward overprediction in the simple methods, the tendency is to overbuild the structures designed to provide for future demands. Because such structures usually involve economies of scale in construction, it is optimal to build them ahead of demand, so that predictions cannot be checked until resources are committed. The resulting distortions can sometimes be concealed by promotional pricing of project outputs, but such practices only create more trouble for the future by artificially inflating current demand and the rate of growth of demand. Because capital unnecessarily sunk into dams, canals, water transfer facilities, and the like, could be used to meet other social needs, and because many of the world's governments seem to be feeling the pinch of inflation and taxpayer restlessness, the importance of avoiding these distortions is growing.

While it is impossible to avoid mistakes about the future, it is possible to improve the odds that a particular prediction will be close to correct. In the business of projecting water demands a major improvement can be made by correcting the bias mentioned above—the bias toward overprediction. This bias arises from the common assumption that the price or cost of water does not matter to users. These users are implicitly or explicitly assumed to have inflexible *requirements* for water (per unit of output, per hectare irrigated, per household member per day, or whatever). It is a major message of this book that this assumption should be abandoned and the economic concept of water *demand* substituted for it. The next sections of this chapter expand on this idea.

Definitions for the Analysis of Water Demand

A useful way into the problem is to examine the definition of relevant terms, especially requirements and demand, the price of water, demand elasticity, and dimensions of water demand.

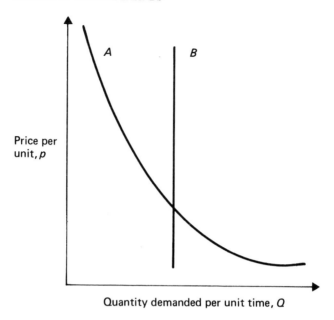

Figure 1.2. Demand functions.

Demand versus requirements

The term "demand" is often used interchangeably with "requirement" in discussions of water use, but this confuses two ideas usefully kept separate (see, for example, Hanke and Boland 1971). Demand is a general concept used by economists to denote the willingness of consumers or users to purchase goods, services, or inputs to production processes, since that willingness varies with the price of the thing being purchased.

A commonsense notion (but one elaborated and refined in many ways in economic theory) is that for any single consumer or group of consumers and almost anything we can imagine him or them purchasing, the quantity demanded will increase as the price (cost) per unit decreases. The demand function A in Figure 1.2 conforms to this expectation of a negative relationship between price and quantity demanded.

A "requirement" is something that does not obey this commonsense rule: no matter what the price, the same quantity is purchased, as illustrated by B in Figure 1.2.[1] Now, of course, it is also commonsense that there do exist

[1] It has already been implied that water demand is also a function of several factors other than price. Figure 1.2 illustrates only quantity–price relationships, provided all factors other than quantity and price are held constant.

minimum requirements for many things in life that are unresponsive to price (imagine B in Figure 1.2 moved left close to the origin). Our bodies need some minimum input of food, and some minimum levels of clothing and shelter if we are to survive. Our production processes likewise, at any given time, have irreducible minimum input levels (as fossil fuel in electricity generation). Even water, at certain levels of use, is a requirement. But it is very seldom that one is actually talking about questions relevant to requirement levels. Almost always the notion of demand is what is relevant. In agriculture and industry, too, the true "requirements" are usually only a small part of observed water use, and are almost never what giant projects are built to supply. For example, in the production of beer and soft drinks, there is no substitute for that portion of water intake that is incorporated in the product. Similarly, in the production of canned fruits and vegetables, there is no substitute for that portion of water intake that is used to make the syrup or brine that is included with the product in the cans. On the other hand, in industrial cooling it is possible to substitute physical capital for water by building closed cooling systems with non-evaporative towers (analogous to auto engine cooling) and, by varying the extent to which this is done, to vary the use of water (in terms of withdrawals from a watercourse or evaporation) down almost to zero (Abbey 1979).

Similarly, in agriculture it is well known that there are at least two ways of substituting away from water quantity in irrigation. One way is by changing or improving the irrigation system, e.g. by lining canals, changing from flooding to sprinkler or drip methods. The second is by investing in the care and timing of water application—by taking advantage of careful analysis of plant needs and soil moisture conditions to estimate the optimal quantity to apply rather than to follow a traditional rule of thumb. Therefore, to treat all existing and future uses as requirements is to ignore important possible methods of substitution and adjustment that will be seized upon as the cost of water to users goes up.

Demand elasticity

One of the most important concepts in demand analysis is the elasticity of demand. The elasticity of demand of an activity or user, with respect to a demand-determining variable such as price P, is the percentage by which the quantity demanded by the user Q changes for a 1% change in the variable. The price elasticity, PE, which describes this relationship, may be defined as:

$$PE = \frac{\text{percentage change in } Q}{\text{percentage change in } P} = \frac{\Delta Q/Q}{\Delta P/P} \simeq \frac{dQ/Q}{dP/P} = \frac{P}{Q}\frac{dQ}{dP}.$$

For example, if the price elasticity of demand for water is -0.5, this means that a 1 % increase in the price of water will result in a 0·5 % decrease in water demand, with all other factors held constant.[2] It should be noted that price elasticity is not the same as the slope of the demand function shown in Figure 1.2, dP/dQ.

The concept of elasticity can be used in relation to any one of a host of demand-determining variables; but price and, for consumption of goods, income, demand elasticities are the measures of most importance. As noted earlier, it can be said that the demand for a commodity having no close substitutes is likely to be inelastic, i.e., an absolute value of $PE < 1\cdot0$. Perfect price inelasticity (zero elasticity) means the good, service, or input in question is a requirement. In general, the more easily available substitutes are, the greater is the elasticity of demand.

The concept of elasticity, even of price elasticity alone, involves more complications than can be fully dealt with here; however, a particular good or service does not come with an elasticity attached to it independent of context. For one thing, "the" elasticity of demand for a particular good in a particular market will usually vary with price. For another, elasticity will depend on the definition used: the demand for automobiles in the UK, for instance, will display certain elasticity properties (if we can estimate it). But the demand for any particular automobile make or style (all other prices held constant) will have a very different elasticity pattern. The narrower the definition, in general, the greater will be the elasticity because the field of substitutes will be larger.

When the commodity or service in question is an input to the production process, the demand for it is called "derived" demand because it is derived from the demand for the final output of the production process. The elasticity of derived demand is determined by the characteristics of that production process and of the fundamental demand for the output. In particular, the elasticity of derived demand for a factor input is a function of the share of the relevant factor in total production cost, the elasticity of substitution between the relevant factor and other inputs, and the elasticity of demand for the final product (see, for example, Bronfenbrenner 1961.)

It is also important to distinguish between long- and short-term elasticities of water demand. As noted by Carson (1979), "a change in the price of water may have a very small instantaneous effect on demand, but as time passes and the home-owner fixes his leaks, the industrial plant installs a recirculating

---

[2] The expression given above for price elasticity pertains only to the situation where price–quantity data pairs are close to each other, or where a smooth demand function be satisfactorily fitted to the data that are known. As stressed by Carson (1979), the analyst should carefully check if the data available to him satisfy these requirements. Although the concept of "arc elasticity" does exist to deal with the situation when the only data pairs known are widely separated points on the demand function, the predictive value of this measure is generally considered to be small.

system, or the farmer adopts sprinklers or drip irrigation instead of flood irrigation, water demand tends to respond to price changes." Hence, in the long term, demand is *more* elastic than in the short term, because greater time allows for more opportunities to adjust, and thus presents more options for substitution.

Establishing the price of water

Because historically water, in many of its uses, has had a zero price, it is reasonable at this point to look a little more closely at the idea of "the price of water" and to ask where such a price does, or could, come from. In principle, there are two ways in which water prices may be established. One is through the interaction of supply and demand in an open market, and the other is through administrative decisions. In practice, neither way is used in its "pure" form.

The first option, by definition, does not apply to centrally planned economies. Owing to the predominantly public ownership of the means of production and the absence of free markets, centrally planned economies have no automatic mechanisms for determining resource prices. In search of the optimal plan, the central planning authority, often using a system of balance calculations[3] and mathematical programming methods, tries to equilibrate supply and demand on a macroscale in the interest of society as a whole. This search, or as Kantorovich (1965) describes it, "competition among plans", involves the application of the "programming prices", which recognize the scarcity of resources and their marginal rates of substitution for each other in production. It is also necessary to distinguish between the "programming prices" used by the central planner and the purchase, wholesale, and retail prices used in the actual exchange of goods and services (Belousov 1979). The purchase, wholesale, and retail prices are used as an instrument for implementation of the centrally determined economic and social policies. The responsibility for establishing these prices, however, including the price of water, if any, rests with the government authorities.

Even in the predominantly market economies, there are often no "markets" for water either in withdrawal or in-stream uses. Howe (1976), for example, points out that in the USA, the prices charged for irrigation water provided by public agencies are usually nominal and unrelated to either the costs of

---

[3] A system of balance calculations is utilized in the formulation and verification of the national plan, as well as in ensuring its fulfillment. These calculations take into account the "resources" (supply) available to the national economy on the one hand, and the "uses" (demand) on the other.

supply or the values derived. Others, including Milliman (1963), Warford (1966), and Hanke and Davis (1973), have noted that prices charged for domestic water supply or sewage disposal are seldom arrived at through a market-type interaction between suppliers and users of such services. There are many possible reasons for this situation, including the fact that in most societies the services of natural watercourses, such as the ability to remove and dilute wastewater, are not privately owned. Further, the services with which these waste removal services compete, such as the provision of recreational opportunities, are also usually considered the property of society at large (so-called common property). Furthermore, there often exists a view that a certain level of water service should be provided at nominal cost to ensure that public health standards are maintained.

The second option, setting water prices by administrative decisions, underlies most of the water pricing schemes in existence. In this case, the questions of primary importance are how the price is to be administered, how high it should be, and to what extent the price should be varied in time and space. For optimal allocation of resources, the price water users pay for their marginal units of water withdrawal, consumptive use, and wastewater disposal services should reflect the marginal costs of supplying these units. The practical implementation of this principle presents several difficulties, and readers are referred to studies on water pricing policies in the US by Gysi and Loucks (1971), Hanke and Davis (1973), Gibbs (1978), and Saunders *et al.* (1977). Similar problems have been studied in the UK by Rees (1974), in France by Fiessinger and Teniere-Buchot (1976), in Poland by Symonowicz (1976), and in the USSR by Fedenko (1966) and Loiter (1967).

A water user may, of course, face not one price for water, but several prices simultaneously. For example, if the user purchases water from the municipal water authority and discharges wastewater to a municipal sewage system, he may pay a price for each unit of intake water purchased, a price for each unit of wastewater discharged, a price for each unit of biochemical oxygen-demanding (BOD) material or suspended solids material discharged. The user may also face prohibitions on the discharge of certain materials or constraints relating to other indicators of water quality—a requirement that pH must be between 5·5 and 9·5, for example.

The foregoing discussion has concentrated on water prices established externally to the water-using activity. But in many cases a water user has additional options, for example: to turn to his own sources of supply, such as wells; to build his own facilities for modifying wastewater before discharge; and to add facilities for recirculating water within his activity. Given the *externally* established prices and the *internally* established costs for different water supply and wastewater discharge options, the rational user compares the total costs of different water supply and wastewater discharge options, and selects a combination that best satisfies his criteria of choice. Thus, a water user is responding to a *set* of prices and costs, not to a single price.

In some cases, there may be no externally established water price. It is then necessary to use the available data to derive a rational price reflecting the costs society imposes on itself by deciding to use a further quantity of water in a particular way. Such a rational price is often called a "shadow price". The calculation of shadow prices for water uses of various kinds in various places may be the business of water management agencies or of central planners, depending on the country and the context. In other cases, even though real prices exist (whether market or administered) they may be rejected by planners as not reflecting the true *social* marginal cost of the water being used. This would be true, for example, if a local public agency were selling groundwater pumped from an aquifer it shared with other jurisdictions. If the extra pumping costs of its withdrawal and reduced withdrawal potential imposed on the others were not reflected in its price, then its consumers would be responding to a socially incorrect signal. Calculations introducing such neglected elements of social cost would have the effect of producing shadow prices.

The dimensions of water demand

The discussion so far has referred rather generally to the use of or demand for water by industrial plants, farms, and households, though more specific dimensions of demand have been mentioned in passing. For later clarity it will be useful to distinguish six separate dimensions of water demand:

(1) quantity of water withdrawn at the intake(s) of a given activity (withdrawals);
(2) total quantity of water used, including any recirculation (gross water applied);
(3) quantity of water evaporated, incorporated in a product, or otherwise lost before discharge (consumptive use);
(4) quantity of water discharged (discharge);
(5) quality of water discharged (wastewater disposal services demanded); and
(6) the time patterns of each of the above dimensions.

The first four dimensions are illustrated by the simplified production process shown in Figure 1.3. These dimensions are relevant both to self-supplied activities, e.g., water users that provide their own water and disposal services (as illustrated in Figure 1.3), and to various activities that are provided with water supply and wastewater disposal services by a communal

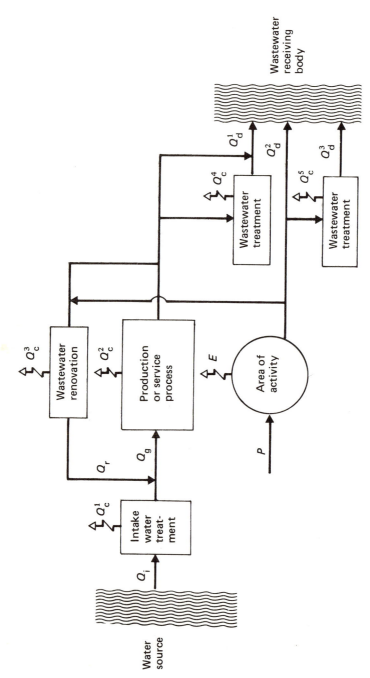

Figure 1.3. Schematic diagram of water intake, consumptive use, gross water applied, and wastewater disposal points (self-supplied individual water-use activity). Water and wastewater circuits in relation to unit processes within the activity are not shown.

Q_i = intake water (withdrawals)

Q_c = consumptive water use ($Q_c^1 + Q_c^2 + Q_c^3 + Q_c^4 + Q_c^5$)

Q_g = gross water applied

Q_r = recirculated water

Q_d = wastewater discharge ($Q_d^1 + Q_d^2 + Q_d^3$)

P = precipitation

E = evaporation.

(municipal) agency or enterprise. The key relations between the dimensions are as follows:

● Gross use equals net withdrawal plus recirculation:

$$Q_g = Q_i - Q_c^1 + Q_r.$$

● Discharge equals withdrawal less consumption plus net additions from the precipitation collection system:

$$Q_d = Q_i - Q_c + P - E.$$

● Recirculation equals gross use adjusted for losses and net additions from precipitation:

$$Q_r = Q_g - Q_c^3 - Q_c^2 + P - E - (Q_d + Q_c^4 + Q_c^5) = Q_g - Q_i + Q_c^1.$$

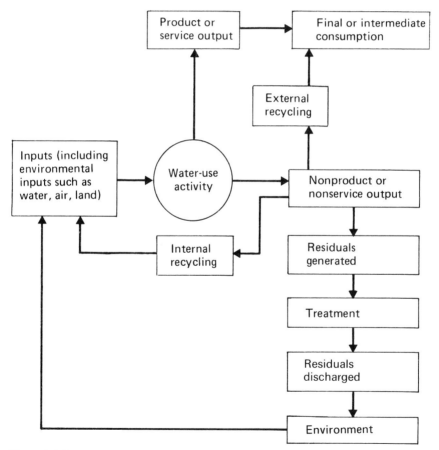

Figure 1.4. Input–output relationships for a water-use activity.

The quality of water discharged

In discussing the quality of water discharged, it should be emphasized that all water-use activities discussed in this book result in the generation of "residuals", as shown in Figure 1.4. No production or service activity transforms all of its inputs into the desired products or services and these remaining flows of material and energy from the activity, the nonproduct outputs, are called residuals if their economic values are nil or are less than the cost of collecting, processing, and transporting them for input into the same or another activity. Hence, whether a nonproduct output is a residual or not depends on existing technology, relative prices, and on various governmental policies, all of which can change over time. It should be stressed that there are technological, physical, and economic interrelationships between two basic types of residuals—materials and energy; and between the three states of the former—liquid, gaseous, and solid (Bower 1977). For example, a residual generated in one state can be transformed into one or more residuals in another state. Indeed, such transformations are the essence of wastewater treatment methods.

Temporal variability of water demand

The time dimension of water demand may exhibit: (1) variations within a day and from day to day; (2) variations by season; and (3) variations from year to year. Daily variations in intake water are illustrated in Figure 1.5. In industrial activities, they may result from random changes in such demand-determining variables as raw material quality, operating rate, product mix, weather, as well as breakdowns and spills.

Seasonal variations in water demand (defined as a seasonal average) often exhibit some regularity in that certain activities take place each year during a certain season, although the specific beginning and ending dates and levels of activity can vary from year to year. For example, the times when the product mix in a petroleum refinery shifts from more fuel oil to more gasoline in the spring and back in the fall depend on the weather. Water demand for cooling varies with season, as a function of ambient temperature. And irrigation in most areas occurs only during certain months.

Water demand (defined as the annual average) also varies from year to year as a result of such factors as weather variability, population changes, levels of activity in an industrial operation, or changing cropping patterns in an agricultural operation. For example, cropping patterns change in accordance with planned rotation, and in years of below-average precipitation there tend to be larger water demands for lawn sprinkling. Levels of production in industrial plants change with business cycle conditions and with structural changes in industrial composition. Municipalities grow and decline, gain and

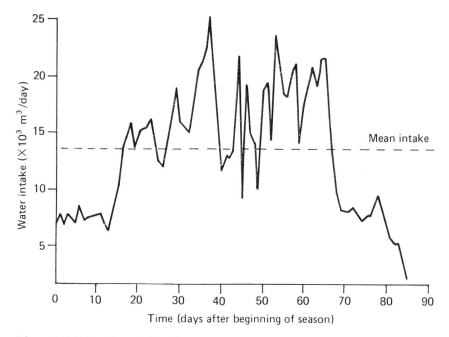

Figure 1.5. Diurnal variations in water demand for one California cannery (from Sewell *et al.* 1968).

lose acreage under lawns, and build and abandon swimming pools, fountains and other water-using facilities.

As the reader will have noted, temporal variations in water demands can either be stochastic (e.g., tied to probabilistic processes such as the weather) or deterministic (e.g., determined by production or service process technologies). Taking either kind of variation into account on any of the possible time scales is difficult. But reflecting stochastic variation in a useful way is generally harder than reflecting deterministic changes.

Three other points relating to temporal variations in water demand merit mention. First, not all parts of an activity necessarily have the same temporal pattern of water demands. An agricultural operation with crop and livestock production is a typical example. Whereas the requirements for livestock may be fairly constant over the year, those relating to the production of particular kinds of crops may have accentuated seasonal peaks.

Secondly, there can be secular trends in some water demands for a given activity with fixed technology—such as an existing power plant—as a result of deterioration of equipment (even with good maintenance). For example, the heat production rate of a power plant increases over time, thereby requiring more water for cooling for the same net energy output. A similar situation exists in an agricultural activity. The management practices used, such as the weight of equipment used, amounts and types of pesticides and fertilizer applied, cultivation practices, etc., are likely to modify the soil system itself. For example, the layer of topsoil may be lost due to erosion, a compacted subsoil layer may be formed, and the amount of biological organisms in the soil profile may be reduced. These changes in the soil system in turn affect irrigation water demand.

Thirdly, the discussion so far has concentrated on temporal variations in intake water demand for an activity. Significant variation also occurs in wastewater discharges. For example, irrigation return flow may vary over time for any of the three reasons: (1) over-irrigation; (2) rainfall during the irrigation season; and (3) rainfall during the nonirrigation season. The load of residuals generated at a petroleum refinery varies with the product mix being refined (and similarly for other multiproduct industrial plants). The quantity of municipal waste will of course, vary with population (as with long-term growth and decline and short-term variations due to tourism).

Modeling Water Demand Relations

If we take seriously the idea that water in its several dimensions as a consumption good and as an input to production is *demanded* rather than required, then it makes sense in the context of water resources management to try to understand and capture in mathematical form these demand relations. Our approach to baseline forecasting, policy impact assessment, and the balancing of demand and supply will thereby be undertaken from a firmer base and with a correspondingly higher chance of success. Efforts to understand water demand and to describe it mathematically we shall call "modeling", and these are the principal subject of this book. Because Chapter 2 discusses two alternative approaches to building models of water demand by water-using activities, while Chapters 3–7 offer several examples of actual modeling efforts, it is not necessary here to go into detail about concepts or techniques. A few things are, however, worth saying right at the start.

First, the essence of a water demand model is that it contains the price of water as a variable explaining demand. This price may, as already remarked, be a market price, an administered price, an internal use cost, or even a shadow price (although, of course, if there is no current price or measurable internal cost per unit, there will be no data from which to estimate the demand elasticity). Secondly, we do not wish to give the impression that only complex and mathematically sophisticated structures count as water demand models. The essence of modeling is the art of cutting and simplifying, and an elegant model is one that helps us to understand and predict with a minimum of fuss and extraneous detail. On the other hand, modeling artistry usually arises out of long experience with building and applying models, and the newcomer to the field is well advised to avoid self-discovered shortcuts and to begin at least with attempts at fairly complete representation of the activity or system of interest. Then, the management use of the model may dictate simplifications in the model structure; simplifications that can be undertaken with a better understanding of the price paid for them (see Vaughan and Smith 1980 for a discussion of the simplification of a complex steel mill model, and Chapter 6 below for another technique). Chapter 7 makes the point that, in the context of an interest in national aggregates, it may be appropriate to summarize quite complex models as single coefficients.

Finally, it should be recognized that any attempt to influence and improve decision making in water resources management by modeling water demands must pay careful attention to practical issues, must take into account the political, institutional and legal constraints under which water systems are planned and operated, and must clearly show the value of these models *vis à vis* conventional approaches. Otherwise, the impact of modeling water demands will be less than that which analysts might have wished or expected. Many models will remain academic exercises and will be seldom used. Future improvements in modeling water demand complexities and in algorithms for solving such models, while possible and of scientific value, will by themselves not have much of an impact on management decisions. The analysts must learn more about how to implement models within the decision-making process relevant to the problem being addressed. How can we develop and apply our models in a manner that will increase their utility to water resources planners? The demand for information that can be derived from models exists, but we have to communicate with individuals other than fellow modelers in a way that they can understand, critically appreciate, and act upon.

Levels of analysis and the plan of the book

The last observation above raises the issue of the level of water demand analysis required for the water resources management task at hand. We can distinguish four such levels: (1) the individual water-use activity; (2) the aggregated water-use activity; (3) the region; and (4) the nation. Figure 1.6 illustrates schematically how the demands of individual water-use activities are built up into the demands of aggregated activities, regional water demands, and, finally, national demands for water and water-related services. These aggregation processes are pursued more thoroughly in Chapters 6 and 7.

Individual water-use activities are decision units such as farms, factories,

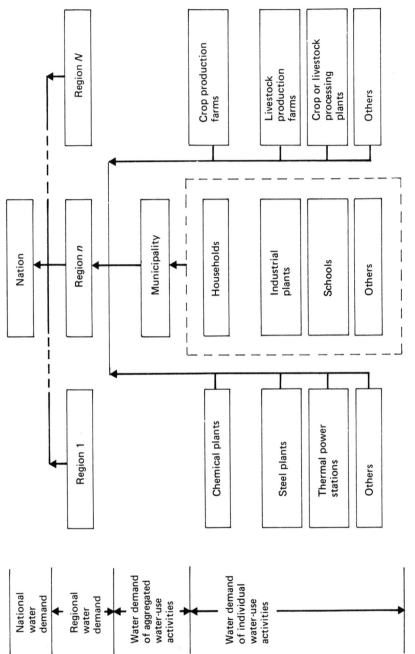

Figure 1.6. The different levels of water demand analysis.

and households.[4] Chapter 3 describes the modeling of industrial water demand; and agricultural demand is the subject of Chapter 4. Household water demand is treated as part of aggregated municipal demand in Chapter 5. Aggregated water-use activities comprise individual activities served by a common system, such as all of the activities receiving water through the distribution system of a municipal water supply agency, or all of the activities discharging wastewater into a common sewerage system. The most familiar aggregate of individual water-use activities is the municipality or metro-politan area, in which residential, commercial, institutional, industrial, and recreational water-use activities are served by water from and/or discharge wastewater to communal systems. Other types of aggregated water-use activities include industrial complexes in which multiple industrial activities discharge wastewater to a common system, irrigation districts consisting of a number of separate agricultural operations, and agricultural complexes con-taining a number of different operations under a single management.

The estimation of water demands of entire regions has to take into account how individual and aggregated water users interact to the extent that they share sources of water and sinks for residuals discharges. In this case, the dimensions of water demand, discussed above in relation to individual and aggregated water users, must be reinterpreted to reflect these interactions through the natural environment. For example, for most purposes, the sum of withdrawals in a region is of no particular interest because such a figure implicitly ignores the water re-use practiced when upstream and downstream users share a watercourse, and because it may miss local problems in which some subset of withdrawals exceeds or is dangerously close to common low stream flows at a particular point. These matters are discussed in Chapter 6.

Water demand at the national level comprises the demands of all regions located within the boundaries of a nation, and although national demand totals in particular types of water-use activities generally have little signi-ficance for specific management decisions, they may be helpful in providing a perspective for policy actions. It may be important to know, for example, the principal water uses in a country and the trends in their demands for additional supplies. This may provide critical information when allocations of capital are to be made, or decisions as to agricultural or industrial policy are at issue. How the national macroeconomic and social policies affect water demand modeling efforts at a lower level of aggregation is discussed in Chapter 7. At this point it is only to be mentioned that regional or basin-wide demand analyses carried out without national policies being properly taken

---

[4] Virtually all these water use activities comprise several *unit processes*, many of which use water and generate liquid residuals. As will be shown in the following chapters, close examination of the water demands of these unit processes is often required.

into account may be totally misleading because of several problems that could seriously bias the results. As pointed out by Tate (1978), "these problems include local optimism in regard to new developments, a tendency to assume that new supply systems will be required before they actually are, and a tendency to build in excess capacity in order to attract new industry." Therefore any regional water demand analysis may have to be approached in several iterations involving regional and sectoral disaggregation of national policies and estimation of regional water demands, which may then be aggregated to give the national picture of the water demand situation.

In the final chapter some general reflections on the subject of this volume are presented. The potential role of water demand modeling is discussed, together with some factors that are responsible for its limited use in the current practice of water resources management planning and policy making.

2 Methodological Framework*

In Chapter 1 the importance of analyzing water use was discussed, the notion of water demand was introduced, and water demand modeling was described very generally. Now, the discussion will go more deeply into this last subject as a means of laying a foundation for the case studies set out in the following chapters. This discussion will concentrate on two broad approaches to water demand modeling, *statistical* and *engineering*, and for each the techniques involved, their conceptual underpinnings, data needs, and some special problems will be examined. Verification is a step common to all modeling work and is so treated here. But at the application stage it is again possible to draw some useful distinctions between the statistical and engineering approaches.

It should be stressed once more that water demand modeling may be informal—an art rather than a formal technique. There is very little one can say to assist such enterprises, except to produce a catalog of rules of thumb. The authors aim to help those who suspect that some formal analytical techniques may be useful, and who would like to know more about some generally recognized guidelines and warnings concerning application of these techniques.

Characterizing the Two Approaches

The statistical and engineering approaches to producing water demand relations involve two quite different responses to perceived problems and opportunities. They begin from different views of what it is that one wishes to model; they involve the use of different types and amounts of data; and, of course, they are based on sharply contrasting computations. In general, one even finds that they appeal to different people. Nonetheless, it is possible to overdo this emphasis on differences, for in fact it is often the case that the methods of one will be found useful in pursuing the other. Therefore, the reader should bear in mind that the drawing of sharp distinctions serves

---

* This chapter was written by J. Kindler and C. S. Russell.

MODELING WATER DEMANDS
ISBN 0-12-407380-8

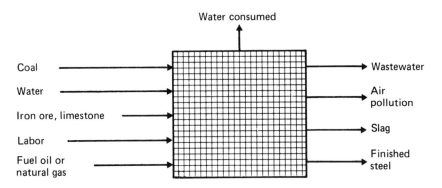

Figure 2.1. A steel mill as a black box.

expositional convenience, but that often in practice the edges between the methods soften and blur.

View of the activity

To begin, the assumption is made that one is interested in modeling the water demand relation(s) for an activity on the scale of a farm or an industrial plant. A household would be another possibility on the same conceptual level, if not the same physical or economic scale. The *statistical approach* begins with a view of the activity as a "black box" with a set of overall inputs, their associated prices or costs, and a set of total outputs, including (for correctness) outputs of pollution, with their associated prices or costs. For example, a steel mill can be viewed as a (simple) black box, as shown in Figure 2.1. Although the activity itself is seen as a black box, that does not necessarily mean the analyst has no interest whatsoever in the contents of this box. The "completely black" box goes with an implicit assumption that there are no internal differences over the sampled activities. If one uses data from activities that are known to be different inside the box, this must be allowed for in the modeling process, as explained below.

The *engineering approach*, on the other hand, fills the black box with individual unit processes, as that of Figure 2.1 is shown filled in for the same simple steel mill in Figure 2.2.[1] Neither approach is intrinsically more correct, although the engineering approach is certainly more complex. And some would argue that learning enough about the activity of interest to fill in the

[1] A real engineer designing a steel mill would have to go to a very much finer level of detail, and then each of the unit processes in Figure 2.2 would become black boxes to be filled in with the pumps, conveyors, vessels, cranes, ovens, generators, motors, etc., etc. Everything is relative—even in water demand analysis.

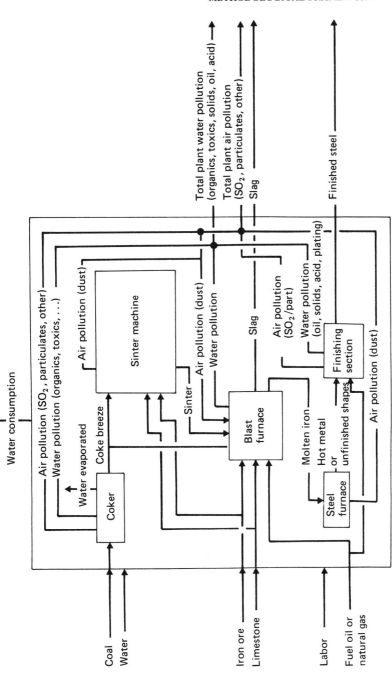

Figure 2.2. A steel mill as a set of unit processes. Note: labor and water inputs go to every process, but for clarity the relevant flow lines have been eliminated.

processes and their linkages is useful even if the statistical approach is to be the method used in model construction.

Data sources and manipulation techniques

The views of the activity contrasted above correspond to contrasting data requirements, and these in turn are linked to contrasting techniques for using the data to obtain a water demand relation(s). The statistical method uses data on inputs to and outputs from the "perimeter" of the activity box. In particular, quantities and corresponding unit costs are the heart of the matter. That method does not require information on the flows between nor the costs and inputs attached to specific unit processes within the perimeter. On the other hand, the statistical method, as its name suggests, thrives on great quantities of data—the more independent observations of flows and prices the better. This is because the method amounts to an attempt to infer from discrete sets of n-dimensional data the parameters of the function "most consistent" with the observations. The method of inference is almost always some more or less elaborate form of multiple regression analysis in which the parameters sought are given by combinations of the statistics of the observations, and these combinations in turn have been derived from some chosen decision rule that takes into account the inevitable "noise" in the data (i.e., the inevitable but not systematic impact of unmeasured influences). Total or unit water demands[2]—intake, gross water applied, consumptive use, wastewater quantity or quality—are regressed against the variables considered to affect a given dimension of water demand. Multiple regression enables the consideration of both quantitative variables, such as level of production, price of intake water, and wastewater disposal charges, and qualitative variables such as the type of production technology (by application of so-called dummy or 0–1 variables, essentially tags that say, "This observation comes from a plant using process X", or "This comes from a plant using process Y").

To return to the steel mill example, suppose one believed, on the basis of a very general understanding of how steel is made, that the quality of wastewater discharge from the mill is determined by what happens at the coker and at the finishing mill. Then, to develop a statistical relation capturing this belief, one would want to find the parameters of a function connecting such variables as the quantity of coal purchased, its carbon and volatile organic content, the extent of the finishing operations conducted (as measured perhaps by the weighted average thinness of the steel sheets shipped), the cost of discharges (if there is an effluent charge or sewer service charge), all to the

---

[2] Per unit of raw material input, per unit of product output, per inhabitant, per patient-night in a hospital, per employee, or per any other similar referent.

quality of the wastewater discharge, as measured by, for example, its bio-chemical oxygen demand.

It is evident from the above that to estimate any functional form and to test any hypothesis about the water demand relation (except a trivially simple one) requires quite large amounts of data. Such data could only come from repeated observation of the same activity over time (say, monthly totals over 10 or 20 years) or simultaneous observation of many activities of the same sort at the same time (say 100 or so plants). For self-evident reasons the first source is known as a time series, the second as a cross-section.[3] Data in these quantities for individual water-using activities are almost unknown, certainly to the independent researcher, probably to the consulting engineer, and in many cases even to the company or agency "owning" one of those activities. (This latter statement generally applies when such measures as water use and pollution loads are in question, for it is only recently that such measurements have become more or less routine). In passing, one may note that it is hard to find such data for an entire activity; how much harder for the unit processes? This is the sense in which data and methodology are intertwined. The black box view of the whole activity is usually the best the statistical data will support.

But even in this case, extreme care must be exercised in the interpretation of the available statistical information, especially of the price–quantity data. Many attempts to analyze water demands are undertaken on the basis of statistical data that do exist, but reveal nothing about price responsiveness of water use. If water users are not charged according to the quantity of water they use (but are charged a flat-rate per unit of *time*), how can one draw any conclusion about their price responses? If average cost pricing is used in a given region (price = total cost of water supply divided by the total quantity of water supplied), and if it is true that the more water supplied by the given system, the lower the average cost, can one draw any conclusion about water users' responses to price? This problem is also encountered in the statistical modeling of electricity demand, where ways have been developed to handle it (see, for example, Bohi 1981).

The engineering approach requires knowledge of what is going on within and among the many unit processes with which it fills up the box. But for any given process it can be content with very little (even no) observed data, for it takes the view that one ought to be able to calculate from first principles and rules of engineering practice just how each unit process would operate under

[3] Under certain conditions and using the correct techniques, it is possible to pool time series and cross-sectional data, so that several inadequate data sets may be combined into one with enough size and variation to be helpful. See, for example: Johnston (1972, pp 192–207), and Balestra and Nerlove (1966). Also see the example in Chapter 5 of this volume.

different assumptions about such details as boiler efficiencies, amount spent on heat exchangers, pressures and temperatures of reactions, pump types, vessel sizes, and so forth. In other words, the engineering approach amounts to an engineering design exercise (albeit a simple one); or, more accurately, a set of alternative unit design exercises which, taken together in different combinations, can produce a large number of alternative activity designs. These in turn can be used to define water demand relations for the activity.

For the steel mill example we have been following, the engineering approach would involve a study of each unit process, alternative designs for it, alternative inputs to it, and alternative operating conditions in it. Any particular combination of assumptions about these features would imply a set of outputs and a set of "utilities", including those of special interest to the reader: water use and wastewater generation. Connecting all units together in a consistent way (e.g., the sulfur content of the coal input to the coker must be consistent with the sulfur content of the coke input to the blast furnace, given the effect of coking on sulfur content), one can produce an activity model *in toto*, with inputs, outputs, and the dimensions of water demand. In a real sense one can view this approach as the result of "data malaise". Because data in sufficient quantity and detail for real plants do not exist, or at least are almost unobtainable even by public water management agencies, the only possible way to understand water demand relations is to start from scratch—from what ought to be—and to build an artificial but completely accessible "activity".[4]

There are two principal ways of analyzing an activity using the engineering approach: (1) engineering design, and its extension (2) mathematical programming. Up to a certain point both ways follow the same path. The preliminary investigation of the activity, the development of material and energy balances for unit processes, the specification of factor inputs and their costs, the calculation of residuals of interest, always comprise necessary steps for developing water demand models by the engineering approach. Following identification of the technological options available for changing water use and the estimation of costs of making such changes, the next step is to determine whether the savings in costs of intake water and wastewater discharge justify the increased costs associated with making the change. It is in the method of seeking an answer to this question, in whatever specific guise it appears, that the design and programming approaches differ.

---

[4] Indeed, the obvious leap from accessibility back to statistical analysis has been exploited by energetic researchers who have used some of the big water demand models to generate what they call "pseudo-data", which they then use to test a range of ideas about various kinds of aggregation, the difficulties introduced by pollution discharge limits, and the general accuracy of their representations of complex production function surfaces (see, for example, Griffin 1978, 1980).

The goal in most cases is to find the optimal response of the activity to a change in the cost of water at the intake, to a modification of a certain water quality standard in the wastewater receiving body, or to some other outside influence. If the charge for water withdrawals increases, the question arises as to whether it is cheaper to continue using the same amount of water or to spend money to reduce water intake. Similarly, if residuals discharge standards become more stringent or an effluent charge is imposed, the problem is to determine the least-cost way of meeting the standards or the best reaction to the charge (where the sum of the cost of discharge reduction plus the remaining charge payments is a minimum). The analyst must determine how flows and waste loads can be reduced, what the different levels of such reductions would cost, and how such changes would affect the demands for other factor inputs in the production of service processes. The decision rule is usually to change water-use patterns and other factor inputs to minimize the total cost of producing the output.[5]

The major problem is how to consider a wide range of possible combinations of alternative unit process configurations. An exhaustive search for the least-cost solution at any given level of output can be very long and complex. For example, the analyst may be interested in the least-cost solutions associated with different prices of water, different prices of energy, different specifications of final products, alternative recirculation systems, alternative production technologies, and so on. If there are n unit processes with m alternatives for each process, there are m^n possible chains of unit processes to be analyzed.[6] In this situation rules are required to limit the number of combinations to be analyzed, because it is usually impossible to investigate the entire response surface.

Much computational effort can be saved if it is possible, on the basis of systematic sampling, to disregard several different ways of producing goods or services and various water utilization system alternatives, and to focus the greater part of the effort on those combinations of unit process that are most likely to contain the solution maximizing or minimizing a certain objective function. In a sense this is a step towards the application of mathematical programming, which involves the use of optimization techniques (such as

[5] The actual problem will usually involve such complications as the desire to maintain the quality of water used in certain ways (such as boiler feed water) and the need to meet a specific time pattern related to each water-using unit process. Subject to quality demanded, recirculation of water and cross-connections among uses are possible. Relationships between extent of recirculation and cost, and extent of recirculation and consumptive use should be developed for each unit process, in order to have the base for the analysis of possible substitutions among elements of the activity's water utilization system and between that system and the production process.

[6] Just to strengthen the point, note that if m is only 3 and n is only 10, there are 59 049 possible combinations or chains.

linear and mixed integer programming) for analysis of combinations of unit production or service processes of an activity and the associated water utilization system. Application of mathematical programming supplements an engineering design procedure with a systematic search method for determining the optimal chains of unit processes and the associated water demand (see, for example, Dorfman 1953, Baumol 1961, Hillier and Lieberman 1974). One advantage of the engineering/programming model[7] over the statistical one is that costs and prices (including the price of water) may be allowed to vary beyond their values recorded in the past and the resulting prediction of the demand for water (one of the factor inputs) may be accepted with reasonable confidence. The statistical model results must be treated very gingerly when the exogenous variable values used are outside the ranges of the observations. Another advantage of the engineering/programming model over the statistical approach is that the former allows one to introduce new technologies into the problem explicitly, once their characteristics are known, and hence explicitly model technical change.

The Statistical Approach

As discussed above and illustrated in Figure 2.1, in the statistical approach each activity whose water demand is being modeled is conceptualized as a black box. There are, however, different ways of looking at the black box representations. In Figure 2.1 all inputs and outputs follow the physical reality. Water is withdrawn by the activity, part of it is consumed, and finally wastewater is discharged by the activity along with product or nonproduct outputs. In Figure 2.3 the black box inputs and outputs are arranged in a different way as required by the statistical analysis.[8]

The variables shown as inputs to the box represent the *explanatory* variables; those shown as the outputs are *dependent* variables. Among the explanatory variables one should distinguish the so-called exogenous variables that have an effect on the dependent variables but which are not explained by the model. These include administered prices, environmental

---

[7] The models involving application of mathematical programming will often be referred to in the following as "engineering/programming models".

[8] This discussion of the statistical approach is designed to provide a general feeling for what is involved. This is not a how-to-do-it manual. Such a manual would be far beyond the scope of this book, not to say the authors' talents. The reader interested in pursuing a statistical model is referred to some of the basic textbooks on statistics and in particular on regression analysis (e.g., Draper and Smith 1966) and numerous contributions to this topic offered by econometricians (e.g., Pindyck and Rubinfeld 1976, Kmenta, 1971, Intrilligator 1978, Maddala 1977). Some water demand studies using the statistical approach are also discussed in Chapters 3 and 5.

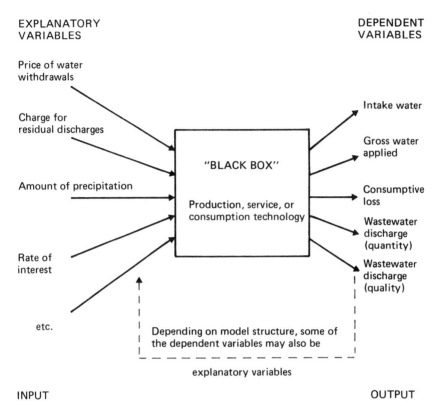

EXPLANATORY
VARIABLES

DEPENDENT
VARIABLES

Price of water
withdrawals

Charge for
residual discharges

Amount of precipitation

Rate of
interest

etc.

"BLACK BOX"

Production, service, or
consumption technology

Intake water

Gross water
applied

Consumptive
loss

Wastewater
discharge
(quantity)

Wastewater
discharge
(quality)

Depending on model structure, some of
the dependent variables may also be

explanatory variables

INPUT

OUTPUT

Figure 2.3. Representation of the black box concept in the statistical approach to modeling water demand relationships.

standards, amounts of precipitation, and government subsidies to a particular type of production or service. As shown in Figure 2.3, depending on the model structure, some of the dependent variables may also become explanatory variables (see the following discussion of interdependence and simultaneity of water demand dimensions).

The modeling process usually proceeds by a series of iterations through the following steps:

(a) choosing the model structure, i.e., selecting variables, and hypothesizing structural relationships, including whether or not simultaneous determination is involved for two (or more) variables;
(b) choosing functional forms;
(c) estimating model parameters;
(d) verifying and validating the model; and
(e) using the model.

The following discussion is concerned with some important subjects which bear on the conduct of the first three steps above. Model verification and validation is a step common to all modeling efforts; therefore, it is discussed later jointly for both statistical and engineering approaches. The application of models developed by the two approaches is also discussed jointly at the end of this chapter.

Specifying the model

In general, a statistical model of a water demand relation can be written as:

$$Q = f(X_1, X_2, \ldots, X_n) + u, \tag{2.1}$$

where $f(.)$ denotes the function of explanatory variables $X_1, X_2, \ldots, X_n$, and u is a random variable describing the joint effect on Q of all factors that are not explicitly taken into account in the form of explanatory variables.[9] The stochastic error term is almost always assumed to have the following properties:

- the expected value of u is zero;
- the variance of u is a constant;
- looking across observations, the errors are uncorrelated, i.e., the expected value of the product $u_i . u_j$ is zero.

There is usually no correct *a priori* analytical form for the function f. In practical applications, however, water demand models are commonly assumed to be either additive, multiplicative, or a combination of the two. These possibilities translate into linear, full logarithmic, or semilogarithmic forms:[10]

$$\left.\begin{array}{l} Q = a_0 + a_1 X_1 + \ldots + a_n X_n + u \\[2ex] \ln Q = b_0 + b_1 \ln X_1 + \ldots + b_n \ln X_n + u \\[2ex] Q = c_0 + c_1 \ln X_1 + \ldots + c_n \ln X_n + u \end{array}\right\} \tag{2.2}$$

or

or

[9] If it is desired to distinguish between specific observations, it is possible to write

$$Q_i = f(X_{i1}, X_{i2}, \ldots, X_{in}) + u_i$$

for the relationship involving the ith observation of $Q, X_1, \ldots, X_n$.

[10] The usual method of dealing with nonlinear relations is to seek an initial transformation of the data such that the relationship between the transformed data appears approximately linear. Recent work in econometrics has involved the use of more and more general functional forms. The most important varieties for the analyst of water demand relations are discussed in Intrilligator (1978, Chapter 8).

where Q is the total or unit amount of water or wastewater disposal services demanded; $a_o, \ldots, a_n, b_0, \ldots, b_n$, and $c_0, \ldots, c_n$ are the structural parameters of the alternative models, $X_1, \ldots, X_n$ are explanatory variables, and u is the random error term. These forms are convenient because they allow for easy estimation of model parameters by use of the ordinary least-squares method, provided it can be assumed that the explanatory variables are determined independently of the dependent variable. It should be noted that this condition is not satisfied if the set of explanatory variables includes other dimensions of water demand, the values of which are determined in the same process as that producing the observed values of Q (the simultaneous determination problem). If Q were the quantity of water demanded in a market for water, and p were the price of water, p and Q would also be simultaneously determined. When this is the case, more complicated estimation techniques must be used (see the next sections).

At this point, the issue of interdependence should be distinguished from that of simultaneity of determination in the context of water demand dimensions. All such dimensions are of course interdependent; they are tied together by the material balance conditions as shown in Chapter 1. These conditions do not indicate, however, direct causality. The causal forces are *economic*. Water intake is not caused by gross water applied. Rather, both are determined by costs. Gross water applied is determined by the economics of production, process alternatives, and the cost of water delivered to the process. This cost is determined by an economic balance between the costs of direct water intake and water recirculation. The same kind of argument applies to the discharge end of an activity. The potential discharge depends on gross water applied, but the actual discharge depends on the relative economics of effluent charges/constraints, end-of-pipe treatment, and recirculation. If all unit costs for water handling by the activity are constant, there is no simultaneity of determination among the different dimensions of water demand. Interdependence, in the sense described above, does, however, imply its own estimation problems, and special techniques exist for dealing with situations in which several dependent variables are interdependent.[11]

Now suppose that the costs of either or both of water intake and recirculation vary with quantity (i.e., rate of flow). Then one must substitute a unit cost equation for the constant unit cost factor assumed above. Economically, the cost equation is equivalent to a supply equation, and now there is a problem of determining a point of equilibrium between the demand equation and the cost (supply) equation. This yields a problem in true causal simultaneity, cost and quantity being jointly determined as discussed below. The economic balance between water intake and recirculation now also depends on the

---

[11] See, for example, Pindyck and Rubinfeld (1976, pp280–2) on Zellner estimation.

quantity of whichever (or both) has nonconstant cost. This means that the composite unit cost of water delivered to process (gross water applied) is also dependent on its quantity. Under such circumstances, the identity relating intake, recirculation, and gross water applied becomes important, since it makes the cost term in the demand equation for gross water applied dependent on the quantity of this water; that is, gross water applied is also determined as a point of equilibrium between cost and demand functions.

Simultaneity and identification

When two or more variables are jointly or simultaneously determined, as is the case for price and quantity of a good sold in a classical market situation or cost and quantity in the example cited above, there arises the possibility that it will be impossible from available data to sort out what is going on; that is, to identify the true demand and supply equations. This is logically prior to the estimation problem, which is discussed in the next section. An easy way to see how such a problem might arise is to look at the data that would be generated if only observed price and quantity data were available, even though some other conditions were causing the demand and supply curves to shift, thus generating the data. This is illustrated in Figure 2.4, where the circled points

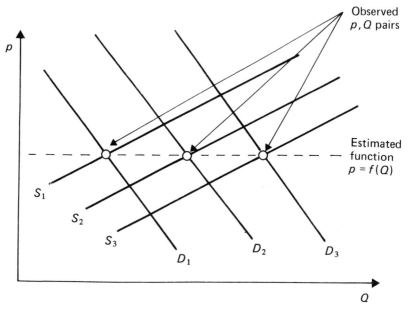

Figure 2.4. Shifting of demand and supply functions.

of intersection of the shifting demand and supply functions are the observed points (the data) and the estimated function $p = f(Q)$ is shown as a dotted line—and is *neither* a demand *nor* a supply function.

Could one sort things out if there were information available on the forces shifting the functions? The answer at a first approximation depends on whether the shifts in demand and supply curves occur because of the same variables or are independently caused by different variables. To see this, consider an algebraic version of the sketch in Figure 2.4:

$$\text{demand function:} \; p = f(Q, X_D) \tag{2.3}$$

$$\text{supply function:} \; p = g(Q, X_S), \tag{2.4}$$

where X_D and X_S are the *exogenous* or shift variables. If X_D and X_S are the same, then there is no way of untangling their effects. For example, let the demand function be:

$$p = a + bQ + cY \tag{2.5}$$

and the supply function be:

$$p = d + eQ + kY, \tag{2.6}$$

where Y is income.

To see that these equations cannot be identified from information on p, Q, and Y, it is convenient to define the *reduced-form* equations: i.e., those in which each endogenous (simultaneously determined) variable is expressed as a function of the exogenous (predetermined) variables. Here the reduced-form equations are:

$$Q = \frac{k-c}{b-e} Y + \frac{d-a}{b-e} \tag{2.7}$$

$$p = \frac{kb-ec}{b-e} Y + \frac{db-ae}{b-e}. \tag{2.8}$$

These functions can always be estimated, but what one has after the estimation is *combinations* of the parameter values actually sought; that is, combinations of the values a, b, c, d, e, k, the structural parameters, that characterize the demand and supply equations themselves.[12] One way of looking at the identification problem is in the form of the question: Is it possible to disentangle the structural parameters from the reduced-form equation parameters [e.g. $(k-c)/(b-e)$]? In the simple example set out above, the answer is no. Neither the demand nor the supply equation is identified.

[12] The reduced form may suffice if one is interested in simple prediction.

If, however, the demand and supply shifts occur independently, under certain circumstances either or both the demand and supply equations may be identified. In the simple context pursued above let the demand function be:

$$p = a + bQ + cY \qquad (2.9)$$

and the supply function be:

$$p = d + eQ + kW, \qquad (2.10)$$

where W is weather, and all else is as defined above. Then demand shifts because of income only and supply shifts because of weather only. Here the reduced-form equations are:

$$Q = \frac{k}{b-e}W - \frac{c}{b-e}Y + \frac{d-a}{b-e} \qquad (2.11)$$

$$p = \frac{bk}{b-e}W - \frac{ec}{b-e}Y + \frac{db-ae}{b-e}. \qquad (2.12)$$

A few minutes with pencil and paper should convince the reader that the parameters of these reduced-form equations are sufficient to calculate *all* of the structural equation parameters. For example, using a "hat" to indicate "estimate of", $\hat{b}$ can be estimated as

$$\hat{b} = \left(\widehat{\frac{bk}{b-e}}\right) \Big/ \left(\widehat{\frac{k}{b-e}}\right), \qquad (2.13)$$

and $\hat{a}$ as

$$\hat{a} = \left(\widehat{\frac{db-ae}{b-e}}\right) - \hat{b}\left(\widehat{\frac{d-a}{b-e}}\right). \qquad (2.14)$$

Hence, the parameters of both structural equations are identified.

Intuitively, what is involved is the presence in each equation of shifters (exogenous variables) that do not appear in the other. More formally, the necessary condition for an *equation* to be identified is that the number of predetermined variables excluded from that equation must be greater than or equal to the number of *included* endogenous (jointly determined) variables minus one. In the last example, both the demand and supply equations had two endogenous variables, p and Q, and each equation had excluded from it one variable that appeared elsewhere in the system. Thus both exactly meet the criteria for identification (are exactly identified).[13] If there is more than enough independent information to identify the structural coefficients of a

[13] The necessary and *sufficient* conditions for identification of equations in equation sets are much more difficult to state (see, for example, Pindyck and Rubinfeld 1976, pp 292–8).

basic equation (i.e., they can be calculated in more than one way from the reduced-form parameters), then the equation is said to be over-identified.

Parameter estimation

The ordinary least-squares method is the most commonly used technique for estimation of model parameters. It can be shown that—under assumptions about the properties of the already mentioned random error term u, and provided that causal independence of variables can be assumed—the ordinary least-squares method yields the best estimates of the model parameters. They are of course *best* only to the extent that the defined structure of the model is accurate.

As discussed earlier, sometimes it may be necessary to build a more complicated, multi-equation model in which at least some of the dependent variables serve as explanatory variables for other dependent variables. It has been shown (e.g., Goldberger 1964, Theil 1978) that in the case of such interdependent models, the use of ordinary least-squares equation by equation leads to systematically "biased" and "inconsistent" parameter estimates.[14] Special methods of estimation (i.e., maximum likelihood or two-stage least-squares) must be used in these cases. For details the reader is referred to the two monographs cited above. It is sometimes possible to avoid this serious complication by recognizing that causality runs in one direction only, so that there is a "first" dependent variable which in turn helps to determine a second, those two helping to determine a third, and so on. This is called a recursive system.

Mathematical Programming

The initial discussion of the engineering approach to water demand modeling ended by indicating the possibility of applying mathematical programming methods to the analysis of combinations of unit production or service processes of an overall activity and its associated water utilization system. Here a particular mathematical programming technique, linear programming, is described in the context of water demand modeling.

---

[14] For a parameter estimator to be unbiased means that if we could find a large number of sets of data and use each set to estimate the structural parameter the expected value of the parameter estimates obtained in this way would equal the true parameter value. Consistency is a property defined in terms of the size of the data set used in any particular estimation. Its intuitive meaning is that as the amount of data grows without limit, the consistent estimate gets closer and closer to the true value of the structural parameter of interest. If an estimator is inconsistent, this does not happen.

The purpose of the model and its structure

A linear programming (LP) model of an activity is a combination of unit processes, including those relating to the water utilization system, written in the form of a set of linear inequalities, where the variables are the levels of operation of the processes, and the inequalities express requirements (constraints) on the overall system or its parts. For example, one requirement might be that total production be so many units per period; another might be that wastewater discharge be less than a specified volume. The "objective function" for the model represents the criterion for choosing the optimum combination of unit processes, the measure that must be minimized or maximized. In water demand analysis it is most common to find that the objective function represents cost. In such cases the problem is stated as "minimize cost subject to certain constraints", in particular to a minimum constraint on acceptable output. (The choice of the appropriate objective function is a much more difficult and delicate matter than is indicated here, and is discussed further at the end of this chapter.)

Cost-minimizing solutions to the model may be calculated for each specification of effluent (or ambient environmental) standards, water prices or charges, water availability, availability or prices of energy and feedstocks, etc. This process is technically called parametrization, and involves repeated solution of the model under successive changes in level of an input price or a constraint. This is the way one explores the model's response patterns and extracts information from it. The model may be designed so that each optimal combination of processes gives, among other results, the amount of water withdrawn, applied, consumed, and discharged; the quantity of each pollutant discharged, and the amount of wastewater (residual) disposal services demanded. In this manner, alternative values of unit and total water demands by activity may be generated for further analysis and use.

In LP models the unit processes are included as vectors and are characterized by fixed proportions between inputs and outputs. The elements of these vectors are called "technical coefficients". A modeled activity has only a finite number of processes available to it (which it is convenient to think of as the alternative unit processes from an engineering unit process analysis) and each process may be operated at any non-negative level as long as the necessary inputs are available and all constraints are met. When the level of a process is changed, the consumption of all its inputs changes in the same proportion. It is also assumed that the various processes may be operated simultaneously. (To impose the requirement that the model choose *either* process X or process Y *but not both* requires the use of integer programming.)

The beauty of the LP technique is that there is available an algorithm or rule (the simplex method) for moving systematically from any initial trial solution that satisfies the constraints, to the optimal solution.[15] This algorithm has been programmed, and modern computers can very quickly find the optimal solutions to problems in which there are literally millions of possible combinations (chains) of unit processes.

If the levels of the unit processes in the overall activity are denoted by vector x, then the LP model associated with a cost-minimization objective would have the following symbolic form:

$$\min Z = c\,x$$

subject to
$$(2.15)$$
$$Ax \geqslant b \qquad x \geqslant 0$$

where

- Z is the value of the objective function, the quantity to be "optimized"—in this case minimized;
- c is an $(1 \times n)$ vector of unit prices and costs associated with the $(n \times 1)$ vector x of unit processes distinguished in the model. These costs detail the process operating costs, and where relevant, the associated capital charge;
- A is an $(m \times n)$ matrix of technical coefficients that identify the amounts of inputs required and outputs produced per unit of each process;
- b is an $(m \times 1)$ vector of requirements that must be satisfied by the linear combinations expressed by the corresponding rows of the A matrix multiplied by the x vector. These coefficients (usually called "right-hand sides") represent for example, resource availability, mass balance requirements, and production or service requirements.

A special feature of LP models is the automatic computation, along with the optimal levels of all unit processes, of a corresponding set of *shadow prices*, each associated with a particular constraint in the model. The shadow price concept is of special importance in water demand analysis because it can help in situations in which market prices are hard to visualize. The shadow price associated with a constraint that curtails the availability of a certain resource measures the economic cost (to the modeled activity) of that constraint. For instance, a shadow price associated with an environmental standard for maximum allowable concentration of toxic materials in the receiving water can be used to determine the marginal cost of such a standard. If a constraint is not binding, its shadow price is zero.

The general structure of an LP water demand model is well illustrated by concrete applications described in Chapters 3, 4, and 6 of this volume.

[15] On solving linear programs, see, for example, Gass (1969). A widely used and highly regarded algorithm package is the MPSX available from IBM.

Model building

The primary task in the development of an LP model of a water-use activity is the construction of the activity vectors—columns in the **A** matrix. By assumption, the coefficients of each column are independent of the coefficients of every other column. Therefore, it is not necessary to know in advance which processes the model will select in its optimal solution. Rather, it is necessary to attempt to model as plausibly as possible all possible processes, and then let the model choose the best (cost-minimizing or benefit-maximizing) subset. But the modeling effort generally proceeds most efficiently if the following steps are followed.

First, a flow diagram of the activity is prepared which identifies not only the basic system components necessary to produce the desired output(s) of product(s) or service(s), but also as many production process and water utilization alternatives as are to be considered. This diagram establishes both the system configuration and level of detail to be modeled, and explicitly indicates linkages and interrelationships between system components. For example, in Figure 2.2 a simple flow diagram associated with steel production was shown.

Secondly, each modeled process and each alternative for that process is identified separately and described in terms of its technical coefficients, prices, and costs. (The number and nature of row constraints in the model and the set of coefficients that must be defined are determined together in anticipation of the overall model's structure.) At this point, the level of engineering knowledge required depends upon the level of detail and degree of accuracy desired in the model. This is usually a rather involved and time-consuming task, but the same is basically needed in the conventional engineering design calculations. To assist the reader in gaining a feel for this part of the process, several examples of deriving technical coefficients in industrial and agricultural applications of the mathematical programming approach are presented in Chapters 3 and 4.

Finally, when all technical coefficients, prices, costs, and right-hand sides have been identified, the individual processes are fitted into the structure of an LP model. Each modeled process (or combination thereof) becomes a column in the A matrix; each constrained input or output or material balance requirement implies a row constraint in the matrix. These constraints may be structured to require purchase (without limit) of all input required by the solution; or to place an upper limit on resource availability or use.

The LP framework can be elaborated to encompass those processes of the activity that are of particular interest in the analysis of water demands. The basic procedure is to account for all the important inputs and outputs of each process in the set of constraints, explicitly including all dimensions of water demand. The objective function should include the prices and costs associated with water withdrawal, gross water use, consumptive use, and disposal into the environment of all residuals of the production or service activity. In this formulation of the model, the (row) balance constraints require that for each resource or input used by the activity, the total input to all processes equals the amount "purchased" plus the amount produced within the plant; this total must in turn equal the amount consumed plus any amount "sold" and the amount released to the environment.

Model Verification and Validation

But before one proceeds to use a water demand model, developed either by the statistical or the engineering approach, a fundamental question has to be answered: How much confidence does one have in the model? This is the question of model verification and validation. These two terms are easily confused, and both have come to be interpreted in several different ways.

In this book, "verification" is understood as the determination of whether or not the correct model has been developed from a given *single* set of data describing water demand relations. The notion of "correctness" carries some ambiguity, but it will hopefully be clarified in the following discussion. Model "validation" is the testing of the model's adequacy against one or more *independent* sets of data. It is the process of acquiring increasing confidence from the fact that the outputs of the model conform to reality in the required range. A model can never be completely validated: one can never prove that its results conform to reality in all possible data ranges; it can only be invalidated by failure in one instance. Validation is a step in water demand modeling which, unfortunately, is rarely attempted, principally because data are scarce and of limited quality, as discussed earlier.

Although verification and validation are common steps in all modeling efforts, operationally these two terms have a different meaning, depending upon whether one deals with the statistical or engineering/programming model of water demand.

In the case of a *statistical* model estimated by application of multiple regression analysis, verification involves computation of various goodness-of-fit measures (e.g., multiple correlation coefficient, coefficient of determination), application of several statistical tests of significance (e.g., F-test for the overall significance of the regression equation, t-tests for the significance of the individual regression coefficients), and checking of the extent to which some basic assumptions of multiple regression are met (e.g., linearity, independence of residuals, constancy of residuals' variance, normality of residuals).[16] In addition, the model builder usually also involves himself in the qualitative verification of the model which, first of all, consists of ascertaining whether the regression coefficients have correct signs.

To give the reader a general idea of this qualitative type of model verification, an example of a water intake demand function may be considered. In this equation the regression coefficient on water intake price (and probably on wastewater disposal price) should be negative, because higher prices generally induce lower water intake and wastewater discharges (although consumptive use of water could increase, depending on the options available to the plant). The signs of the regression coefficients for other factor input prices can be either negative or positive, depending upon whether they are complements or substitutes (relative to water), respectively. If one of the explanatory variables is the level of output (or size of activity), the estimated regression coefficient for that variable (which measures the effect on unit demand of the scale of production) could also be either negative or positive. For example, there may be economies of scale—at least up to a certain level—for internal recirculation of water, such that the unit water intake and wastewater discharge would decrease in association with an increase in the level of output. On the other hand, plant size may be positively correlated with water demand, because, e.g., greater water demand is typically associated with greater complexity, and complexity with size. If the signs of the estimated parameter values are correct in the sense of being in agreement with theory and common sense, then one can say that the model is verified from the qualitative point of view.

The validation of a statistical model entails using a new set of data and testing the values of dependent variables derived by application of the model against the observed values of these variables. However, in the statistical modeling of water demand, all the available data are usually too few for the model-building phase, and there is simply no additional data to speak of.

The *engineering/programming* model is a totally different type from that just discussed; therefore, its verification and validation must also be viewed differently. In this case, there are no standard procedures to be followed, and in fact, the distinction between verification and validation is no longer a sharp one. Verification of the "correctness" of the model probably means not much more than carefully checking results of experimental model runs for their completeness and internal consistency. A model can sometimes also be checked (if not formally verified) by submitting selected process components for evaluation by a sort of higher-level expert (say, a specialist in coking or blast furnaces at a steel mill). The model can also be applied to particular

---

[16] At this point, the reader is referred to any standard textbook on mathematical statistics or econometrics, e.g., Johnston (1972).

activities of the type modeled, and after tailoring inputs, sizes, processes, output mixes, costs, and prices, to the extent possible on the basis of available data, one can compare predicted water demands with the actual ones.

Thus far, verification and validation of the model as a finished product have been emphasized. In fact, modeling, and especially model verification, are continuous processes in time. When preliminary runs are performed with a computer-implemented model, one usually finds several clues to possible model improvements, and verification should rather be viewed as an integral part of the whole modeling process. As far as model validation is concerned, the critical question for the advancement of water demand analysis is not whether the demand models currently in use can simulate everything of interest about water demands. One can assume with a high degree of certainty that they are not capable of doing that, primarily because of the usually poor data base and the overall complexity of the demand generating factors. Hence, the question seems to be whether the model provides a rigorous and systematic framework for further investigations (including data collection programs), and whether one can use the model for the purpose for which it was originally conceived and designed. Virtually every aspect of model building depends on the purposes for which the model was designed, and this observation leads to the next section concerning model applications and use.

Model Applications

Three specific problems for water-use analysis and application of water demand models were mentioned in Chapter 1. These were:

● baseline forecasting;
● policy analysis (where either direct, intentional, or indirect, unintentional policy impacts may be of interest); and
● demand/supply balancing.

A few more words about these applications and about matching models and problem application will round out this general discussion of methodology.

Baseline forecasting of water demands may be thought of as an exercise in translating forecasts of other social and economic measures into future water use. For example, national level water withdrawal forecasts might involve using a statistical reduced-form equation connecting national aggregated withdrawals with such variables as gross national product, population, urban population, the size of the agricultural sector, water recirculation factor, and the importance of manufacturing as opposed to service industries. A baseline forecast of water use would involve predicting future values of the explanatory variables over the period of interest, and then producing a water withdrawal forecast by inserting these predicted values of the explanatory variables in the reduced-form equation. The adjective "baseline" is applied because the forecast does not reflect any direct policy interventions designed to change future levels of water withdrawals. It implicitly assumes no change in the policies pursued during the period over which the relation was estimated.

Any attempt to forecast the future on the basis of the past is fraught with obvious dangers in the form of discontinuities in technology, and economic and institutional structures. But it is really impossible (and inefficient) to avoid using the past as a guide to the future, and a formal forecasting procedure may be thought of as an attempt to improve our chances of being close to correct. By taking account of many more or less independent explanatory variables one may increase the chance of uncovering and taking into account some *predicted* break in past patterns, such as a predicted spurt in the growth rate of agriculture. If the break really does occur it will be reflected in the withdrawal forecasts—subject to the caveat that the underlying relationship reflected in the estimated equation parameters and functional form may be changing as well.

The analysis of the impacts of public policies on water demands may conveniently be thought of as an elaboration of baseline forecasting, the elaboration taking the form of making allowance for changes in policy variables (or instruments). These may be policy instruments designed to influence water demand levels directly, such as water prices, standards controlling wastewater discharge, or requirements that water use in certain shortage periods be reduced. The policies to be analyzed may, on the other hand, be those having only an indirect connection with water use; for example, farm subsidies, energy pricing, or air pollution control. In either case, one obvious measure of the impact of the policy is found through comparing water demand forecasts with and without the policy change(s). To be able to make such alternative forecasts the water demand relations must be developed so that values for the relevant policy variables may be included. This requirement may, as discussed below, have important implications for the relative suitability of the two modeling approaches for the analysis of particular policies at particular levels of analysis.

The balancing of water supply and demand is yet a more complex application of water demand relations.[17] In its most complex application it may be seen as iterative forecasting of demand subject to iterative adjustment of a mediating variable, depending on supply-side choices, the most obvious choice for which is price or cost to the users. Thus, for a municipal water system, one might first propose a plan of capacity expansion over time. Then

---

[17] By one route it is not complex at all. The traditional approach to balancing might in fact be called increasing supply to meet the baseline forecast of water use.

a trial time path of prices to be charged could be inserted in the system demand relation. The resulting path of demand could then be compared with the capacity expansion path (neglecting for purposes of exposition the uncertainty problem). This demand path may be inconsistent with the supply plan for the trial price set. So another price set must be chosen and tried. Whether the process will converge to a balance in a reasonable number of trials—or, indeed, whether convergence is to be expected at all—will depend on the shapes of the relevant cost and demand functions, even though these may remain implicit for large regional balancing problems (for the mechanics of such a procedure, see Hanke 1978).

Model application and choice of model type

The choice between model types depends on such factors as data availability, skills and interests of the modeling team, and access to computational facilities. But this choice is also linked to the intended application of the model(s) to be constructed. That is, for some applications, statistical models seem more promising; for others the engineering approach with application of mathematical programming is to be preferred. One way of summarizing the links between application and preferred model type is to look at combinations of the two principal characteristics of specific application: the level of analysis, and the problem to be addressed. However, the variety of situations under which demand analysis is required is so large that there is simply no way to provide a clear-cut general recommendation of the "best" way to proceed.

Thus, where the individual industrial plant (like the large coal-fired power plant discussed in Chapter 3) or farm is concerned, the engineering/programming models seem better suited for all three problem types. This is partly because the data problems of the statistical approach leave one almost inevitably with a rather crude average representation of the activity in question, and a representation not easily tailored to particular circumstances. Thus, if the statistical water demand relations for a petroleum refinery could be based on cross-sectional data over many different refineries at different locations, of different vintages, mixes of operations and products, types of crude oils used, and so forth, these relations might allow the modeler to come very close to specifying a particular refinery demand relation by specifying the relevant shift variables. As a practical matter, however, it is likely that the refinery data base available even to a government or industry modeler will be substantially less complete than that just assumed.

The engineering approach, on the other hand, though not entirely free of the "tailoring" problem, at least allows the construction of models that are in principle flexible, for what one includes or excludes by way of specific detail is more often a matter of choice than of necessity forced on the modeler by data gaps.[18] The problem here is that the actual job of tailoring may be very difficult, involving many changes to the coefficients of the programming matrix. Thus the choice for individual water-use activity models comes down to a choice based on expected data availability.

When the analysis is concerned with municipal water use, and especially with the household water demand involving many small, individual users, like in the city of Malmö, Sweden discussed in Chapter 5, the model of choice is usually the statistical one. Here the key variables (such as climate, average lot size, water price, wastewater charge) are likely to be both easy to measure and actually measured. Furthermore, the results of the measurements are likely to be matters of reasonably accessible record. Such systems offer many advantages to the statistical modeler and do not for the most part conceal the sorts of interactions that are best handled by the engineering approach.

When the *problem* at hand is one of baseline forecasting, especially for levels of analysis above that of the individual activity, the statistical approach comes into its own. Then, even if the analysis begins with models of the individual activities, the necessity for highly differentiated data (the tailoring problem) is less serious, for a set of "average" petroleum refineries may not work out badly as a representation of a regional situation—and is indeed the essence of the national aggregates. Perhaps even more to the point, it may be possible to apply statistical analysis directly at the level of interest, bypassing modeling the individual activities completely, as was done for the case of the Dutch paper industry described in Chapter 3. This is more likely to be the case for the national than the regional level, for that is the level at which many public data are aggregated.

There will, however, be a problem at this level of aggregation with the price variables. In most countries there will be no single price variable to include in an aggregate relation, based perhaps on time series. In these circumstances, the model builder will at best be estimating what amounts to a reduced-form equation. So long as the interest is in baseline forecasting rather than the analysis of alternative pricing policies, this need not be a problem. But the situation may not even be this favorable, and for both baseline forecasting and supply–demand matching exercises at the national level the modeler may be thrown back on the use of coefficients, only some of which will have been derived from water demand models of activities at lower levels of aggregation.

When one is particularly interested in the analysis of policies either directly or indirectly affecting water demand at the regional level (e.g., the Silistra

[18] There are, of course, gaps for the would-be engineering modeler, too. The exact details of some process (e.g., conversion rates for chemical processes, temperatures and pressures, achievable rates of production) may be industrial secrets; and these can usually not be inferred from other known items.

regional study described in Chapter 4 and the Lower Delaware study discussed in Chapter 6), the model type most likely to be useful, at least in the initial phase of analysis is the engineering/programming one. This is again partly a matter of data availability, but it also involves structure. In the first place, most of the policy instruments of special interest in the water field at a given time (such as charges for abstractions from rivers, effluent standards, and requirements for certain conservation actions) have not been used before, or have been used only for short times in one or two places. Thus, there is no statistical record from which to estimate anything.[19]

In the second place, many of these instruments are very difficult to include in the statistically derived estimating equations. For example, consider the regulation of wastewater discharges through the use of standards based on treatment process definitions, as is now the policy in the USA. In principle, the standards apply to all industrial sources of wastewater, but the levels of control actually specified may vary between sources because of such characteristics as age of plant and even the political power of the industry and the region. In order to see how such "a policy" affects water demands other than wastewater assimilation services, it would be necessary to have very detailed plant-by-plant information on the actual workings of the policy in a form that could be used as "a variable". Simple 0–1 variables, or required discharge reductions, will not reflect what is actually happening (see Hazilla et al. 1980).

This situation may be contrasted with that faced by modelers of the macroeconomy. There, many of the most important policy instruments (interest rates, budget deficits, maximal tax rates) are straightforward to measure; have been used for long enough that a response record has been established; and are easy to include in macrolevel equations.

In setting out to find plans that optimally balance demand and supply of water one may want to use either the statistical or the engineering approach depending on the particular context. On the one hand, it may be the case that the interest is in balancing (deterministic) demand and supply of water for a municipal water system's withdrawals at one point in time. Then statistical analysis of demand and supply might allow the analyst to proceed rather directly to the answer. Even if one wished to reflect the stochastic character of water supply and the costs of shortages, the overall system demand relation may still be quite sufficient (see, for example, Russell et al. 1970, where such an analysis makes use of the demand equations of Howe and Linaweaver 1967; for a more recent review, see Russell 1979). If one attempts to do it all at once, however (that is, to include a variable price instrument along with supply expansion possibilities and demand curves), there may be an analytically

---

[19] This problem is analogous to that discussed above for national level water demand modeling where there may exist no meaningful price.

intractable problem, although aggregate statistical relations may still be appropriate for the demand side.

On the other hand, if balancing of demand and supply involves individual water-use activities explicitly, as when the modeler is interested in:

- the balance for streamflow at several points, each affected by a different set of water-use activities, and
- the water quality at various specific points, each of which is again influenced by different wastewater dischargers,

then one must begin with models of the activities, and for this, the engineering/programming approach is preferable. That approach is also preferable where the instruments to be used in achieving the balance do not fit easily into the statistical mold for the reasons outlined above.

The foregoing discussion of model use raises two other fundamental issues that have so far been neglected: the choice of the objective function for individual activity models or for aggregates of such models, and the matter of optimization itself. To this point, the assumption has been that decision makers at every level will find it relevant to look at *costs* and that their aim is to minimize the costs of achieving particular policy aims, such as the production of a given quantity of output at a certain industrial plant or large-scale agricultural enterprise. A first level of complication is to bring in benefits—as might be represented by the demand functions for the output of the plant or farm—and to shift to maximization of net benefits.

Other complications can easily be imagined, and these force a deeper look at the relation between model use and the objective function and choice rule. Indeed, a thorough examination of this area would require a book in itself. However, the would-be modeler can be warned of the kinds of problems likely to be encountered without being lectured on all the relevant subtleties. Further, methods for incorporating some of the complications can be briefly suggested.

One problem with the simple approach is that water-using or managing enterprises are likely to be public (government) bodies with more complex objectives than is implied by single-minded attention to cost, or even to net money benefits. For example, the maintenance of total employment may be an important objective—perhaps even the major objective. Alternatively, water quantity or quality measures may be dominant; for example, perhaps a large state farm has been told to minimize its irrigation water withdrawals. (Even private businesses may not be interested only, or even most importantly, in cost minimization or profit maximization. For example, they may concentrate on total sales or on market share. In the long term, however, it is difficult for firms to survive in a competitive system if they completely ignore costs and profits.) One possible response to such a situation is to construct the model(s) to concentrate entirely on the mandated concern, and this will often, though not always, be technically possible. Thus, the objective function could become employment or energy use, or irrigation withdrawals, or whatever, and the "value" of each unit process would be measured entirely by its contribution to the (nonmonetary) objective.

Such a single-minded approach may not be the wisest course, however, because other aspects of the problem are also likely to concern policy makers. For example, energy use or raw material demand may be important even though maximizing employment is the charge of the decision maker. In such circumstances, the modeler may choose to build a model with employment per unit process in the objective function, but to include constraints on energy or other raw material use. If enough other considerations are important, it may be worthwhile to summarize them in the form of a cost constraint, where energy and raw material use are valued, along with other cost items, at market, administrative, or national shadow prices and a constraint placed on total cost. A fundamental observation, then, is that the problem:

max: employment

subject to: a constraint on total costs

is almost indistinguishable from its so-called "dual":

min: cost of production

subject to: a lower limit on total employment.

Similar observations apply whenever there is more than one concern. Whatever approach is chosen it will usually be possible to lay out schedules of predicted policy results that show the decision maker (an individual or collective body) how much of one important item may be obtained at how great a "cost" in terms of the other concerns (a more sophisticated approach to similar knowledge is multiobjective programming; see, for example, Cohon 1978).

Notice that the possibilities opened up by the above observations are bounded only by the imagination of policy makers and, more to the point, the virtuosity of model builders. If it is possible to connect the modeled activity or set of activities to any social or political concern, it will also be possible to examine the costs of pursuing one goal in terms of other goals sacrificed. Even the distribution of policy costs and benefits over regions or groups within a population can be explored in this way. For one example, see the description in Chapter 6 of a regional model with constraints on the distribution of certain costs.

The second issue mentioned above, the possibility that "optimization" is not the appropriate requirement, is potentially more difficult. Most fundamentally, if policy makers actively reject optimization, there is no obvious basis for a *technical* analysis of the infinite number of possible policies (prices, quantities, standards, or quotas). It is well, therefore, to distinguish between possible causes for the apparent rejection of optimality. For example, the decision maker may *individually* be "boundedly rational", in the sense of Herbert Simon. Practically speaking, this will mean that it is too much trouble for him or her to search for the optimum position, taking into account the full range and complexity of the responsibilities inherent in the office (see, for example, the work of Simon: March and Simon 1958, Simon 1960). Another possibility is that the models available to decision makers do not in fact capture the relevant objectives and constraints, so that the results become more or less irrelevant and decisions appear to reject optimality when what they actually do is recognize the existence of a different problem. Finally, there may be philosophical objections among the audience for the model's results to using, or at least to appearing to use, the crassly materialistic output of any applied cost benefit study or model (e.g., Kelman 1981). These people may embrace "spontaneity" as a value in itself and thus be averse to "calculation" of any sort. Or they may feel that some things are, or should be, priceless—by which they may mean either infinitely valuable or freely available at zero price. Whatever the specific arguments used to support the rejection, it is very difficult to see how the approach described in this book can be made useful to those who reject cost–benefit types of calculation.

With this background on methodology, data, verification, and application, it is time to turn to the specific case studies so long promised to the patient reader. In Chapter 3 the focus will be on the water demands of the paper industry and for electric power generation (as examples of demand analysis for industrial water use), in Chapter 4 on agricultural water demands, and in Chapter 5 on municipal water demands. Subsequently, there will be an examination of regional (Chapter 6) and national (Chapter 7) levels of analysis.

3 *Industrial Water Demands**

Introduction

Most industrial processes use water as an input, though the purposes to which the water is put vary widely. In some cases water is an input in the classic sense and forms part of the product. The beverage industry is an obvious example, but water or steam is also used as feedstock or processing agent in numerous chemical and pharmaceutical processes. In other plants it is used to convey the product from one stage of production to another. For example, in paper making, pulp is carried in slurry form from the pulping operation to bleaching and paper-making. In the canning industry fruits and vegetables are often transported through the production process in a water stream.

Where excess or unwanted heat is generated by a mechanical process or chemical or nuclear reaction, water is the obvious choice as the heat removal medium. This use is nearly universal, but is on an especially grand scale in the steam-electric power generating industry.

Water is used for washing and cleaning throughout industrial facilities. In the canning industry fruits and vegetables are washed with water at the beginning of the production process; hydraulic debarking in the pulp and paper industry is a standard method for removing the bark and cleaning the dirt from incoming logs; and water is also used to wash final products. Water is, of course, used for personal and plant hygiene and for other overhead purposes such as lawn watering, vehicle washing, and fire protection. Steam may be used for space heating. Moreover, an examination of the water utilization system of an industrial plant may show that water is actually a net output of some stages of the production process as when liquid residuals result from the production of some dry foods. Nonproduct residuals other than energy are also commonly removed from industrial processes in water streams, and the treatment and disposal of the resulting wastewater is a major concern of public policy makers in most industrial nations.

Thus, water demand by an industrial activity is a multidimensional

* This chapter was written by J. C. Stone and D. Whittington.

MODELING WATER DEMANDS
ISBN 0-12-407380-8

phenomenon. At a given point in time, water demands with respect to all six dimensions set out in Chapter 1 are determined by the following interrelated factors:

- production technology;
- product mix and quality specifications;
- qualities and prices of raw materials, including fuel and electrical energy;
- unit values of recoverable nonproduct materials and energy;
- price of purchased water of given quality at the intake to the plant;
- costs of different amounts of self-supplied intake water, e.g., costs of intake facilities, treatment, and recirculation;
- limitations, standards, or unit fees imposed on the discharge of liquid, gaseous, and solid residuals from the plant, either directly to the environment or to some collection and disposal system;
- costs of different degrees of in-plant residuals modification;
- capital availability;
- climate.

Because there are different uses of water within an industrial plant and because of the many factors that affect those uses, the development of specific and accurate relationships explaining water-use patterns is difficult. As discussed in Chapter 2, there are two basic approaches to modeling industrial water demand relationships: statistical and engineering. The latter may further be divided into the engineering design and mathematical programming categories. This chapter discusses and illustrates the statistical and mathematical programming approaches to modeling industrial water demand relationships.

Statistical Approach to Modeling Industrial Water Demand Relationships: The Dutch Paper Industry

The objective of this section is to illustrate some of the pitfalls that await the unwary analyst who sets out to build a statistical model of industrial water demand. The discussion does not attempt to describe the estimation procedures themselves or their limitations; details of these can be found in any number of econometrics texts. The focus is rather on estimating water demand relationships, and a checklist of some of the econometric problems that are most likely to be encountered is provided. Ideally, a review of the professional literature should serve the same purpose, but few examples exist of the application of regression techniques to modeling industrial water use that include a measure of the "price of water" as one of the explanatory variables (Ginn *et al.* 1975, De Rooy 1974, Rees 1969). The vast majority of the existing work in the area of statistical water demand models has focused on domestic water use (see Chapter 5 for a brief review and example; see also Gorman 1980). The following discussion is primarily concerned with the use of cross-sectional samples of industrial facilities because these are the only data usually available. A specific example is utilized—water use and effluent charges in the Dutch paper industry—to show more concretely the difficulties that .arise in the analysis. This example has been developed within the framework of collaborative arrangements between IIASA and the National Institute for Water Supply RID, The Hague, The Netherlands.

Table 3.1. Products, processes, and water intake for 21 plants in the Dutch paper industry in 1974 (from Rijksinstituut voor drinkwatervoorziening, Voorburg, The Netherlands).

Plant number	Annual production (10^3 tons)	Process water intake per ton of output (m^3 per ton)	Age of technology[a]	Type of production process[b]	Product type[c]	Location (urban or rural)
1	43·50	65·54	A	A	3	U
2	133·40	55·83	A	C	1, 3, 5	U
3	91·00	34·69	AD	S	1	U
4	123·00	26·60	AD	A	5	U
5	78·80	71·87	A	A	4, 5	R
6	86·75	47·77	AD	A	4, 5	U
7	175·56	58·34	AD	C	3, 5	U
8	28·20	86·88	A	A	4, 5	R
9	43·00	40·70	AD	S	5	R
10	55·65	51·93	A	A	4	R
11	62·00	79·32	A	A	3, 5	U
12	17·20	38·55	A	S	5	R
13	33·50	30·15	O	A	4, 5	U
14	57·00	20·16	O	S	2, 4	R
15	50·00	21·06	O	S	2, 4	R
16	66·00	85·34	O	C	2, 4	R
17	131·00	26·12	A	C	4, 5	R
18	17·80	28·09	A	S	3, 4, 5	R
19	12·00	41·67	A	A	4, 5	R
20	12·20	68·85	A	C	3	R
21	49·00	45·14	O	A	2, 4	R

[a] Technology: O, old; A, average; AD, advanced.
[b] Type of production process: S, simple; A, average; C, complicated.
[c] Product type: 1, newsprint; 2, strawboard; 3, printing and writing paper; 4, packing paper and board; 5, special paper and board.

In 1974 the Dutch paper industry consisted of 38 plants. Raw materials inputs to the industry consisted of 40% waste paper and 60% pulp, two-thirds of which was imported. Data for 1974 production, process water intake per ton of product, types of product outputs, type of production technology, and location (urban-rural) of 21 of the 38 plants in the industry are shown in Table 3.1. These plants produce approximately 75% by weight of the output of the Dutch paper industry. The plants obtain their water from a combination of groundwater and surface water sources, and from the public water supply system. Of these plants, 11 withdraw some of their water from public water supply systems; 15 utilize some groundwater; and seven use surface water. Thirteen of the plants are located in rural areas.

The types of technology of the 21 plants have been characterized as old, average, or advanced. The types of production process may similarly be characterized as simple, average, or complicated. The types of products produced are newsprint, strawboard, printing paper, writing paper, and board and packing paper. Seven of the plants produce only a single product; the other 14 produce two or three of these products.

All of the plants in the sample are subject to the 1970 Surface Water Pollution Law, which requires a reduction by wastewater dischargers of approximately 90% from their 1970 discharge levels. The legislation also requires that dischargers pay an effluent fee (charge) based upon the bio-chemical oxygen demand (BOD) content of their effluents. The level of the effluent fee varies depending upon whether the discharge is into water administered by the national government (e.g., sea, large rivers, or lakes), or by provincial or local authorities. The level of the effluent fee cannot be easily related to local water quality conditions.

Choice of model structure and its functional form

The most comprehensive approach to the estimation of industrial water demand relationships would be first to estimate a production function for the Dutch paper industry from which the demand function for water (as well as for other factor inputs) could then be derived. A given production function yields specific functional forms for the factor input demand equations, which can also be directly estimated simultaneously. Functional forms for the production relationship commonly used in econometrics include Cobb–Douglas and constant elasticity of substitution. More general forms of the production relationship and the resulting derived demand functions are, however, becoming more widely used (Box and Cox 1964, Corbo and Meller 1979, Berndt and Christensen 1973, Berndt and Wood 1975, Burgess 1975, Fuss 1977, Fuss and McFadden 1978). The duality approach to the theory of production is just beginning to find applications in the area of water and wastewater demand relationships (Sims 1979).

For several reasons, little attention has been given in the literature to the specification of general production relationships for industrial facilities, or to the simultaneous estimation of factor input demand functions (see Pittman 1981 for an exception). First, for a given sample of industrial facilities, there is usually little theoretical justification for selecting one of the general functional forms postulated for production relationships.

Secondly, the estimation of production functions or demand functions for inputs such as labor, capital, energy, and chemicals requires data that are rarely available to water resource planning agencies or authorities. This is true in the example of the Dutch paper industry; information on the costs of capital, labor, and energy were unavailable, so that their collection would have entailed considerable effort. Thirdly, the small sample sizes commonly used by the water resources planner make the estimation of a system of equations (and any significant number of parameters) impossible. For example, the cross-sectional sample used by De Rooy (1974) consisted of 30 observations; that of Ginn *et al.* (1975) contained 20 observations for each of four two-digit standard industrial classification groupings; Pittman (1981) had 30 observations; and the Dutch paper industry example contains only 21 observations.[1]

Given these difficulties, the standard approach in the literature is to estimate a single-equation model, as discussed in Chapter 2:

$$Q_w = f(X_1, X_2, \ldots, X_n) + u, \tag{3.1}$$

where Q_w is the quantity of water demanded, and $f(.)$ represents the functional form of the explanatory variables (output and factor prices). Analysts have generally not been concerned whether the parameters estimated for this single equation are consistent with restrictions imposed by production theory. Since there is little *a priori* reason for selecting one production function over another, there is no preferred functional form of the single-equation water demand model. The choice of functional form is usually determined on the basis of two (sometimes conflicting) criteria: (1) best fit,[2] and (2) ease of estimation. A search for the functional form that yields the best fit can quickly become an exercise with little theoretical content. It is in practice often constrained only by the limited number of functional forms that can be easily estimated. In this Dutch paper industry example, the linear form of the single-equation model for the estimation of a water demand relationship is used.

---

[1] This focus in the literature on cross-section studies also leads to the estimation of long-term water demand elasticities. Statistical analysis of short-term industrial responses to changes in water prices has yet to be undertaken.

[2] Note that the R^2 values for linear and logarithmic functional forms cannot be compared directly to judge the best fit (see, for example, Rao and Miller 1971).

One logical way to extend this single-equation structure is to attempt to model more of the complexity of the water demand relationships within industrial facilities. For example, a plant's water intake may come from several sources such as public water supply, surface water, and groundwater. Although water withdrawals from different sources may be close substitutes, the qualities may not be identical and reliabilities may differ as well. Thus there could be different demand functions associated with each source. As another approach, De Rooy (1974) attempted to estimate demand functions for four categories of water use within chemical plants:

(1) cooling of solutions and thermal control of machinery;
(2) processing, washing, and conveying final products;
(3) steam generation in boilers;
(4) sanitation.

Such a disaggregation by type of use can be valuable when data are available. Three sources of water and four types of water use would, however, yield 12 distinct demand functions if water from each source were used for each purpose. As a practical matter, data are simply not available to estimate statistically water demand functions for more than one level of disaggregation. In the Dutch example, water use was categorized as either cooling or process water. Since many of the plants in the sample did not use water for cooling (according to the definition utilized), it was decided to focus only on process water intake.

The dependent variable in the single-equation industrial water demand model (3.1) is commonly defined as the quantity of water intake (perhaps from a given source or for a particular use) divided by some measure of the level of industrial production from the facility. This is usually weight or volume of plant output, such as tons of steel per month, but the appropriate measure will vary by industry. For instance, the level of production in a petroleum refinery might be indicated in terms of barrels of crude oil *input*, rather than some measure of output.

For some industries the choice of the measure of production level can be particularly difficult, with troublesome implications for the estimation in terms of "errors in variables". For example, the US Environmental Protection Agency (1980) standardizes water intake and wastewater discharged for the microelectronics industry (SIC 3674) in terms of the floor area of the manufacturing plant because there is neither a standard input nor output from the industry. Water use per employee and per dollar value added are other commonly suggested measures. Despite the measurement problems, if the analyst does not standardize water intake when levels of production of different plants in a cross-sectional sample vary significantly, the consequence will be to simply ensure a high R^2 because water intake is usually highly correlated with the output from an industrial facility. In this example of the Dutch paper industry, water intake is standardized by the annual production level in each plant, in terms of tons of final product output. The dependent variable is thus process water intake per ton of final product.

As indicated in Chapter 2, the next step in the statistical approach to modeling water demand relationships is to posit variables that would appear to affect water demand per unit of output. This could be done by intensive visits to various plants in the given industry and discussions with knowledgeable individuals in the industry. Economic theory suggests the following explanatory variables for use in the cross-sectional model of industrial water use:

(a) prices of other factor inputs;
(b) type of technology or production process;
(c) product mix;
(d) output level;
(e) "price of water".

The same set of variables, plus the possibility of lagged values, would be used for a model to be estimated with time series data.

Data on the prices of factor inputs other than water present problems not only because they are hard for water authorities to obtain, but also because they may be difficult for the industrial facilities themselves to calculate. An obvious example is the cost of capital, for which the economist's and accountant's definitions are considerably different. Similarly, for other inputs, the data available are likely to be for average accounting costs, not marginal opportunity costs.

If variables for the prices of other factor inputs are not included in the single-equation model, this will lead to a specification error, and the estimated coefficients will be biased and inconsistent if the factor prices vary between the plants in the sample and are correlated with the explanatory variables included in the model.[3] In the Dutch example, one is forced to live with this specification error. Since the plants are located in a relatively small, homogeneous region, this is not anticipated to be a major concern for such inputs as labor, energy, and other raw materials. The cost of capital, however, could differ substantially between plants in close proximity.

Regarding other potential explanatory variables, one might hypothesize that the type of technology and the type of products would be significant in determining the quantity of water intake. To account for these factors in the

---

[3] One method of addressing the problem of missing prices for other factor inputs that has been suggested (Ginn et al. 1975) is to include in the water demand equation a proxy variable defined as the cost of water as a percentage of the firm's income. The use of such variables should be treated with caution, however.

Dutch example, three dummy variables have been defined: M (age of technology), T (type of production process), and Pr (product type). M and T can each take any one of three values in the single-equation model. Operationally, this means that there must be two dummy variables in the regression equation to represent each of these three-way classifications, and thus each requires the estimation of two regression coefficients. In nine of the 21 plants, the most important product is "special paper and board"; in the other 12 the most important product is something else. The Pr variable is therefore defined so that it can take one of two values—either special paper and board or *not* special paper and board. Hence, only one coefficient needs to be estimated. The use of so many dummy variables is a costly practice in terms of the limited degrees of freedom available with such a small sample, and the interpretation of the results will necessarily be somewhat speculative.

The level of plant output could be hypothesized to affect the standardized water intake if there are economies of scale in in-plant recirculation systems, wastewater treatment, or certain managerial and organizational functions. It is thus included in the model.

The price of water

One of the principle objectives of more explicit modeling of water demand relationships is to incorporate the influence of "price" on the quantities of water demanded and discharged. However, including a "price of water" variable as one of the explanatory variables in the single-equation model is, somewhat ironically, the source of many of the difficulties with the statistical estimation of water demand relationships.

Industries either obtain their water supplies directly from surface and groundwater sources, or from municipal water supply systems. The appropriate treatment of the "price of water" variable in the statistical model depends upon which of these situations (or both) exists for the industrial facilities in the sample. Since in many countries there has typically been no charge for self-supplied surface or groundwater, nor any regulation of the quantity withdrawn, industrial facilities have often faced an *externally* established price of zero. In recent years pollution control requirements have been imposed in many countries, which have increased the costs associated with water intake and wastewater discharge. The precise form of the pollution control requirements (effluent taxes or standards, for either wastewater volume or residual mass) influence the manner in which an industrial facility adjusts its water-use patterns, but, as shown in Chapter 1, more stringent pollution control measures usually reduce water intake and wastewater discharges because the costs of using water are higher.

What price of water should be included in the single-equation model in this situation? Economic theory requires the use of the marginal, not average, price. If average prices or costs are used instead of marginal prices, the model will be mis-specified, and the estimates will be biased (Howe and Linaweaver 1967, Gibbs 1978).

In practice, when an industry withdraws water directly from surface or groundwater sources, analysts have tried to determine an *internally* established price of water (Ginn *et al.* 1975, De Rooy 1974). Such estimates have been calculated by dividing, for example, the total annual capital, and operating and maintenance costs for an industrial facility by the quantity of water intake. This obviously yields an average cost, not the desired marginal cost. For a time series analysis with only one plant, some approximation of the facility's marginal costs might be feasible, but for the water resources planner to attempt such a calculation for each facility in a cross-sectional sample could be quite expensive. Such a task would be greatly complicated by the fact that different plants would use different accounting methods for depreciation and taxes in the calculation of their costs of capital.

Differences in average or marginal costs between plants in a cross-sectional sample could result for several reasons, such as economies of scale in water treatment, variations in water quality between sources, and different depths to groundwater aquifers. As noted in Chapter 2, if the marginal costs vary as the quantity of water changes, two problems arise. First, the use of average or marginal cost in the model as the price of water variable creates a simultaneity problem because the price of water and the quantity of water intake are jointly determined. In this case ordinary least-squares is inappropriate. Instrumental variables or, more generally, two-stage least-squares estimation can be used to address this problem, but unfortunately, in cross-sectional industrial water demand analyses, there is no obvious candidate for an appropriate instrument.

Secondly, if the price variable is endogenous rather than exogenous, the demand function may be unidentified (depending on the specification of the other explanatory variables and the function relating the cost of water to the quantity withdrawn), and additional information may be required to distinguish the demand and supply relationships (see Chapter 2). In this case, the "supply" function is not a market determination, but rather the *internal* cost function for obtaining water.

This question of the identification of the single-equation water demand model should logically be raised prior to its estimation, but analysts have often concluded that the demand function has been estimated if a regression analysis yields a negative coefficient for the price variable. The argument is that an upward-sloping supply or cost function would yield a positive coefficient. Such a conclusion is unjustified in any case, but is particularly suspect if the price of water variable is calculated as an internally established

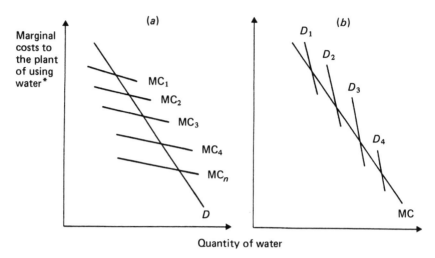

Figure 3.1. (*a*) Estimation of a demand function. (*b*) Estimation of a supply function. *The identification problem would, of course, still arise if the marginal cost curves were upward-sloping.

cost of using water. If there are economies of scale in the use of water, the average and marginal cost curves for water faced by a plant will be downward-sloping.

The reason why this complicates the estimation of the water demand function is illustrated in Figure 3.1. Figure 3.1(*a*) depicts a situation in which the regression model estimates the desired demand relationship. Different supply functions for the sample of plants trace out the downward-sloping demand curve—the higher the marginal costs of water use, the less water is demanded by the plant. Figure 3.1(*b*) illustrates a situation in which the regression model estimates the supply relationship—the more water a facility uses, the lower the marginal costs of water. In this case different demand functions for the sample of plants trace out the downward-sloping marginal cost curve of water. Both situations yield a negative coefficient on the price of water variable in the regression model. Unless the demand function can be properly identified, the analyst cannot determine whether the estimation has yielded a demand function, a supply function, or some combination of the two.

The second situation of interest concerns industries that purchase water from public water systems. Industries on municipal water supply systems typically pay a per unit charge for water intake and often for effluent disposal. Such externally established prices can be based on a variety of types of rate structures, such as flat, uniform, increasing block, or decreasing block. A flat rate is a fixed minimum charge regardless of the quantity of water used (or wastewater discharged), and can be combined with uniform pricing (the per unit charge is fixed regardless of the quantity used) or block pricing (the per unit charge is a step function of the quantity of water used).

The special statistical problems created by the existence of such rate structures have only recently been recognized in the water demand literature (Agthe and Billings 1980, Billings and Agthe 1980, Foster and Beattie 1979, Griffin and Martin 1981, 1982, Griffin et al. 1981, Howe 1982). The marginal "price" is the charge or cost that can be avoided or changed by the industrial facility, and thus reflects the real opportunity cost of using water. When the price of water is *not* a function of the quantity withdrawn (or purchased), the price of water is predetermined, or exogenous, in the model, and the marginal price is unambiguously the appropriate variable. However, when a declining or increasing block rate structure is in effect for an industry purchasing water from a public water supply authority, price is once again a function of quantity withdrawn, and vice versa. This simultaneity problem is likely to be more serious the greater the number of blocks in the rate structure and the closer a facility is operating to one of the changes in the block. The standard practice in the residential water demand literature until recently has been to use the block rate in which each consumer's use falls as the price of water variable (Howe and Linaweaver 1967, Gibbs 1978, Danielson 1979). In the case of a declining or increasing block rate structure, however, Taylor (1975) points out that:

> The use of a marginal price for "the" price variable . . . only conveys part of the information required; for a single marginal price is relevant to a consumer's decision only when he is consuming in the block to which it attaches; it governs behavior while the consumer is in that block, but does not, in and of itself, determine why he consumes in that block as opposed to some other block.

The basic point of Taylor's argument is that the marginal price associated with such residential rate structures (in this case for electricity) does not capture the income effect associated with a change in intramarginal charges. For example, if one consumer faces a declining block rate structure and another faces an increasing block, the marginal price each pays could be the same, but their total water bills could be substantially different. If the quantity of water consumed is a function of both the marginal price of water and income level, the consumer with the declining block rate structure would have a higher water bill, a lower real income, and thus would consume less water. The use of a marginal price variable alone would not adequately characterize the relevant information in the rate structure.

An analogous situation exists with the estimation of industrial water demand relationships when industrial facilities purchase water from public water authorities with declining or increasing block rate structures. A marginal price variable will largely measure the substitution effect of a change in the price of water—i.e., the higher the marginal price of water, the less water will be used for a given output level because factor proportions will shift in response to the change in price. The marginal price variable is not sufficient to capture adequately the output effect; i.e., for a given factor proportion, a higher total water bill leads to higher output prices, which in turn lead to reduced production and less water use.

To measure the effect of intramarginal price changes on the quantity demanded, Taylor recommended the use of a second price variable in the single-equation demand model, which would be constructed as the average price paid over all the steps of the block structure before the marginal step. Nordin (1976) suggested that a better way to construct this second price variable would be to measure the difference between the customer's actual bill and what the quantity used would cost if the consumer paid the marginal price for all units purchased. Billings and Agthe (1980) and Howe (1982) used this difference variable in their estimation of residential water demand relationships.

This elaboration of the water demand model in the context of rate structures has yet to be attempted in the industrial water demand literature. It is not likely to be a fruitful avenue for research with respect to industrial water intake, however, because the costs of water intake are typically a very small fraction of the total costs of water use. By far the largest portion of the costs associated with using water for an industrial facility are usually pollution control costs. On the other hand, if wastewater effluent charges vary as a function of the quantity discharged according to some rate structure, this approach of including a second price variable in the single-equation model has immediate, practical applications.

The price of water variable presents an additional practical difficulty for the analyst. Because sample sizes of industrial facilities are so small, analysts cannot effectively estimate separately all the different dimensions of water demand listed in Chapter 2. Thus, in order to estimate some aggregate measure of responsiveness of water intake to changes in the costs of using water, a common practice has been to construct composite price variables that are the sum of the unit costs of water from all sources (surface, ground, and public water supply) weighted by their relative quantities and the unit costs of effluent disposal. For example, a price of water variable used by De Rooy (1974) was the sum of three unit costs:

(1) the weighted unit cost of intake purchased from a public utility intake pumped from a well or stream;
(2) the unit cost of any treatment prior to use; and
(3) the unit cost of disposal (including any waste treatment).

Such a composite price variable assumes that the relationship between water intake and water discharged is fixed. More importantly, the issues of identification, simultaneity, and the appropriate representation of the rate structure are confounded because some of the unit costs may be simultaneously determined (and thus endogenous), while others may be exogenous.

In the Dutch paper industry example, data for unit costs of water intake from all three sources were average costs and functions of the quantity withdrawn. To include them in the model—individually or as part of a composite variable—would introduce four serious problems:

(i)   average rather than marginal prices would be used;
(ii) prices and quantities would be determined jointly and simultaneity bias would result;
(iii) the water demand function would not be identified; and
(iv) the rate structure of the public water authorities would not be accurately characterized.

Such problems can only be adequately solved by more and better data.

The BOD effluent charges of the Dutch water authorities, however, are fixed regardless of the quantity of wastewater discharged by a facility. They are thus marginal prices and are not jointly determined with the quantity of water intake. Therefore, the effluent charge has been used as the price of water in the single-equation model. The hypothesis to test is thus more restrictive than the general water demand relationship; i.e., whether changes in the effluent charge affect the level of water intake. Another logical hypothesis to test would be whether the quantity of wastewater and its BOD content decrease as the level of the effluent tax increases (Sims 1979). Unfortunately, data were not available on the quantity and quality of the wastewater discharged.

Results of the analysis

Ordinary least-squares regression was used to estimate a linear function relating process water intake per unit of product output to the proposed explanatory variables—effluent charge (price of water), output, type of technology, production process, and product mix. The output and dummy variables for product mix and type of technology did not have significant coefficients and were eliminated from further consideration. Table 3.2 shows the results of the linear estimation with effluent charge and type of production process (as a two-way classification: either "simple" or "average or complicated") included as explanatory variables. This equation was judged to be the best in terms of the test statistics.

Considering first the F statistic for the entire equation, it is possible to reject at more than the 99 % level the null hypothesis that all the estimated coefficients are equal to zero. An examination of the F values for the individual regression coefficients reveals, first, that the coefficient on the

Table 3.2. Results of a regression analysis applied to water demand at 21 plants in the Dutch paper industry.

Regression equation: $(Q_{iw}/P) = \alpha_1 + \alpha_2 \, (p_w) + \alpha_3 \, (T)$

Source	Degrees of freedom	Sum of squares	Mean square
Model	2	3521·0	1760·0
Error	18	4931·0	274·0
Corrected total	20	8452.0	

F value	6·43
Probability $> F$	0·0078
R^2	0·42
Mean of Q_{iw}/P	49·2
Standard deviation	16·6

	Estimate	t for H_0 parameter $= 0$	Probability $> (t)$	Standard error of estimate
Intercept (α_1)	41·0	5·02	0·0001	8·18
α_2	−1·1	−1·95	0·0668	0·58
α_3	24·4	3·06	0·0068	8·00

effluent charge variable is statistically different from zero at more than the 93% confidence level and has the expected negative sign. Secondly, the coefficient on the production process dummy variable is statistically different from zero at more than the 99% confidence level, and is positive, indicating that more complicated production technology requires increased process water per unit of output.

Since the linear functional form was used, the estimated elasticity of process water intake per unit of output with respect to the effluent charge is not constant. At the mean sample value for the quantity of water intake per unit of output $(Q_{iw}/P = 49·2)$ and an effluent charge of 0·11 guilders/m³, this elasticity is −0·25. Given that these facilities have already accomplished substantial reductions in discharge, *a priori* this would be considered a reasonable result (Sims 1979). The R^2 value of 0.42 indicates that there are significant variations in process water intake per unit of output among the plants that are not explained by this simple regression model. This R^2 value is, however, typical of such cross-sectional industrial water demand studies.

Conclusions

One might logically ask how this model could be improved. This section has alluded to several methods, but unfortunately many of these require a larger sample of plants, as well as more data for each plant. Because the mix of raw materials probably varied significantly among plants in the sample, and because water use is affected by the type of raw materials, a raw materials variable could have been included. Because each plant faces effluent standards as well as the effluent fee, one might try to devise an effluent standards variable to include in the equation. If more observations were available, simultaneous equation methods could be used to estimate the water demand function with separate variables for the unit price of process water intake and for the unit fee imposed upon the BOD in the effluent discharge, and to try to determine their impact on different water streams within a facility.

As a practical tool for water resources planners, statistical estimation of industrial water demand relationships is, however, still in its infancy. The small sample sizes commonly available, the lack of necessary data for even those plants in the sample, and the simultaneous determination of the price of water and the quantity of water used pose estimation problems for the analyst which cannot be ignored or treated casually.

Mathematical Programming Approach to Modeling Industrial Water Demand Relationships: Electricity Generation in Poland*

Mathematical programming has for some time been an important tool for modeling industrial operations. Such models have been widely applied to the

* John C. Stone wishes to acknowledge and thank a host of colleagues and friends for their assistance and cooperation in the conception and development of the Vistula case study and its model of electricity generation. From IIASA: Janusz Kindler, Leader of the Water Demand Research Task, for project conception, initiation, and management; Witold Sikorski for technical, system development, and programming assistance; William Orchard-Hays for assistance in model solution; Denise Promper for clerical assistance and logistics; and Christine Swales for editorial assistance. From the Institute of Meteorology and Water Management and other Polish organizations: Zdzislaw Kaczmarek, Director of the Institute; Jerzy Pruchnicki, Deputy Director of the Institute, for air pollution modeling; Mieczyslaw Gadkowski for project conception, technical specification, process configurations and cost estimates; Andrzej Salewicz for technical, system development, and programming assistance; Karol Budzinski for air pollution modeling; Hanna Spoz-Dragan for meteorological/hydrological data; Ewa Czarnecka for clerical assistance, interpretation, and logistics; Aleksander Łaski (Hydroproject) for model review and advice and water policy specifications; and Czestaw Mejro (Warsaw Technical University) for model review and advice. From the University of Houston, Industry Studies Program: Russell G. Thompson, Director for project conception, initiation, and supervision; and F. Dail Singleton, Jr, principal architect of technical relationships and matrix generators for generation and cooling processes.

solution of scheduling, resource allocation, and transportation problems. Models have also been developed for analyzing and forecasting industrial activities under new economic and/or regulatory conditions, and since the early 1970s serious attempts have been made to expand them to include considerations of residuals generation and management. Many of these attempts have their conceptual origins in the work of Russell (1973). Plant-level models of petroleum refining (Russell 1973) and of iron and steel production (Russell and Vaughan 1976) have been developed in the US at Resources for the Future. Plant- and industry-level models have been developed at the University of Houston, Texas, for electricity generation, petroleum refining, and manufacture of several important chemical products, such as chlorine and caustic soda, ammonia and other nitrogenous fertilizers, ethylene and other organic chemicals, synthetic rubber, and certain plastics and polyesters (Thompson *et al.* 1976, 1977, 1978). Plant-level models of paper mills have been developed by Sawyer *et al.* (1976) and Noukka (1978).

The water demand study described here developed as a collaborative arrangement between IIASA, the Institute of Meteorology and Water Management (IMGW), Warsaw, Poland, and the Industry Studies Program of the University of Houston, Texas. The operational objective of this collaborative effort was the development and application of a mathematical programming model of a hypothetical, coal-fired power plant located on the Wisła (Vistula) River in Poland. This choice of focus for the study reflected the recognition that electricity generation is an enormously important component of industrial water demand. The problem, while hypothetical, deals with sufficiently realistic issues to render the results of the analysis useful to Polish decision makers. The objective of the modeling effort was thus analytical rather than predictive—specifically, the development of a tool for quantifying the impact on water demand of alternative resource prices and standards for both pollutant discharges and environmental quality.

Figure 3.2 provides a geographical perspective on the modeled decision problem. The plant is assumed to be located on the middle reach of the Vistula River and has a rated capacity of 3000 MW (net). The potentially substantial water demands of the power plant are supplied exclusively from the river, with the minor exception of slurry water recycling. The significant quantities of coal required to fire the plant are to be transported from the Silesia mining region, approximately 300 km distant. Two alternative grades of coal are available—run-of-mine or "regular" coal, and washed or "beneficiated" coal—and two modes of transport are possible: railroad and slurry pipeline. A third option of barge transport was dismissed as currently uneconomical. The principal economic decisions for the plant are: the mix of coal types to burn, the mode of coal transport, and the design and operation of the plant cooling system.

Figure 3.2. The geographical setting of the modeled problem.

The configuration of the cooling system is the principal determinant of water demand for the plant. Flow levels in the middle reach of the Vistula are not so low as to impose direct restrictions on the intake of water, but problems with heat discharge render it impossible to operate an entirely "once-through" cooling system the whole year round. The problem, therefore, is to determine the optimal design and schedule of operating for a combined cooling system that can operate in an appropriate combination of open- and closed-cycle modes, depending upon the situation (these terms are defined below). This optimal design and pattern of operation are a complicated function of capital and operating costs, meteorological/hydrological conditions, environmental quality standards, and any prices or charges imposed on water withdrawals, water consumption, and effluent discharges.

The provision of boiler fuel is also modeled in some detail, both because of the importance of fuel provision in power plant economics and because of a desire to make the model robust enough to study issues other than water demand. Each of the problems of coal supply, transport, and air emissions control is important enough in its own right, but various water-related aspects of the fuel provision issue also merit consideration in the model.

The problems of water management in a power plant cannot be completely divorced from other aspects of plant design and operation. Water is only one of the basic factors of production, and accurate modeling of the derived demand relationships for water requires due consideration of the full range of relevant factor substitutions in production activities. For electricity generation it is probably sufficient to consider three factors: capital, water, and fuel. To this end, the present study has developed a model of resource use in electricity generation, which is believed to represent the variables and constraints of greatest importance in determining water demand, and also provide a modeling base for analysis of other relevant issues.

The dimensions of water demand in electricity generation

Before proceeding to a description of the model itself, it may prove useful to highlight the various dimensions of water demand as they relate to power plant operations. The discussion in Chapter 1 identifies five static dimensions of water demand (withdrawal, consumption, gross water applied, quantity and quality of wastewater discharge) and adds a sixth dimension pertaining to the time pattern of the first five. The problem of water management in an electric power facility provides an excellent illustration of the high degree of interdependence between these six dimensions.

In a purely static context, it is virtually impossible to reduce any one of the first five dimensions of water demand without thereby affecting (often increasing) one or more of the other four. As an example, reducing water withdrawals by closing the cooling system increases water consumption at the plant through evaporation and drift losses in the cooling tower. This closing of the system also virtually eliminates heat discharges but may increase solids discharges. Reducing heat discharges through the use of a cooling tower increases water losses. Reducing solids discharges by treatment entails certain minor losses in the process but provides a recycle stream that allows for some reduction in water withdrawals. Water consumption is not a flow that can be altered directly, but is a consequence that can be affected by changing the time patterns of withdrawals and discharges. Finally, the impact of any alteration in the pattern of water use on thermal efficiency produces secondary effects on the magnitudes of all flows in the system.

In short, it is inappropriate to consider any one of the first five dimensions of water demand in isolation. The overall pattern of water demand (in all dimensions) is a complicated, *simultaneous* function of the standards and charges pertaining to all six dimensions of water demand (plus everything else in the system). The ability of mathematical programming models to perform this simultaneous determination of optimal flow patterns is one of the key attractions to their use in modeling water demand relationships.

With respect to the time dimension, it is no great revelation to point out the time dependence of the pattern of water use in electricity generation. At a trivial minimum, any idealized model of an industrial operation must define a period of time over which all flows are averaged and measured. Beyond this definitional requirement, however, is the more important consideration of variations over time in the important conditions that influence the pattern of industrial operations, including water use. In baseload electricity generation, the most significant of these time-dependent conditions (which may reasonably be called exogenous variables) are output level, meteorological and hydrological conditions, and specified constraints and charges on resource use, discharges, and other plant operations. The optimal time pattern of the full spectrum of plant operations is a complicated function of the time pattern of variation in the exogenous variables. Thus, the interactions between the five static dimensions of water demand cannot be properly identified and measured without some specification of the relevant time frame for plant operations.

Organization of discussion

The discussion of the case study is divided into three parts. First, a general description of the structure and components of the mathematical model is provided, in essentially nonmathematical terms. Secondly, the process of model construction and specification is outlined, including some comments on the available data for specifying model coefficients and a note on seasonality. The third part is directed to model use and results, including a brief discussion of model operation, size and computability, a description of the kinds of analyses that can be performed with the model, and a summary and analysis of representative model results.

A Nonmathematical Description of the Model

The general formulation of a mathematical programming model has been defined in Chapter 2. This section describes the structure and substance of the model in conceptual terms, without resorting to complicated algebraic notation. The description addresses each of the principal components of the programming model in turn: decision variables, objective function, and constraints. Some discussion is also included of the integer requirements and of the structural representation of seasonality in the model.

The model of resource use in electricity generation belongs to the general class of mixed-integer programming problems. It can be conceptually specified as follows:

minimize
- annual net costs of production
subject to
- seasonal production requirements;
- seasonal constraints on discharges to the water;
- seasonal constraints on discharges to the air;
- non-negativity of decision variables (simple constraints to prevent logical and physical absurdities);
- integer (0, 1) requirements on certain variables.

Decision variables

The set of process variables (columns) in a programming model is typically composed of two classes of model activities: a set of decision variables representing the array of controllable real-world options; and a set of "artificial" variables that perform certain logical, accounting, and integrating functions within the model. This latter set is fairly extensive and quite important in the operation of the model, but merits no particular discussion. The emphasis is more on the process combination decisions that together provide the optimal solution for the plant.

Needless to say, electricity generation is a complex process involving a myriad of decision points in both plant design and day-to-day plant operation. The model developed for this study identifies a limited number of design and operating decisions that are believed to be the most significant determinants of water- and fuel-use patterns in the plant modeled. These key decisions are listed here; a more detailed description is provided in a subsequent section. The principal design decisions modeled are:

- design temperature rise of cooling water across plant condensers;
- capacity of the cooling tower and water treatment facilities;
- capacity of coal slurry transport facilities (if any); and
- height of the stack for diffusing gaseous discharges.

The principal (seasonal) operating decisions are:

- basic flow pattern of plant cooling water, which itself comprises a set of decisions;
- disposition of cooling tower blowdown;
- disposition of slurry water (if any) and other briny streams; and
- mix of alternative coal types burned.

Two other important decisions are predetermined. First, the size of plant is given as 3000 MW net, divided into six basically identical blocks (or units) of

500 MW net each. Secondly, since by its nature the modeled facility is a baseload plant, the level of output is essentially determined by the number of blocks in operation at a given time and the expected rate of utilization for operational units. In a new baseload plant, this rate of utilization will tend to be high, and it is furthermore desirable to keep it fairly constant. For present modeling purposes, therefore, it can be reasonably assumed that the average utilization rate is constant, at least over a short enough period of time. In terms of defining the problem for the present study, this means that the size of plant and level of output (in net terms) cease to be economic decision variables. Gross capacity and output will vary because of the impact of various decision variables on plant efficiency.

Logically, the domain of relevant operating decisions is dependent upon the design decisions, and the impact on operating decisions must be considered in the design decisions. The patterns of water withdrawal, consumption, and discharge are derived results of these operating and design decisions.

Objective function

The cost-minimizing objective function specified for the model may be resolved into the following components:

(1) annual charge for capital investments;
(2) operating costs (or penalties) for the following activities in each season:
   ● electricity generation;
   ● water withdrawals and consumption;
   ● water handling and treatment;
   ● waterborne residuals discharges;
   ● coal supply;
   ● coal transportation and handling;
   ● coal combustion (including sulfur penalty); and
(3) cost reduction applied for extra supplies of coal transported by pipeline (if any).

The annual capital charge of 12% is based on a 4% depreciation charge and an 8% discount rate. The other cost coefficients, as well as the capital investment requirements to which the capital charge is applied, are based on either engineering estimates or policy specifications. While it is not appropriate here to detail the engineering cost estimates, the following policy-dependent prices and penalties are identified, which may be varied by the user for purposes of demand analysis and impact evaluation:

● price of water withdrawals;
● price of water consumption (losses);

- penalty for heat discharges;
- penalty for dissolved solids discharges in excess of a defined standard (except the discharges from open-cycle cooling systems);
- penalty per percent of sulfur per ton of coal combusted;
- price of coal.

A cost-minimization objective is specified in this study for a number of reasons. First, a properly derived demand analysis requires that all factor inputs be evaluated according to a common unit of measure, and monetary cost is a commonly used criterion for analysis of industrial production activities. Secondly, this specification seems to be consistent with the planning structure of the industry and economy. Thirdly, because of the essentially predetermined output profile of a baseload plant, a profit-maximizing objective would reduce to cost minimization anyway. Finally, using monetary cost permits a comparison between the indirect values and prices derived by the model with those of other models and applications using the same measure.

This choice of objective function does not imply that the optimum "social" decision for design and operation of the power plant is necessarily based on production cost minimization alone; this decision may require a much broader purview and consideration of nonmonetary objectives. To some extent, it has been possible to incorporate some of these broader social perspectives and objectives in the form of constraints, prices, and penalties in the programming model. These specifications can in turn be used in performing economically sound analyses of cost and derived demand for use in the social decision process. In other cases, the relevant social considerations may not be so readily parametrized, and analysis proceeds by solving the model under various assumptions (or scenarios) so as to obtain some quantitative measure of the social trade-offs.

Constraints

As is the case with most complex programming models, a significant portion of the constraints set for the model is composed of equations representing logical conditions, performing accounting functions, and assuring proper materials and energy balances. In addition, the model includes three subsets of constraints which, in the more conventional sense of the term, represent actual requirements or limitations imposed on plant activities. Each of these is briefly described below.

Seasonal Production Requirements

The temporal pattern of plant output levels is translated into the model as a set of seasonal production requirements specifying the total number of MW-hours that must be generated (for transmission) in each season. These requirements take the form of a (greater than) row constraint for each season, and the dual values (shadow prices) associated with these rows may be interpreted as marginal costs of producing electricity in each season.

Seasonal Constraints on Discharges to the Water

Four types of constraints are imposed on discharges of waterborne residuals. The first two are based on defined ambient standards, while the latter two are defined standards for the effluent stream itself. These standards may be summarized as follows:

(1) maximum allowable increases in river temperature
   ● 4°C in June, July, August,
   ● 5°C in September,
   ● 6°C in all other months,
(2) maximum allowable river temperature
   ● 30°C,
(3) maximum allowable temperature of plant discharge
   ● 35°C,
(4) maximum concentration of dissolved solids in discharge (except that from open-cycle cooling systems)
   ● 500 mg/l.

In constraint (4), higher concentrations are not strictly prohibited, but a penalty is applied for each kg of excessive solids discharge. In the model, only the stricter of constraints (1) and (2) is specified for a given month. It is not readily determined whether this constraint is more or less strict than constraint (3) in a given month; hence, both constraint (3) and the stricter of constraints (1) and (2) are specified.

The algebraic formulation of these constraints is somewhat complicated because of a need to express quantity-weighted averages in terms of quantities not known until the model solution is calculated. By careful formulation of intermediate accounting structures, however, each standard is ultimately expressed as a single (less than) constraint for each season. Interpretation of the dual values for these constraints requires algebraic manipulation to express them in meaningful terms.

Seasonal Constraints on Discharges to the Air

An ambient standard for the maximum allowable ground level concentration of sulfur dioxide is established by policy. For any given season, the difference between this standard and an expected background concentration may be interpreted as the maximum allowable concentration that may be produced by emissions from the power plant in that season. In order to incorporate the ambient standard in the model, it is necessary to translate this concentration allowance into an emission constraint for the modeled coal combustion activities. This translation has been accomplished with the aid of an atmospheric dispersion model developed by the IMGW. Solutions to this model have determined—for each season and for a range of alternative stack heights over 150 m—the maximum ratio of regular to beneficiated coal that can be combusted at full load consistent with the allowed increment in ground level SO_2 concentration. This ratio can in turn be converted into upper limits on the amounts of regular coal and of total coal—regular plus beneficiated—that can be combusted in a given season at a particular stack height.

In the model, these upper limits take the form of two row constraints for each season. These constraints directly limit the quantities of coal combusted to amounts specified internally by the design choice of stack height; that is, for each additional meter of stack height constructed, an increment is added to the allowable amounts of regular and total coal combustion. The dual values for these constraints, only one of which can be binding in any season, represent the potential savings to the plant of burning one more ton of coal given a fixed stack height as determined in the solution.

Integer requirements

A limited number of integer $(0, 1)$ variables are included in the model to impose certain logical constraints on plant design and to ensure proper consideration of economies of scale in slurry pipeline construction. Because the capacity of the power plant is predetermined, scale economies can be properly accounted for by calculating costs appropriate to an installation containing six 500 MW blocks. It is important, however, to ensure that only one "type" of power plant is constructed with respect to the design temperature rise across the condenser; this requires integer variables. A similar integer control structure is required to ensure complete and exclusive construction of only one size of slurry pipeline instead of linear bits and pieces of various sizes.

Seasonal structure

The time dimension is incorporated in the model by dividing the year into seasons and modeling plant operations in each season in accordance with seasonally specified values for exogenous variables. These seasonal operations are tied together by certain annual resource constraints, and a fixed design decision is a function of the operating conditions in all seasons, while the optimal pattern of operations in a given season is dependent upon the operations in all other seasons through the common demands on annual resources and the design configuration. Again, the optimal overall decision requires a simultaneous determination of the design decision and all seasonal operating decisions, consistent with the seasonal time pattern of specified exogenous variables.

The essence of this interdependence and simultaneity must be incorporated in the mathematical structure of the model; fortunately, this is not especially difficult. Seasonality is handled in a straightforward manner by defining separate column variables and constraints to represent plant operations in each season. The structures of the seasonal submatrices are virtually identical, but for each season a separate set of parameters represents charges for water use and residuals discharges, available supplies of water and other resources, and allowable discharges to the air and water. The coefficients of the electricity generation processes also vary, thus reflecting the impact of output level and of meteorological and hydrological factors on the operating conditions of the power plant and cooling system. A careful distinction is made between activities representing the provision of capital capacity for a given process (a one-time occurrence) and the operation of that process in each defined season. In each seasonal activity, capital capacity (if relevant) is treated much as any other required input, and a separate (one-time) activity is modeled jointly to provide capital capacity for all defined seasons.

Model Construction and Specification

This section describes the construction and specification of the model, following a typical logical sequence in the development of a programming model. First, the basic process options are identified and depicted, where helpful, in the form of flow diagrams. Secondly, modeling correspondences are established between the components of the flow diagrams and the rows and columns of the model matrix. Thirdly, model activities and constraints are logically and algebraically formulated, and, fourthly, the coefficients of model column activities are specified. The section concludes with some comments on data availability (an issue that must always be kept in mind when developing the structure of a model), and a note on seasonality.

Basic process options

With the aid of three flow diagrams, the basic process options represented in the programming model are outlined. Figure 3.3 gives an overview of processes and materials flows with emphasis on activities outside the basic electricity generation processes. Figure 3.4 displays in greater detail the

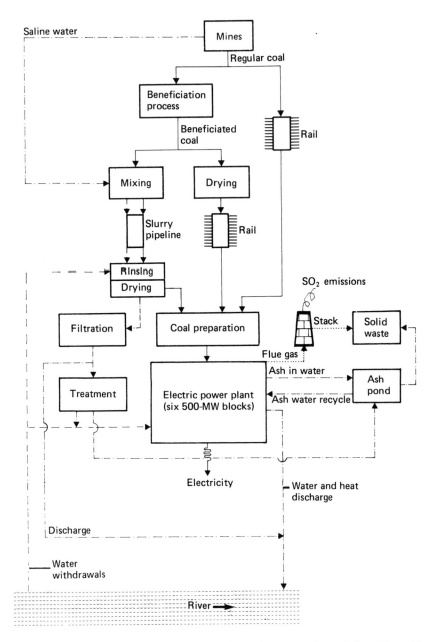

Figure 3.3. Flows of processes and materials in the generation of electricity with emphasis on coal handling and combustion, where – – – denotes river water, – · – denotes polluted water, —— denotes coal, and · · · · denotes flue gas or solid waste.

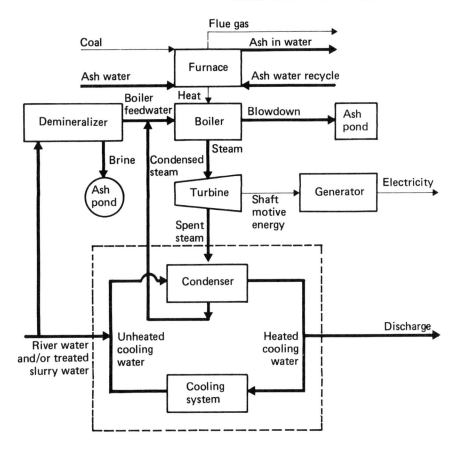

Figure 3.4. Basic unit processes for the electric power plant.

processes contained in the box for the electric power plant in Figure 3.3, identifying the major flows of water, steam, and fuel-related materials. Figure 3.5 shows the alternative configurations for the plant cooling system and is essentially a detailed expansion of the processes and flows in the dashed rectangle of Figure 3.4. A more comprehensive discussion of the process options may be found in Stone *et al.* (1982).

Fuel Provision Activities

Figure 3.3 gives an overview of the entire operation, with emphasis on the activities related to fuel provision. The coal supply for the modeled plant is assumed to be obtained from four Silesian mines with a combined annual

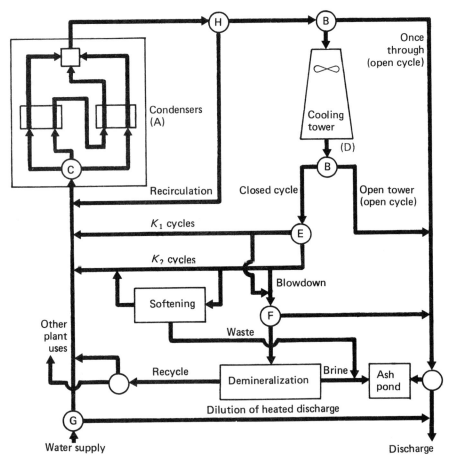

Figure 3.5. Cooling system options.

capacity of perhaps twice the expected coal requirement for the power plant. Mined coal may be transported directly to the plant site by rail, or may be beneficiated (crushed, washed, and gravimetrically separated) to produce a coal of higher heat content and lower ash and sulfur content. The beneficiated coal may be transported to the plant site via rail or slurry pipeline. The slurry transport of regular (run-of-mine) coal or barge transport of either grade of coal are not modeled because preliminary cost calculations showed these options to be currently uneconomical in all circumstances.

None of these mining, beneficiation, or transportation processes is modeled in any great detail. Emphasis is on accurate representation of the costs of these operations and the water balances for the slurry pipeline. A one-to-one ratio is assumed for the water/coal mixture in the slurry; and IMGW estimates water losses—primarily through absorption—at 12%.

Another consideration concerning cost and water use involves water management in the mining region. Planners believe that the water used for slurry preparation and transport could be supplied from the large volumes of saline wastewater generated in mining operations, but a major technical question to be resolved with respect to this option is the corrosive potential of such wastewater on the pipeline itself. If saline water use proves feasible, a significant disposal problem will be alleviated as some of the wastewater can be transported away from the mining area, where river flow is naturally low. From a social point of view, the economics of slurry pipelines should incorporate these benefits, and the model includes an appropriate reduction in the operating costs of the pipeline to account for them.

The cost to be balanced against this benefit arises from the logical consequence that, at the plant site, slurry-transported coal must be dewatered, and the separated water must be discharged or treated for use in plant operations. While the flow of slurry water is not great, its high dissolved solids concentration renders its disposal a nontrivial water management consideration. The optimal decision depends upon the price of water withdrawals and on any environmental standards or effluent charges on dissolved solids discharges. The management of slurry water is thus one of the areas of interaction between the issues of water demand and of the provision of boiler fuel.

Another area of interaction relates to the impact of the cost of boiler fuel on the economic substitutability of cooling systems. The reductions in plant thermal efficiency attributable to the utilization of a cooling tower results in a higher fuel requirement per net kilowatt-hour of power generated. This energy penalty must be considered along with the additional capital requirements, in the comparative economics of open- and closed-cycle cooling systems. Proper evaluation of this energy penalty in turn requires consideration, at least to the extent of costing, of the full range of fuel provision activities from coal supply, to transport, to combustion, in accordance with applicable standards for gaseous residuals discharges.

The available alternatives for the "control" of air emissions are the mix of run-of-mine and beneficiated coal combusted—the plant cannot operate entirely on regular-grade coal because of SO_2 standards—and the stack height, which affects the dispersion of gaseous discharges rather than emission levels. The disposal of solid waste from coal-handling and combustion operations are considered only to the extent of assignment of costs.

Electricity Generation Processes

Figure 3.4 illustrates the major interrelationships between the most basic processes for power generation. Flows to and from the boundaries of this figure directly correspond to the flows entering and leaving the power plant in Figure 3.3. Figure 3.4 shows the basic water-use patterns for process cooling, boiler make-up, and ash removal. Certain other minor uses, such as cleaning water for the boiler, are omitted from the figure but are included in the modeling analysis. Of the three types of water uses depicted, the boiler make-up and ash water flows are fairly small. The more substantial flows used in process cooling and the alternative configurations of the cooling system merit further consideration.

Cooling System Options

Figure 3.5 shows the eight major cooling system options (A to H) considered in the study. The basic options are characterized as follows:

(A) temperature rise across condenser;
(B) type of cooling system;
(C) single or series condensers;
(D) wet bulb approach factor for the cooling tower;
(E) cycles of concentration in the cooling tower;
(F) treatment of cooling tower blowdown;
(G) dilution of heated discharge; and
(H) recirculation for temperature maintenance.

(A) *Temperature rise across condenser.*   The process of heat exchange in a condenser condenses the turbine exhaust steam at the expense of an increase in the temperature of cross-current cooling water. The magnitude of this increase in cooling water temperature (ΔT) is a design decision variable which, for a given rate of waste heat removal, determines the necessary rate of flow of cooling water across the condenser. Cooling water flow is a decreasing function of ΔT.

As an additional important consideration, an increase in ΔT decreases the pressure drop across the turbine, with a resultant loss of generating power. This reduction in thermal efficiency results in an increase in both water and fuel requirements for a given level of net output.

Because both of these effects influence operating conditions throughout the plant, and because a condenser and its accessories must be designed for operation over a fairly narrow range of flow rates and ΔT, the choice of ΔT is a fundamental decision variable in plant design. The present study considers three discrete options for ΔT; only one of these options may be chosen by the model.

(B) *Type of cooling system.* The two decision nodes B in Figure 3.5 represent the second fundamental choice in the cooling system configuration. Depending upon the flow routings at each of these points, the resulting configuration may be classified as one of the following basic types, or a combination of the three:

(1) open-cycle system
    (*a*) "once-through"
    (*b*) "open-tower"
(2) closed-cycle system.

In open-cycle systems, river water is pumped directly across the condensers and then discharged back to the river. In the once-through case, the discharge to the river is direct, and the temperature of the discharge stream is essentially the same as that at the outlets to the condensers. In the open-tower case, the condenser outlet water is pumped through a cooling tower before being discharged; this lowers the temperature of the discharge stream to that in the cooling tower basin.

The recycle flow pattern of a closed-cycle system reduces the potential discharges from the system to the amount of "blowdown" collected at node F. This small blowdown stream is extracted from the recirculating cooling tower in order to maintain an acceptable concentration of dissolved solids in the system. The only withdrawal requirements of the closed-cycle system are a make-up stream to account for evaporative and drift losses and blowdown extraction.

The operation of cooling towers increases water losses through drift and evaporation and also has two effects on plant thermal efficiency. First, the additional energy requirements for the pumps and fans increase the gross energy generation necessary to produce the same level of net output. Second, to the extent that the temperature of the water from a closed-cycle cooling tower is higher than that of the river water, the plant suffers a loss in thermal efficiency relative to an open-cycle system. (This is because, for a given ΔT, the higher-temperature cooling water decreases the pressure drop across the turbine.) Of course, any reduction in plant efficiency increases all water demands per unit of net output.

The essence of the water management problem at the power plant is to determine an optimal combination of the three "pure" types of cooling system described above. This decision is an operating decision as well as a design decision, because the flow patterns through existing equipment can be altered to fit a given situation. As a very simplified generalization, it is presumably necessary to construct a large enough cooling tower to assure compliance with heat discharge standards during low river flow and high temperature conditions. Beyond that, the tower capacity may be expanded and/or the time pattern of flows in the cooling system may be altered in optimal response to the time pattern of other environmental quality constraints, of meteorological and hydrological conditions, and of prices and charges for water withdrawals, water consumption, and effluent discharges.

(C) *Single or series condensers.*   In the normal mode of operation for the cooling system, the flows through the condensers of the various blocks (or units) are independent (although they may share the same water intake and discharge channels). This "single condenser" mode of operation is represented by the outer flow lines at node C in Figure 3.4. Under certain conditions, however, it may prove advantageous to route the heated cooling water from the outlet of one condenser to the inlet of a paired condenser, as represented by the outer flow lines at node C in Figure 3.5. Under certain conditions, operation has two economic and water use advantages. First, the cooling water requirements for the paired condensers are only a little over half those for singly operated condensers. Secondly, in the case of open-tower and closed-cycle systems, the increased outlet temperature from the second of the paired condensers results in a greater temperature drop across the tower and thereby more effective heat rejection. This improvement may allow for construction of a smaller cooling tower. The optimal configuration decision must weigh these advantages against the decline in thermal efficiency implied by the higher cooling water temperature in the second of the paired condensers.

(D) *Wet bulb approach factor for the cooling tower.*   The difference between the water temperature in the cooling tower basin and the wet bulb atmospheric temperature is a so-called wet bulb approach factor, which depends upon cooling tower design, fan speed, and other considerations. As a proxy decision variable, this wet bulb approach factor affects the efficiency of heat rejection in the cooling tower—and therefore its necessary size—as well as the temperatures of the discharge stream in open-tower operation and of the recycle stream in environmental quality and thermal efficiency implications, as discussed above. Four alternative values of the wet bulb approach factor are incorporated as options in the model, and mixtures of these options serve to represent the flexibility in design and operation of the cooling tower.

(E) *Cycles of concentration in the cooling tower.*   The make-up water requirements for a closed-cycle system are a function of the evaporative losses in the cooling tower and a so-called cycle factor associated with the amount and dissolved solids concentration of cooling tower blowdown. In particular, blowdown and make-up requirements decrease with K, while the blowdown solids concentration increases with K.

A base value of $K_1 = 3$ is essentially determined by the concentration and composition of dissolved solids in the make-up water from the river and the allowable build-up of solids of that composition in the cooling system. As an alternative, this base value of K_1 can be doubled to $K_2 = 6$ by softening an amount of recycle water equal to the make-up requirement.

(F) *Treatment of cooling tower blowdown.*   The cooling tower blowdown collected at node F must be disposed of in an optimal manner consistent with liquid effluent discharge standards and effluent charges. This blowdown may be discharged or, alternatively, demineralized (in whole or in part) to produce a clean recycle stream for plant use. Demineralization of all of the cooling tower blowdown essentially eliminates discharges from a closed-cycle cooling system.

(G) *Dilution of heated discharge.*   Under certain conditions the temperature of the cooling water discharge may exceed the standard imposed on discharges. In this case it may be advantageous to use a certain amount of river or other available water to "dilute" the heated discharge to an acceptable temperature. This procedure does not, of course, change the value of the total heat load added to the river; it just reduces the temperature differential at the discharge outlet.

(H) *Recirculation for temperature maintenance.*   The design of the condenser is such that a minimum inlet temperature of 10°C must be maintained. During some parts of the year, however, the temperature of the river—and even that of the recycle stream from a closed-cycle system—may fall below 10°C. In such a situation, the minimum inlet temperature can be maintained by recirculating just enough of the heated outlet water from the condenser to bring the inlet water temperature up to 10°C. Logically, the remaining flow of water proceeding to discharge or cooling tower circulation is reduced by the amount of this recirculation. Water withdrawals are similarly reduced, although the effect is somewhat complicated in the case of a closed-cycle system.

Correspondence of Flows and Processes to Model Rows and Columns

Once the relevant material flows and unit processes have been identified (see Figures 3.3, 3.4, and 3.5), the next task is to develop a correspondence between these flows and processes and the rows and columns of the mathematical programming model. There are any number of ways in which this can be done. At one extreme, a one-to-one correspondence may be developed between each material flow and a model row and between each unit process and a model column. At the other extreme, an entire complex operation can be represented by a single column, with rows defined only for those materials with a net flow across the boundary of the operation. In practice, the correspondence employed is usually a compromise between the two extremes, and the modeler's choice depends upon a number of modeling and budgetary considerations. Four of these—model size, extent of true options, identification of important flows and process options, and linear and integer relationships—are identified here because of their general applicability and because of their particular importance in the formulation of the model.

The first consideration is *model size*. Budgetary or data processing limitations almost inevitably constrain the size of model that can be manageably manipulated and successfully solved. Generally, a trade-off must be made between manageability/computability and the degree of material flow and process detail explicitly represented in the model. This directly conditions the kinds of correspondences that can be made between material flows and rows and between unit processes and columns. This is particularly so in models that attempt to capture the time dimension by representing flows and processes in each of a number of specified time periods. This trade-off regarding model size is an important factor in the resolution of the next two considerations.

The second consideration is the *extent of true options* in the flow and process configurations modeled. Given the model size consideration, it makes little sense to represent explicitly unit processes (and related flows) whose activity levels relative to other processes are logically fixed rather than being actual decision variables. In some cases the distinction is dictated by the basic technical relationships of the modeled technology; in other cases it is a consequence of a decision not to model certain design or operating options. This leads to the third, related, consideration that is an identification of the *important flows and process options*. Here, too, it makes little sense to expand the size of the model with detail on flows and processes that do not significantly interact with the principal decisions, constraints, and flow patterns that are the target of the modeling analysis. In many cases, the flow diagrams themselves are an early stage in this simplification; the figures presented thus far already reflect considerable simplification of the water, energy, and residuals flows in the power plant.

The fourth consideration arises from the representation of power plant activities in terms of *linear and integer relationships*. Such a representation is motivated by the powerful algorithms and software available for solving linear programs and so-called mixed-integer programs with a manageable number of integer variables. This is not to say that the underlying relation-ships of electricity generation are linear (indeed, they are not), but rather that for a given application, these relationships may be adequately approximated by well formulated linear relationships, possibly supplemented by integer variables. The implication for model formulation is that the correspondence between unit processes and model columns should be defined so that the cost and input–output coefficients of linear model columns are independent of the activity levels of all model columns. As illustrated later, these corre-spondences may subsume in one column highly nonlinear relationships. Supplementary integer variables may be used to incorporate such considera-tions as mutual exclusiveness or "all-or-none" decisions, and they may further be used to ensure that the linear segments of a piece-wise approximated relationship are selected in the proper order.

General structure of the model

The end result of developing modeling correspondences is the representa-tion of the modeled operations by a matrix or tableau of numbers. In such a tableau the columns represent modeled activities or accounting variables, and the rows represent imposed constraints or logical conditions. By sign conven-tion, a positive coefficient in a column indicates an output, while a negative coefficient indicates an input.

The matrix structure for the model is depicted in highly aggregated form in Table 3.3. In this tableau each column or row (with three exceptions) represents an entire class of columns or rows in the model. (The exceptions are the "annual capital charge" column and the "cost" and "capital invest-ment" rows.) In particular, those classes of columns and rows identified as seasonal in the tableau are replicated (as a class) in the model as many times as there are seasons defined. At this level of aggregation, it suffices to indicate positive and negative coefficients in the model by + and −, respectively.

A salient feature of Table 3.3 is that many parts of the matrix have little or no interaction with other parts. This so-called sparseness is typical of large mathematical programming models. Areas of the matrix exhibiting high interaction correspond to particular subsystems of the modeled operations, such as fuel provision and combustion or electricity generation and cooling flow. The representation of these subsystems can be examined by means of partial matrix tableaus which focus on a subset of rows and columns from Table 3.3 and expand the selected row and column classes to a more disaggregated form.

We shall not present such an in-depth analysis of model structure here. The interested reader is referred to Stone *et al.* (1982) in which each subsystem is examined in detail.

Specification of model coefficients

Once the row and column structure for the programming model has been established, matrix coefficients must be specified. This task may vary greatly

Table 3.3. Overview of model structure.

		Annual capital charge	Coal supply and transport	Coal combustion	Air emissions accounting
		Logical	Annual	Seasonal	Seasonal
Cost (objective function)	Annual minimum	0·12	+	+	
Capital investment	Logical $= 0$	-1			
Coal	Annual $\geqslant 0$		+	$-$	
Air emissions constraints	Seasonal $\leqslant 0$			+	
Air emissions accounting	Seasonal $= 0$			+	$-$
Air emissions accounting	Annual $= 0$				+
Heat to boiler	Seasonal $\geqslant 0$			+	
Intake water	Seasonal $= 0$			$-$	
Water handling capacity	Seasonal $\geqslant 0$				
Electricity generation	Seasonal $\geqslant 0$				
Wastewater	Seasonal $= 0$		+		
Water discharge constraints	Seasonal $\leqslant b$				
Water use accounting	Seasonal $\leqslant 0$				
Water use accounting	Annual $= 0$				
Integer control rows	Logical $\leqslant 1$		+1 Slurry		

in complexity from one sector of the model to another. In many cases coefficient specification amounts to little more than arranging basic data in a manner that is consistent with respect to units and the period of time over

Air emissions accounting	Plant construction	Electricity generation and cooling	Water discharge	Water treatment	Water use accounting	Water use accounting
Annual	Build	Seasonal	Seasonal	Seasonal	Seasonal	Annual
+	+	+		+		+
	+					
	Stack −					
−						
		−				
		−		+	+	
+		−				
	ΔT options −	+				
		+	−	−		
			+/−		+/−	
			+/−		+/−	
					+	−
	ΔT options +1					

which flows are averaged and measured. Such is the case, for example, with most of the coefficients for coal transportation and combustion and with the coefficients for water use accounting and discharge constraints. In other cases, however, coefficient specification is computationally complex because the coefficient represents the net effect of many technical relationships. Such is the case with the coefficients for allowable coal combustion in the stack-building column variables and with most of the coefficients for activities related to electricity generation and cooling. The procedures developed for specifying these coefficients are central to the modeling analysis, but their details will not be discussed here.

Use of Matrix Generators

Operationally, the coefficient matrix for the programming model is specified through the use of so-called matrix generators. Essentially, a matrix generator is a specialized computer program designed to accept raw data and instructions from the user and to calculate (according to specified mathematical and logical relationships) the input–output coefficients for each of a specified set of column variables in the programming model. Utilization of such a program is particularly useful (often necessary) when calculations are numerous and/or complex and especially when such calculations must be performed repeatedly according to different specifications of the arguments. For the present model, the seasonal and other multiple-option structures give rise to a high degree of repetition for calculations ranging from trivial to extremely complex (even iterative). In short, the model developed for this study could not be specified without the aid of matrix generators.

Five independent (FORTRAN-coded) matrix generators have been developed to produce the entire programming model matrix. One of these programs specifies the column variables related to coal transportation and combustion. Three key programs specify the large number of column variables representing electricity generation and cooling, as well as the columns representing disposal of cooling water effluent. A final program generates everything else, primarily additional water-handling activities, certain construction activities, and accounting procedures for the constraints and charges on waterborne discharges.

Data availability

Aside from its educational value, a mathematical programming model is only as good as the economic and technical data available for defining its coefficients. In the present case, a fairly complex programming model has been constructed because the data were deemed good enough to justify it. For the most part, the data base was collected by the IMGW research team and is specific to Polish conditions. Where gaps appeared during the course of model development, technical information based on similar technologies in the USA was employed, but the use of cost data from the USA was successfully avoided.

Some of the more important components of the collected data base include the following:

(1) a set of highly detailed specifications for the design characteristics of the power plant;

(2) engineering cost estimates for the construction and design of power generation and water treatment processes;

(3) a tabulation of average monthly values for a wide range of meteorological and hydrological variables needed in the analysis, including a monthly specification of low flows in the river (flows exceeded 90 and 95 % of the time);

(4) a set of relationships and parameters for calculating the size of cooling tower required to dissipate a given amount of waste heat under specified meteorological conditions (plus the costs of tower construction);

(5) a specification of the physical, chemical and combustion properties of the two available grades of coal;

(6) engineering cost estimates for the various coal handling and combustion processes;

(7) an assessment of the Upper Vistula water management benefits accrued from the use of saline wastewater in the slurry pipeline;

(8) a full specification of relevant environmental standards and constraints; and

(9) a set of relevant prices and penalties for various aspects of water and coal use, along with ranges of variation in these values for use in water demand and other analyses.

On the whole, the data base is more than sufficiently reliable to produce sound modeling results. Those aspects of the data base in greatest need of further refinement are: (i) the cost structures for coal beneficiation, slurry transport, and certain incidental water treatment processes; and (ii) the benefit assessment for use of saline wastewater in the slurry pipeline.

Seasonality

Throughout this discussion the concept of seasons has been frequently employed, but generally with an intentional vagueness as to number and duration. The key determinations that must be made in defining model seasons are: (a) how short a time period is necessary to accurately capture the important time-dependent variations in operating conditions; and (b) how short a time period can be manageably considered in the modeling analysis (which involves not only model size but also data collection and interpretation of results). In general, there must be some trade-off between accuracy of representation and manageability. For reasons to be outlined below, the present study defines 12 "seasons" corresponding to the months of the year.

Treating the time-dependent conditions in order of increasing complexity, policy specifications tend to show the least time-dependent variation. In the present case, a month-by-month specification of charges and standards is perfectly adequate and manageable. Output levels for a baseload plant may also be reasonably assumed constant over a short enough period of time; the most significant variation is caused by the schedule of planned plant maintenance, which calls for shutdown of each block at least once a year. In the present case, the knowledge that these shutdowns are concentrated in the summer months and require an average of six weeks for completion allows a straightforward specification of the fraction of plant capacity in operation in a given month. Applying a constant baseload utilization rate to this operating fraction provides a monthly time pattern of plant output levels.

As is to be expected, the time pattern of meteorological and hydrological conditions demonstrates the shortest period of variation. Ultimately the availability of data and the manageability of the problem formulation dictates the choice of time period. For the present study, monthly data are available for the most important meteorological/hydrological conditions, and careful design renders the problem manageable at this level of detail.

The model specifications for the defined time periods need not be based on average values, nor is it necessary to define approximately uniform time periods. These can be varied according to the analyst's conception of the proper context for optimizing plant design. Perhaps the most sophisticated treatment would involve an optimization of design and operation in accordance with a time pattern of both average and critical conditions, with time periods for each defined in relation to expected frequencies of occurrence of the various sets of operating conditions. In the present case, manageability and data considerations have so far dictated a composite approach employing monthly time periods, average meteorological factors, and low flow in the river defined as that with a 90% probability of being exceeded monthly. The model structure is sufficiently flexible, however, to allow for easy redefinition of time periods and operating conditions.

Use of the Model

The previous sections have dealt primarily with a description of the model and its development; this section deals with three aspects of model use. First, a few comments are made on the operation of the model, its size, and its computability. Secondly, a brief discussion is provided of the kind of information available from the model and its potential uses. Thirdly, some representative results are presented.

Model operation, size, and computability

In its present form the model encompasses 12 month-long seasons, three options for condenser ΔT, four options for the wet bulb approach factor, two coal types, and three slurry pipeline options. In addition to these specifications, the model includes the full range of fuel provision and water management options selected for this study. At this level of detail, the model contains approximately 350 rows and 1400 columns.

These dimensions do not constitute an especially large problem, and continuous (linear programming, LP) solutions posed no particular difficulties on an IBM 370/168 computer employing the SESAME LP system. An integer algorithm, however, was not readily available within the time constraints for the study. Fortunately, because of the limited number of integer variables, it was possible to heuristically determine optimal solutions—often by inspection and occasionally, in case of doubt, by limited enumeration. On the whole, the computing experience with the model has been highly favorable.

Information available and potential uses

One of the major advantages of programming models is the wealth of information which can be derived from well conceived patterns of model solutions. The present model can be straightforwardly applied to estimate capital and operating costs, as well as the resource demands and pollution loads that result from operation of the power plant under a wide variety of conditions. Standard parametric and ranging techniques can be employed to test the sensitivity of these estimates to model assumptions and specifications. Using such techniques to identify the important constraints and cost values conditioning the model's solution not only contributes to an understanding of the real-world system but also indicates which aspects of model development should be most closely double-checked for accuracy and reasonableness.

The potential also exists for expanding the boundaries of the problem to include a direct interface between the programming model and models of water and air quality (see Chapter 6). The present study employs such environmental models in the background as a means of calculating rigid discharge constraints, but makes no attempt to determine the environmental impacts of relating or tightening those constraints, or to compare such impacts with the economic effects on power plant operations. Such an approach can be a useful means of evaluating public policy and the costs of environmental protection.

The primary purposes of this case study and model were to investigate the patterns of water use in a power plant on the Vistula River and to estimate the demands for water, both as a process input and as a medium for disposal of process wastes. IMGW therefore developed a slate of variants for the seasonal charges for water withdrawals, water losses, heat discharges, and dissolved solids discharges. Some fraction of the many possible combinations of these variants can be investigated to determine the induced changes in optimal plant design and operation. These changes map out derived demand functions for water in its various capacities; such functions may be determined jointly or independently. Shifts in these functions brought about by changes in model constraints or parameters can also be studied, both for their own sake and as a means of identifying important interdependencies among various water uses or among water use, fuel use, and air pollution considerations.

Representative model results

Model analyses performed at IIASA were directed almost exclusively to the impact of variations in the charges (prices) for water withdrawals and losses, although some less extensive variations in the penalty for heat discharges and the price of coal were also investigated. No analysis was made of the impact of changing the constraints on discharges to the water and air or the penalty on excess dissolved solids discharge. While key results of these limited analyses are summarized in this section, it is important to remember that model solutions contain a great deal more information than is presented here.

The (base) price for water withdrawals was varied in fixed steps over a range from 0·0 to 5·0 zloty (Zl) per m^3 (1·0 Zl = 100 groszy $\cong$ 0·03 US$, at the time of the study). The charge for water losses was fixed at 25 times the price for water withdrawals. Initial penalties for heat and excess dissolved solids discharges were set at 0·5 Zl/10^6 kcal and 0·5 Zl/kg, respectively. Alternate heat discharge penalties of 1·0 and 2·0 Zl/10^6 kcal were investigated at three different water prices. The minemouth price of regular grade coal was specified as 320 Zl/tonne for most of the modeling analyses, but this price was increased to 1000 Zl/tonne (at three different water prices) to investigate the interaction between thermal efficiency and water use. All model constraints were held constant throughout the analyses.

A few generalizations are possible about the model results. First, the maximum-size slurry pipeline proves to be the preferred mode of coal transportation in all cases. This consistently preferred option underscores a need to carefully verify the cost and feasibility assessments reflected in model specifications. Ideally, an investigation should be made of the range of costs over which the slurry (at any size) remains the preferred option.

Secondly, the maximum of the three specified options for condenser ΔT proves to be the preferred option for plant type in almost all model solutions. This preference arises both from reduced water flows and from lower capital costs relative to the other two options. A sharp rise in coal prices, however, shifts the preference to the middle option, indicating a dominance of the improvement in thermal efficiency over both increased water flows and capital costs. More sophisticated sensitivity analysis would be required to determine the precise switchpoint and to determine the relative importance of water flow versus capital cost in the choice of condenser ΔT. It also seems that future analysis would be improved by providing a yet higher option for ΔT and removing the lowest option.

Thirdly, the model solutions show great variation in the patterns of water use and in the marginal costs of electricity from season to season (i.e., from month to month). This is, of course, the expected result given the considerable seasonal variation in operating conditions, constraints, and prices and penalties. As a weak generalization, the open-tower cooling configuration seems to be a preferred option for complying with heat discharge constraints. The costs specified for make-up water treatment (even at three cycles) render a closed-cycle system the option of last resort. This sensitivity points to a need to verify carefully the treatment costs applied in the model.

Rather than presenting more specific results by season, the "flavor" of the model results can be communicated by using certain annual totals or weighted averages. Since withdrawal and loss charges and heat discharge penalties are not applied in certain seasons, the annual results presented must inevitably dilute somewhat the impact in price-sensitive seasons; impacts are nonetheless quite visible.

Figure 3.6 illustrates the derived demand relationship for water withdrawals, given the standard specifications for coal price and heat discharge tax. The axes are defined according to the convention in economics, even though price is specified and quantity observed. Withdrawal quantity is the annual total expressed in m^3/sec; this expression allows for a comparison with river flow over the middle reach of the Vistula. Mean annual flow is $297 \, m^3/sec$, and low flows with a 90% probability of being exceeded range from as low as $89 \, m^3/sec$ in fall and winter, to $249 \, m^3/sec$ in the spring.

Line segments connecting observation points in the graph are provided as an aid to visualizing the general shape of the relationship. They do *not* represent the response surface of the programming model. This response surface is actually a step function following the basic pattern indicated in the graph.

This limitation notwithstanding, the basic price sensitivity of withdrawal demand is readily apparent in Figure 3.6. Withdrawals decrease significantly as price is raised from 0·0 to 0·6 Zl/m³, but higher prices produce only modest reductions on an absolute scale. On a proportional scale, the pattern is roughly similar, but the change at 0·6 Zl/m³ is not as abrupt. This can be seen in Figure 3.7, in which the same results are plotted on a logarithmic scale.

The significance of a logarithmic plot is that the slope of a demand curve (or, more precisely, the reciprocal of the slope) can be interpreted as a price

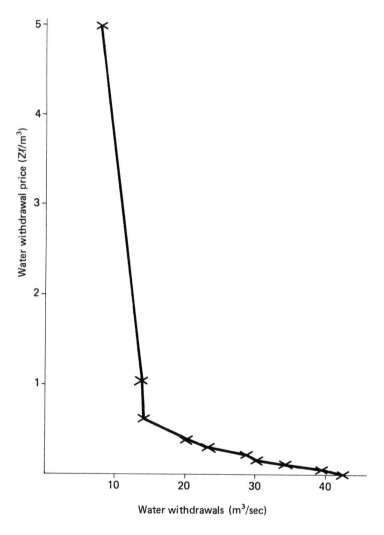

Figure 3.6. Derived demand for water withdrawal.

elasticity of demand. For larger variations in price, the so-called arc elasticity of demand defines an average elasticity between two price–quantity points (see Chapter 1). This is the most appropriate quantitative measure for the presented results, while the logarithmic plot aids in their visual interpretation.

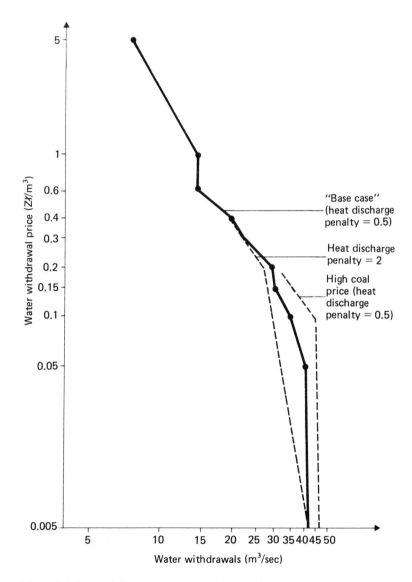

Figure 3.7. Derived demand for water withdrawal (logarithmic plot).

(Note that because the underlying model response surface is a discontinuous step function, the elasticity interpretations must be rather loose.)

Over the price range 0·0–0·5 ZI/m³, the arc elasticity is merely −0·02, confirming the visual impression of an inelastic range. Demand becomes more elastic over the price range 0·05–0·6 ZI/m³, for which the arc elasticity is −0·56. The apparent changes in elasticity over this range are typical of LP model response surfaces, but no rigorous interpretations can be made here because the observation points do not necessarily represent switchpoints in the model solution. Demand again becomes quite inelastic over the price range 0·6–1·0 ZI/m³ (and possibly beyond), but a less inelastic range is indicated somewhere between 1·0 and 5·0 ZI/m³.

Figure 3.7 also shows shifts in the derived demand relationship for water withdrawals brought about by separate increases in the heat discharge penalty and the coal price. A higher coal price brings about increased water

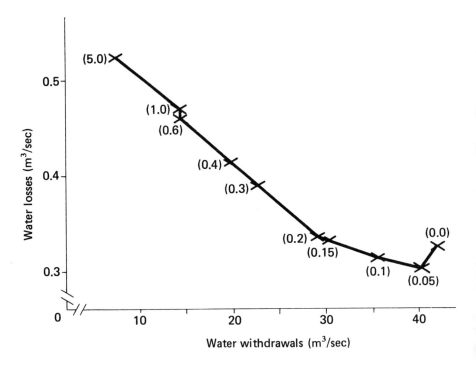

Figure 3.8. Water losses versus water withdrawals. Water withdrawal prices are shown in parentheses.

withdrawals at each price investigated. This substitution of water for energy reflects the lower value of condenser ΔT chosen at the high coal price. Although higher water prices were not investigated at the high coal price, the near convergence of the graphs at a water price of $0 \cdot 2 \, Zl/m^3$ supports the logical prior hypothesis that the graphs will approach each other as higher water prices dictate greater and greater use of closed-cycle cooling. Higher water prices may also raise the value of condenser ΔT chosen under a high coal price.

These results reflect the logical complementarity between water withdrawals and heat discharges. With a few minor exceptions, the process substitutions to decrease (increase) withdrawals simultaneously decrease (increase) heat discharges—and vice versa. The opposite relationship is for the most part demonstrated between water withdrawals and water losses (principally because of the losses in cooling towers). Figure 3.8 shows the general increase in water losses as the process configuration responds to higher and higher prices for water withdrawal. (The initial decrease in water losses results from a shift to a higher wet bulb approach factor in open tower cooling flows. This shift lowers the temperature differential across the tower and decreases evaporative loss.) The largest part of the increase in water losses occurs over the range in which once-through and then open-tower flows are progressively replaced by closed-cycle configurations. Interestingly, the relationship is linear over much of the response range investigated, with incremental increases in water losses amounting to around 1 % of incremental savings in water withdrawals.

The above discussion and graphs have focused exclusively on water use relationships without any indication of the cost consequences of the changes in process configuration. Since it is a cost minimization, after all, that determines patterns of water use (subject to the defined constraints), these cost consequences are also of interest. In the end they must be borne by someone, whether or not model prices permit an interpretation of the costs as proper social costs. As an indication of these cost consequences, Figure 3.9 shows the average and marginal costs of plant operation as water withdrawals are varied in response to the programmed variation in withdrawal prices. Both cost figures include the outlays for withdrawal and loss charges and for penalties on heat and excess dissolved solids discharges. Average costs are significantly higher than marginal costs because the model structure and solution essentially treat the costs of plant installation and slurry operation as fixed-cost components. As the construction of the cooling tower, water intake station, blowdown demineralizer, and combustion stack are modeled linearly, the capital costs of each of these units are reflected in the marginal cost for at least one season; this cost in turn shows up in the (weighted average) marginal cost of Figure 3.9 as well as in the average cost.

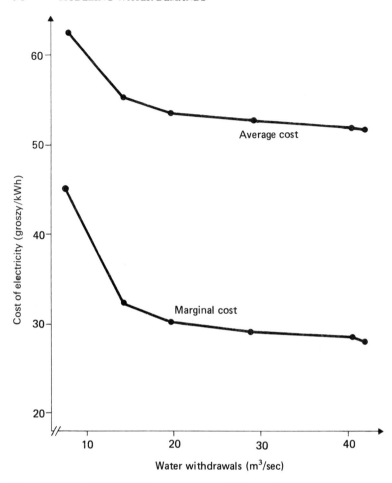

Figure 3.9. Cost of electricity versus water withdrawals.

Figure 3.9 shows that an initial 66% decrease can be attained in water withdrawals at a fairly minor increase in electricity cost; average costs increase by only 7% while marginal costs increase by 15%. In absolute terms, electricity costs per kWh increase by less than 0·16 groszy for each m^3/sec of reductions in water withdrawals. The final steep increment is considerably more costly in both absolute and relative terms. The incremental cost per m^3/sec of withdrawal savings is over 1·1 gr/kWh in this range, and the proportional cost increases are approximately threefold higher than those observed over the flatter range. This result is properly reflective of the economic law of diminishing returns, and identification of this high-cost region is essential to any cost-based determination of the socially optimal rate of water withdrawal.

While many other economic and resource use relationships are contained in the analyses performed, it is hoped that the results selected for presentation here sufficiently illustrate the analytical potential of the programming model. In particular, these results should demonstrate the usefulness of programming models for extracting information about water demand relationships that might not be available in the statistical record.

Conclusions

In this section the mathematical programming approach to modeling industrial water demands has been illustrated at some length. In particular, the objectives, structure, and development of a mixed-integer programming model of a hypothetical coal-fired power plant on the middle reach of the Vistula River in Poland have been addressed. While this application is quite specific, the basic methodology is inherently general and the modeled operations and issues are typical of those involved in the construction and operation of any power plant. Because of the basic homogeneity of power plant technologies, it is reasonable to expect that both the elaborated model structures and the qualitative nature of model results are relevant to other locations and other fuel types.

To be sure, the development of a sufficiently "realistic" mathematical programming model requires specialized expertise and a great deal of cost and technological data. These necessary data are, of course, only a subset of the data required to construct and operate the modeled facility anyway, but this does not mean that such data are easily collected. In addition, the development and operation of a model typically requires considerable outlays in terms of both human and computer time. Finally, the communication of model workings and results to relevant planners and decision makers may be the most difficult task of all.

The above obstacles notwithstanding, the advantages of a mathematical programming model are significant. First, it is future-oriented and permits an integrated analysis of new or hypothetical situations and technologies about which there may be no information in the statistical record. Secondly, its construction is step-by-step and verifiable. The focus is on systematically characterizing specific processes and constraints, a task which is far more easily and reliably contemplated than deriving (second-guessing) the "optimal" decisions directly. The "optimal" decisions are obtained as a *result* of model solution in accordance with user-specified objectives, constraints, and resource prices. Such solutions properly consider the significant interrelationships between the various dimensions of water demand and between water use and other aspects of plant operation.

Finally, in the context of planning and social decision making, the fact that a mathematical programming model (even of many sectors) cannot adequately address all of the objectives of social policy is no argument against its use in the decision process. A stand-alone power plant model may not be able to determine whether a plant should be built at all (or what size or where), but it does reveal the minimum cost design and operation of a fixed-size plant in a particular location and the associated implications for capital investment, water and other resource use, and waste discharges. A plant model cannot by itself determine socially optimal effluent discharge constraints or penalties, but it can internalize such social perspectives in its structure and estimate the "hard" economic costs of their imposition. In short, to the extent that social decisions are not made in an informational vacuum, mathematical programming models of industrial operations (and water demands in particular) have a valuable role to play in providing quantitative input to social decision processes.

4 Agricultural Water Demands*

Introduction

In most countries agriculture consumes more water than all other sectors of economy combined. The US National Water Commission (1973) reported that 77% of global water withdrawals and 87% of global consumptive use occurred in agriculture, and these can be expected to rise in the future. The UN Food and Agriculture Organization (FAO 1977b) has estimated that a US$100 billion investment program in irrigation will be required to provide adequate food supplies for the world's population by 1990. However, not all this investment is intended for development of new irrigation areas; $23 billion would be allocated to improving existing irrigation schemes and $14 billion to the provision of drainage.

Where water is plentiful irrigation efficiency is often low. Overwatering commonly leads to waterlogging and the need for drainage systems. Although effective irrigation methods are well known, they require large capital investments, and it is not always clear whether these investments are justified.

Water quality is becoming an increasingly important factor in determining the levels of agricultural water use. Salinity is well recognized as an issue, and many irrigation areas have been abandoned through excessive soil salinization. Sediment, fertilizers, and pesticides in irrigation runoff are also of concern. Although livestock water demands are small compared with those for crops, the resulting wastewater can be highly polluted, especially from feedlots and piggeries.

The nature of agricultural water uses varies widely with location. In Finland about 30 mm is applied to grain crops once a year by sprinkling, while in the Far East rice is usually flooded to a depth of 50 mm throughout most of the growing season. In Czechoslovakia's semi-humid climate irrigation supplements rainfall in the growing period in dry years, while in the arid climate of Arizona (USA) many crops could not be grown without irrigation. The basic management unit may control less than one hectare in some countries, and as much as thousands of hectares in others.

*This chapter was written by I. V. Gouevsky and D. R. Maidment.

MODELING WATER DEMANDS
ISBN 0-12-407380-8

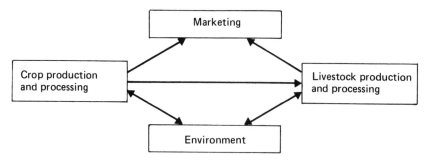

Figure 4.1. Basic agricultural subsystems.

As with many other sectors of the economy, the agricultural sector consists of several complex, interacting subsystems. In a very aggregated way agriculture can be schematically represented as shown in Figure 4.1. The two basic subsystems, crop production and processing, and livestock production and processing, are the major water users. Their water demands depend not only on the production processes but also on the various interactions with the marketing and environmental systems.

In the conventional approach to estimating agricultural water demands these interactions are often ignored. Instead, for the case of crop production, the area to be developed for irrigation is specified and multiplied by a coefficient reflecting the volume of the water required per unit area, thus giving an estimate of the water requirements. Such coefficients may be found from past experience, as, for example, in the Canterbury region of New Zealand where a coefficient of 0·7 l/sec/ha is used on the basis of 40 years of irrigation practice.

While the water-use coefficient approach has a certain value, it is often found inadequate in the face of the difficult decisions and controversies that may be encountered in water resource system planning. Could water demands be reduced in the future by the introduction of more efficient technologies? What will be the impact on water demands of changes in agricultural production, such as changes in cropping patterns or in the types of animals raised? What effect will rising energy costs have? Should the water be allocated to this use or to another? Is storage needed to increase water supply? In order to answer these questions adequately, more sophisticated approaches are being developed, some of which are described in this chapter.

To provide a basis for the discussion, the methodological framework set up in Chapter 2 is used. According to Chapter 1, water demands in agriculture can be estimated on the following levels:

- *Unit processes*, which refer to a field in crop production and to an animal in livestock production (water demand per hectare (ha), or per animal).

- *Individual agricultural activities:*[1] this level is characterized by increasingly complex agricultural systems, with each of the activities including several unit processes. The individual activity is a basic decision unit, often managed by one person or a unified administrative body (e.g., farm, enterprise).
- *Regional agricultural activities,*[1] which involve hierarchical management within an agricultural complex, or interacting individual farms and enterprises; this level of demand analysis can be conceptually extended to a region, or even to a nation.

Agricultural water demands on each of these levels have five dimensions: (a) water withdrawn at the intake of a given supply system; (b) the quantity of water consumed by crops or livestock; (c) the quantity of water discharged; (d) the quality of water discharged; and (e) the time pattern of each of the above dimensions.

The focus of the following discussion is first a brief review of unit processes; then, water demands of individual and regional agricultural activities are considered, using as an example a linear programming (LP) model dealing with a simplified agricultural system consisting of one type of crop and one type of animal. Finally, a case study of the Silistra region in Bulgaria is described, which deals with the modeling and forecasting of agricultural water demands in a large agroindustrial complex.

Water Use by Agricultural Unit Processes

The correct determination of water use by agricultural unit processes plays an important role in carrying out a successful analysis. To estimate these water uses, the methods range from assuming simple water-use coefficients (amount of water per hectare or per animal) to more sophisticated analyses based on climatological, soil, and crop growth data.

Water use in crop production

Water can be considered as one of the inputs to crop production, along with soil, seeds, fertilizers, pesticides, labor, machinery, and solar radiation. Any discussion of demand for these inputs must be based on some knowledge of input–output relationships, although unfortunately this is usually incomplete, especially for crop production involving several inputs. Consequently, the extent to which water application–crop yield relationships can be

[1] The word "agricultural" is usually omitted in the rest of this chapter.

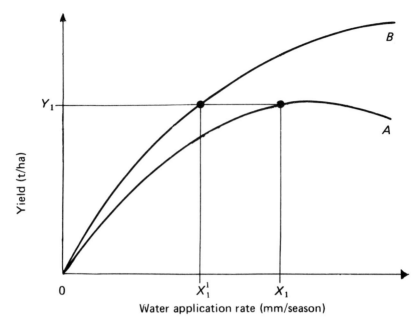

Figure 4.2. Hypothetical relationship between water application and crop yield (from Hexem and Heady 1978).

estimated depends on the overall knowledge of crop production processes and data availability.

Crop yield is, under given conditions, a function of the amount of water applied during the growing season, as shown in Figure 4.2. In this simplified example, taken from Hexem and Heady (1978), assume that the input–output relationship is known with certainty so that OX_1 of water applied is expected to produce OY_1 output. An agricultural producer planning to operate along OA in Figure 4.2 must, however, be aware that this curve corresponds to the fixed use levels for an unspecified number of other inputs that *jointly* generate a crop yield. Improvements on inputs other than water may permit the agricultural producer to move to the OB curve where each water input level results in crop yields above those realizable with OA. Alternatively, OY_1, for example, can be generated with OX_1^1, thereby freeing $X_1 - X_1^1$ units of water for other uses.

Although it would be desirable to have such functions as those shown in Figure 4.2 for all crops considered in a given water demand study, they are rarely available for all crops under the conditions of the region where the demands are to be estimated. Under such circumstances, empirical methods must often be used to compute the amount of water needed at each stage of crop growth to sustain maximum production (given a chosen set of other inputs). This in itself is a complex task, but is well described in a number of textbooks and related papers on irrigation (e.g., Israelson and Hansen 1962, Hagan *et al.* 1967, FAO/UNESCO 1973, Doorenbos and Pruitt 1977, Doorenbos and Kassam 1979, Dastane 1974, Bos and Nugteren 1974, Palacios and Day 1977, Yaron *et al.* 1972, Maas and Hoffman 1977, Ayers and Westcot 1976).

Water use in livestock production

The next important subsystem in the agricultural sector is livestock production and processing. Although livestock processing uses considerable amounts of water, it is not discussed in this chapter as it is considered an industrial activity.

The unit process water use in livestock production refers to the amount of water needed to sustain a given animal provided all other inputs are kept constant. Such water use can be divided into two categories: drinking water consumption and other water needs.

Drinking water use varies with the type, age, and environment of the animal. Animals obtain water from three sources: water that is directly consumed; water contained in the feed; and water made available through metabolic processes. The amounts of water needed depend on various factors such as animal species, size, age, sex, amount and content of feed, accessibility of water, and air temperature. Air temperature has a substantial impact on livestock drinking water consumption.

Other livestock water needs are mostly concerned with on-farm production processing and effluent disposal. These include: daily sanitation (utensil cleaning, parlor washdown); waste disposal (manure disposal, animal wash and dips, disinfectant sprays, cleaning and sanitizing equipment); cooling (milk, air temperature for hogs and poultry); and water losses.

The disposal of animal wastewater has become an issue of increasing importance in recent years. More intensive livestock production has led to concentration of large numbers of animals in barns and feed lots, with resulting problems of solid and liquid waste disposal (e.g., see Loehr 1977).

Modeling Water Demands of Individual and Regional Agricultural Activities

To account for the great diversity of problems in determining agricultural water demands by individual and regional activities, a number of different types of models have been developed. Models used in agricultural water demand analysis vary in complexity and methodology, ranging from statistical analysis of past trends—followed by adapting concepts for changing of the demands in the future—to more complex ones based on simulation or mathematical programming techniques. (Although there have been a considerable number of simulation models formulated for studying individual soil–crop unit processes, very few of these models have been spatially integrated to represent water use by individual or regional agricultural activities.)

Statistical methods are universally employed when analyzing measured historical data. However, statistical methods have not been widely used for modeling water demand relationships in agriculture. For example, Bain *et al.* (1966) used regression to relate water withdrawals for irrigation (W) to prices charged (p) in various irrigation districts of northern California (1958 cross-sectional data). They found that

$$\lg W = 1 \cdot 74 - 0 \cdot 64 \lg p, \tag{4.1}$$

which gives a price elasticity of demand of $-0 \cdot 64$ This equation accounts for 48 % of the variance in the data. To use regression models for prediction purposes with confidence, the model should account for at least 70–80 % of the variation in the data. Clearly, in this case, factors other than price cause significant variations in water withdrawals. Farm-level LP models applied in a part of the same area gave demand curves with a price elasticity of $-0 \cdot 19$. The discrepancy between these two estimates of price elasticity draws attention to a major problem in water demand analysis. That is, prices actually charged for water withdrawn are usually very low so that the observed price range never includes the equilibrium, market clearing price.

Mathematical programming models: A linear programming example

Mathematical programming is a planning tool that can aggregate the various agricultural subsystems into a single system by specifying a certain objective function and a number of constraints. The objective function in the mathematical programming reflects the decision maker's view of the goal of the system, which could be, for example, to minimize the total cost of production or to maximize the net benefits of the system. The constraints in mathematical programming take care of production requirements, availability of various resources, and interrelations within and between the subsystems. If both the objective function and constraints are linear, mathematical programming is called linear programming (LP), the main idea and mathematical format of which were described in Chapter 2.

The first step in an analysis of water demands of an individual or regional activity, using the mathematical programming approach, is to identify the system that will be of primary concern in the subsequent study. As was pointed out earlier, the agricultural sector has a complicated structure with a number of interacting subsystems. The resulting interdependencies require more modeling effort, but provide opportunities to substitute one input resource or output product for another.

The basic notion in LP is a unit process. In the crop production system one may identify such unit processes as, for example, wheat planting on an irrigated area with no fertilizer application or wheat planting on an irrigated area with fertilizer, and so on. In general, if one process differs from another in the type, proportions, or timing of the inputs they use, they are treated as separate processes in the LP framework.

To set up an LP model of the type discussed in Chapter 2, one has to

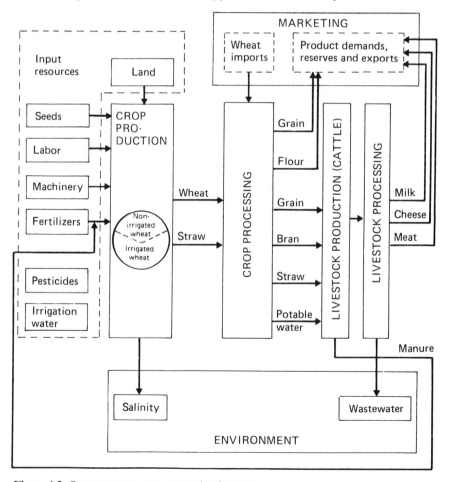

Figure 4.3. One type crop, one type animal system.

identify unit processes of the given agricultural activity and estimate technical coefficients describing inputs to and outputs from these activities. Unfortunately, this is a rather involved and time-consuming task. To assist the reader

Table 4.1. LP tableau of one type crop, one type animal agricultural system.

i / j	Irr. wheat area (ha) x_1	Nonirr. wheat area (ha) x_2	Required fertilizer (kg) N x_3	P x_4	K x_5	Total irr. water (m³) x_6	Irr. water saline (m³) x_7	Irr. water good (m³) x_8	Wheat (t) x_9	Straw (t) x_{10}
Objective function z (unit of activity)	−112·78	−64·22	−0·31	−0·28	−0·19	−0·007	−0·0542	−0·062	−1·67	−1
1 Seeds (t)	0·12	0·10								
2 Labor tractors (man-hr)	2·276	2·10								
3 Labor harvesters (man-hr)	0·455	0·364								
4 Machinery, tractors (No.)	0·032	0·03								
5 Machinery, harvesters (No.)	0·011	0·009								
6 Fuel (l)	72·75	69·67								
7 Fertilizer N (kg)	79·2	69	−1							
8 Fertilizer P (kg)	68	60		−1						
9 Fertilizer K (kg)	17·6	14·4			−1					
10 Pesticides (kg)	2·5	2·5								
11 Irr. water (m³)	1200					−1				
12 Water balance (m³)						1	−1	−1		
13 Saline irr. water (m³)						−0·3	1			
14 Wheat yield (t)	4·8	3·2							−1	
15 Straw yield (t)	45	45								−1
16 Land balance (ha)	1	1								
17 Wheat balance (t)									1	
18 Flour prod. (t)										
19 Bran prod. (t)										
20 Cattle DN (t)										0·03
21 Protein from cows (t)										0·0001
22 Cattle water req. (l)										
23 Milk (l)										
24 Beef (kg)										
25 Cheese (kg)										
26 Cattle manure N (kg)										
27 Cattle manure P (kg)										
28 Cattle manure K (kg)										
29 Wastewater (m³)										
30 Flour needs min (t)										
31 Flour needs max (t)										
32 Min number of cows										

in this respect, a step-by-step procedure for modeling a simple agricultural (one type crop, one type animal) system is presented below. As illustrated in Figure 4.3, this system encompasses the entire process of producing wheat, its

Imp. wheat (t)	Exp. grain (t)	Pop. grain (t)	Flour (t)	Bran (t)	Feed grain (t)	Cows (No.)	Milk (l)	Meat (kg)	Cheese (kg)	Manure (kg) N	P	K	Waste-water (m^3)	RHS
x_{11}	x_{12}	x_{13}	x_{14}	x_{15}	x_{16}	x_{17}	x_{18}	x_{19}	x_{20}	x_{21}	x_{22}	x_{23}	x_{24}	b_j
−240	140		200			−37·5		3	4				−0·09	
														≤ 120
														≤ 280
														≤ 500
														≤ 4
														≤ 2
														≤ 7000
										−1				= 0
											−1			= 0
												−1		= 0
														≤ 250
														= 0
														= 0
														≤ 0
														= 0
														= 0
														≤ 100
1	−1	−1			−1									= 0
			0·78	−1										= 0
			0·18		−1									= 0
				0·30	0·52	−3·0								≥ 0
				0·08	0·05	−0·686								≥ 0
						50								≤ 10000
						3000	−1							= 0
						220		−1						= 0
							0·2		−1					= 0
						0·01				−1				= 0
						0·04					−1			= 0
						0·07						−1		= 0
						40							−1	= 0
			1											≥ 5
			1											≤ 6
						1								≥ 25

processing and product marketing, including alternative uses of some products for feeding livestock (cattle) and livestock processing. Although the
process is somewhat artificial (a cow could not eat just wheat and produce all
specified products), it has all the subsystems discussed in the beginning of this
chapter.

The first and most important step in modeling is to define the objectives
that the decision makers want to achieve. In this particular example the
objective function is to maximize net benefits from agricultural production. In
other words, the difference between the gross benefits and the costs of
production in the system is to be maximized.

The next important step is to identify the decision variables. These can
include each of the inputs to or outputs from the six agricultural subsystems
shown in Figure 4.3. If one input or output differs from another by type,
proportion, or time, the two should be treated as separate decision variables.
The LP format also allows for the modeling of some nonlinear relationships
by piecewise linearization in which each of the linear segments is represented
by a separate decision variable.

In the model discussed here there are 24 decision variables denoted by
$x_1, x_2, \ldots, x_{24}$ (Table 4.1). The constraints in LP quantify the various
physical, economic, and environmental relationships and restrictions in the
system being modeled.

In mathematical terms the problem of modeling the system and its
associated water demands can be expressed as follows. Find that set of values
of the decision variables $x_1, x_2, \ldots, x_{24}$ that maximizes the objective function[2]

$$z = \max \left(\underbrace{\sum_{i=12,14,19,20} c_i x_i}_{\text{benefits}} - \underbrace{\sum_{i=1}^{11} c_i x_i - c_{17} x_{17} - c_{24} x_{24}}_{\text{costs}} \right), \tag{4.2}$$

subject to the following set of constraints:

(1) The amounts of input resources required cannot exceed the amounts
available:

$$a_{1j} x_1 + a_{2j} x_2 \leqslant b_j; \qquad j = 1, \ldots, 6, \tag{4.3}$$

where x_1 and x_2 are irrigated and nonirrigated areas, respectively, planted
with wheat; a_{1j} and a_{2j} are the respective rates (unit of resource/ha) of a given

---

[2] Note that: (a) in Table 4.1, cost coefficients associated with the variables $x_1, \ldots, x_{11}$,
x_{17}, and x_{24} already have negative signs; (b) wheat grain to be used domestically, x_{13},
and milk, x_{18}, do not have benefits associated with them because these products are
transformed into flour, x_{14}, and cheese, x_{20}, respectively; the same applies to bran,
x_{15}, and feed grain, x_{16}, because they are fed directly to cattle.

resource shown in row j of the LP tableau; and b_j is the amount of input resource j available shown in row j of the right-hand side of Table 4.1. The j resources are: seeds, labor for tractor operation, labor for harvesting, tractor numbers, harvester numbers, and fuel.

(2) The amount of nitrogen (N), phosphorus (P), and potassium (K) fertilizers used must be provided either from manure or by purchase:

$$a_{1,7}x_1 + a_{2,7}x_2 - x_3 - x_{21} = 0$$

$$a_{1,8}x_1 + a_{2,8}x_2 - x_4 - x_{22} = 0 \qquad (4.4)$$

$$a_{1,9}x_1 + a_{2,9}x_2 - x_5 - x_{23} = 0,$$

where x_3, x_4, and x_5 are the amounts of N, P, and K fertilizers to be purchased; and x_{21}, x_{22}, and x_{23} are the equivalent amounts of fertilizers produced by cattle manure and spread onto the land.

(3) The amount of pesticides used cannot exceed the amount available:

$$a_{1,10}x_1 + a_{2,10}x_2 \leqslant b_{10}. \qquad (4.5)$$

(4) The amount and type of irrigation water applied must satisfy three requirements:

$$a_{1,11}x_1 - x_6 = 0$$

$$x_6 - x_7 - x_8 = 0 \qquad (4.6)$$

$$-a_{6,13}x_6 + x_7 \leqslant 0.$$

The first of these constraints indicates that the total amount of irrigation water, x_6, must equal the product of the irrigated area, x_1, and the amount of water demanded by 1 ha of land, $a_{1,11}$. The second equation requires that total irrigation water applied, x_6, be equal to the sum of saline water, x_7, and water with more appropriate quality characteristics, x_8. Finally, the last inequality specifies an upper limit on the amount of saline water in the total amount of irrigation water. (It is assumed that if the ratio between x_7 and x_6 is kept at the level $a_{6,13}$, water salinity will not have a negative impact on wheat production.)

(5) Wheat and straw must be produced on the area available:

$$a_{1,14}x_1 + a_{2,14}x_2 - x_9 = 0$$

$$a_{1,15}x_1 + a_{2,15}x_2 - x_{10} = 0, \qquad (4.7)$$

where $a_{i,j}$ are rates of wheat and straw yield per ha; and x_9 and x_{10} are amounts of wheat and straw produced, respectively.

(6) The acreage used cannot exceed the available area of arable land:

$$x_1 + x_2 \leqslant b_{16}. \qquad (4.8)$$

The variables $x_1, \ldots, x_{10}$ and the constraints (4.3), ..., (4.8) describe the crop production subsystem and part of the environmental subsystem shown in Figure 4.3. The next three constraints and six variables are associated with the crop processing system and marketing of crop products.

(7) The grain exported, used domestically, and fed to cattle, must be provided either by production or import:

$$x_9 + x_{11} - x_{12} - x_{13} - x_{16} = 0. \tag{4.9}$$

(8) Flour production, x_{14}, is limited by the amount of wheat used domestically:

$$a_{13,18}x_{13} - x_{14} = 0. \tag{4.10}$$

(9) Similarly, for bran production, x_{15}:

$$a_{13,19}x_{13} - x_{15} = 0. \tag{4.11}$$

It can be seen from Table 4.1 that $a_{13,18} + a_{13,19} = 0.96$, i.e., 4 % of the wheat by weight is lost during milling into flour and bran. The last eight variables $(x_{17}, \ldots, x_{24})$ and constraints (4.12), (4.13) and (4.14) describe the livestock production and processing systems, as well as the rest of environment and marketing.

(10) The total digestible nutrients and protein required by cattle, x_{17}, must be provided by straw, x_{10}, bran, x_{15}, or feed grain, x_{16}:

$$a_{10,j}x_{10} + a_{15,j}x_{15} + a_{16,j}x_{16} - a_{17,j}x_{17} \geqslant 0, \quad j = 20, 21. \tag{4.12}$$

(11) The drinking water required for cattle must not exceed the amount of water available for this purpose:

$$a_{17,22}x_{17} \leqslant b_{22}. \tag{4.13}$$

(12) The amounts of various outputs from cattle are determined by the number of cattle raised, x_{17}:

milk:	$a_{17,23}x_{17} - x_{18} = 0$
meat:	$a_{17,24}x_{17} - x_{19} = 0$
cheese:	$a_{18,25}x_{18} - x_{20} = 0$
manure (N content):	$a_{17,26}x_{17} - x_{21} = 0$
manure (P content):	$a_{17,27}x_{17} - x_{22} = 0$
manure (K content):	$a_{17,28}x_{17} - x_{23} = 0$
wastewater:	$a_{17,29}x_{17} - x_{24} = 0.$

(4.14)

Table 4.2. Tractor and harvester requirements (man-hr/ha) and related fuel needs (l/ha).

	Tractors						Harvesters	$a_{1,2}$	$a_{1,3}$
	Plowing	Cultivation	Planting	Fertilizer and chemical spreading	Irrigation	Harvest	Harvest	Total tractors harvesters (man-hr/ha)	Total Total tractors harvesters (man-hr/ha)
Tractors and harvesters (man-hr/ha)	0·55	0·149	0·148	0·315	0·5	0·614	0·455	2.276	0·455
Fuel (l/ha)	19·80	4·62	3·70	2·80	1·40	13·57	10·06		

(13) The last three constraints specify the minimum and maximum flour needs and the minimum number of cattle in the system:

$$x_{14} \geqslant b_{30} \qquad x_{14} \leqslant b_{31} \qquad x_{17} \geqslant b_{32}. \qquad (4.15)$$

The objective function coefficients $c = \{c_i\}$, $i = 1, \ldots, 24$, the right-hand side vector $b = \{b_j\}$, $j = 1, \ldots, 32$, and the coefficients a_{ij}, $i = 1, \ldots, 24$; $j = 1, \ldots, 32$, must be estimated before proceeding to the next step of running the model. They can be derived from the information already available for the entire agricultural process. In case of limited local data one can adopt available data from other agricultural systems with similar characteristics. Regardless of the way in which the data are obtained, however, they must be carefully checked for consistency, e.g., ensuring that they are all expressed in consistent units.

The ways of deriving the coefficients can be illustrated by considering the coefficients relating to the decision variable x_1 (area of wheat planted on irrigated land).

The seeding rate coefficient, $a_{1,1} = 0 \cdot 12 \, \text{t/ha}$, can be obtained from agricultural manuals taking into account the site-specific conditions of the crop production system.

To determine $a_{1,2}$ and $a_{1,3}$, at least two kinds of information are needed: the types of tractors and harvesters to be used, and the schedule of field operations. An example of operations required to produce wheat is given in Table 4.2. (If the type of machines is not known in advance more variables may be introduced to allow for different machines to be used and, for each of these variables, coefficients similar to $a_{1,2}$ and $a_{1,3}$ would be incorporated in the matrix.)

Having obtained the coefficients $a_{1,2}$ and $a_{1,3}$ for a given type of equipment, one can proceed to determine $a_{1,6}$ (fuel rate per ha) using the second row of Table 4.2:

$$a_{1,6} = 19 \cdot 80 + 4 \cdot 62 + 3 \cdot 70 + 2 \cdot 80 + 1 \cdot 40 + 13 \cdot 57 + 10 \cdot 06 + l_w \cdot a_{1,14} = 72 \cdot 75 \, \text{l/ha},$$

where l_w is the amount of fuel required to dry one ton of wheat, $l_w = 3 \cdot 5$; and $a_{1,14}$ is the crop yield (t/ha), $a_{1,14} = 4.8 \, \text{t/ha}$; $l_w \cdot a_{1,14} = 16.8$.

To obtain the coefficients $a_{1,4}$ and $a_{1,5}$ (numbers of tractors and harvesters, respectively) the critical time of field operation as well as the type of machines must be determined. (The critical time is when all tractors or harvesters are pressed into operation.)

The coefficients $a_{1,7}$, $a_{1,8}$, and $a_{1,9}$ can be set up in the model in two ways: either as active ingredients N, P, and K (the amount of nutrients removed by the crop), or in amounts of fertilizers. In Table 4.3, the first method is employed in order to account in the same way for the active ingredients N, P, and K in cattle manure. Hence, $a_{1,7}$, $a_{1,8}$, and $a_{1,9}$ can be obtained from any agricultural manual after making them consistent with the type of soil of the crop production system. This way of computing required fertilizers implies that the obtained results for the variables x_3, x_4, and x_5 have to be modified to obtain fertilizer requirements by taking into account the application losses and the proportion of active nutrient in each of the fertilizers. The same procedure can be followed to determine the rate of pesticide use ($a_{1,10}$), which depends primarily on the types of weeds and insects that have negative impacts on the crop.

The last three coefficients $a_{1,11}$ (crop unit water demand), $a_{1,14}$ (wheat yield), and $a_{1,15}$ (straw yield), may sometimes have to be derived from special auxiliary models. This is true in particular for the crop unit water demand, which depends on a number of stochastic variables (rainfall, temperature, solar radiation, wind speed, quality of water, etc.). A method for deriving these demands is discussed below in the description of the Silistra case study.

The only coefficient pertaining to x_1 that still has to be determined is c_1 (the coefficient in the objective function associated with the variable x_1); c_1 represents the costs involved in crop production using x_1. The first step to be taken in determining c_1 is to decide which costs one has to consider. If some of the input resources, or the production outputs, are identified as separate variables, the unit costs associated with them can be assigned to those variables' cost coefficients. This then enables the impact of those unit costs on the model solution to be investigated.

The cost associated with each variable can be subdivided into two categories: fixed costs, including capital investment depreciated over time; the variable costs that include resources (not concerned with capital investments); and the cost of various activities such as equipment maintenance, labor, etc.

Table 4.3 summarizes the procedure for obtaining $c_1 = 112 \cdot 78 \, \$/\text{ha}$ attached to activity. It should be pointed out that Table 4.3 gives only an idea for the procedure of calculation of the objective function coefficients. In real world studies there may be a number of other costs associated with running a given activity such as, for example, the depreciated cost of land. A comparatively complete description of all coefficients in the LP tableau is given in Nicol and Heady (1974) for a national water demand model.

After all the coefficients have been identified, they are arranged in a matrix form (Table 4.1). The matrix provides the basic information for introducing the data into the computer and carrying out the actual computations. Standard LP packages are generally available for that purpose. The most advanced packages utilize matrix generators, which considerably reduce the amount of time required to arrange an LP tableau and to ensure that the coefficients $a_{i,j}$ are put in the right place.

Table 4.3. Derivation of the coefficient c_1 in the objective function.

Variable cost	Cost assigned to variable x_1	Cost assigned to other variables
1. Seed: seed rate (t/ha) × cost of seed ($/t)	$0.12 \times 185 = 22.20$	
2. Labor: tractor man hr/ha × cost of labor ($/hr) + harvester man hr/ha × cost of labor	$2.276 \times 2.50 +$ $0.455 \times 3.00 = \quad 7.05$	
3. Fuel fuel rate (l/ha × cost of fuel ($/l))	$72.75 \times 0.35 = 25.46$	
4. Fertilizers: (a) cost of fertilizers ($/kg active ingredient) N P K (b) spreading on the field ($/ha)	3·00	0·31 (assigned to x_3) 0·28 (assigned to x_4) 0 19 (assigned to x_5)
5. Chemicals: chemicals rate (kg/ha) × [cost ($/kg) + cost of spreading ($/kg)]	$2.5 \times 0.24 + 0.08 = \quad 0.62$	
6. Machine operation cost (repairs) ($/ha)	2·50	
7. Irrigation: (a) Maintenance and repair parts $\dfrac{\text{cost per sprinkler (\$)}}{\text{area covered by sprinkler (ha)}}$	$\dfrac{120}{10} = 12.00$	
(b) Maintenance vehicles (labor, repairs) $\dfrac{\text{hours per sprinkler (hr)}}{\text{area covered by sprinkler (ha)}}$ × cost of labor ($/hr)	$\dfrac{18}{10} \times 2 = \quad 3.60$	
(c) pumping cost volume of water (m³/ha) × cost of pumping ($/m³)	$1200 \times 0.02 = 24.00$	
8. Transportation to drying ($/t)		0·50 (assigned to x_9)
9. Transportation of straw to storage ($/t)		1·00 (assigned to x_{10})
10. Grain drying operation cost ($/t)		1·17 (assigned to x_9)
Total variable cost assigned to x_1	100·43	
Fixed costs (capital investment depreciated over time)	12·35	
Total fixed and variable cost assigned to x_1 (value of c_1)	112·78	

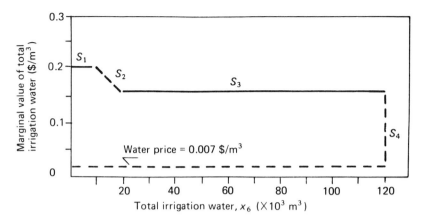

Figure 4.4. Demand function for the total irrigation water withdrawals. The individual segments of the demand function are:

S_1 the highest marginal value of irrigation water; wheat is imported to sustain livestock production;

S_2 the amount of imported wheat decreases; wheat begins to be irrigated;

S_3 imported wheat completely drops out of the solution;

S_4 water is no longer a constraining factor on the system.

Among the information that can be derived from this simple one type crop, one type animal model is the demand function for total irrigation water withdrawals shown in Figure 4.4 (total water demand as a function of the marginal (dual) value of irrigation water). In a similar fashion, the demand function for wastewater discharges could be derived by plotting the dual value of constraint 29 against the optimal value of variable x_{24} when it is constrained.

Table 4.4 represents a sample of some of the results obtained for the one type crop, one type animal system when the total amount of irrigation water is varied. The results serve to illustrate the method and also indicate a certain pattern of behavior of this system when irrigation water is scarce. For example, one can see structural changes in the crop production system (amount of irrigated and nonirrigated area versus irrigation), as well as in the crop processing systems (wheat is imported when levels of irrigation water are low). The reason for having idle land for values of irrigation water equal to 20 000, 40 000, and 115 460 m³ is that fuel is a constraining factor (see the marginal values of fuel in Table 4.4).

Overview of the models

Over the past 20 years there has been considerable interest in developing models of agricultural activities that, among other things, are able to answer

Table 4.4. Sample of results for one type crop, one type animal agricultural system.

	Designation in the model	Total irrigation water available (m³)				
		0	10 000	20 000	40 000	115 460
Objective function ($)		56 469	58 522	60 263	63 417	75 320
Irrigated wheat area (ha)	x_1	0	8·33	16·66	33·33	96·22
Nonirrigated wheat area (ha)	x_2	100	91·66	83·07	65·66	0
Required N fertilizer (kg)	x_3	6899	6984	7051	7170	7620
Required P fertilizer (kg)	x_4	5999	6065	6116	6205	6541
Required K fertilizer (kg)	x_5	1438	1464	1487	1530	1691
Good quality irrigation water (m³)	x_8	0	7000	14 000	28 000	80 224
Saline irrigation water (m³)	x_7	0	3000	6000	12 000	34 639
Marginal value of total irrigation water ($/m³)		0·2053	0·2053	0·1577	0·1577	0
Marginal value of fuel ($/l)		0	0	8·2	8·2	10·8
Wheat production (t)	x_9	320	333·33	345·82	370·13	461·85
Wheat imports (t)	x_{11}	18·56	5·23	0	0	0
Grain exports (t)	x_{12}	0	0	0	0	0
Feed grain (t)	x_{16}	332·15	332·15	339·41	363·72	455·44
Cattle (No.)	x_{17}	25	25	26	27	34
Milk (t)	x_{18}	75 000	75 000	76 582	81 883	101 880
Meat (t)	x_{19}	5500	5500	5616	6004	7471
Cheese (t)	x_{20}	15 000	15 000	15 316	16 376	20 376
Wastewater (m³)	x_{24}	1000	1000	1021	1091	1358

questions concerning economic demand for water. Because of their great complexity and the planner's need to find "the best" solution in a set of feasible solutions, LP models have been employed from the very beginning. The models can be grouped into three categories: national, regional, and farm-level models. One of the first families of national models was developed at the Center for Agricultural and Rural Development (CARD) at Iowa State University in the US beginning in 1954 (Heady and Agrawal 1972, Heady and Srivastava 1975, Nicol and Heady 1974). These models simultaneously consider (a) exogenous variables affecting food requirements; (b) government programs to control supply and increase food exports; (c) technological advances; and (d) the pricing of water through public investment in irrigation development. The models minimize total crop and livestock production costs over a 25-year time horizon. Duloy and Norton (1973) employed a similar concept in developing a model for the agricultural sector in Mexico. This model maximized the sum of the producer and consumer surpluses in national crop production. A similar model was also developed by the UN Food and Agriculture Organization (FAO 1977a) in order to identify policy options for an optimal crop mix pattern in long-term planning in Iraq.

Regional models receive the greatest attention in the literature. For example, Gisser (1970), Mohammadi-Soltani (1972), Voropaev (1973), Dean *et al.* (1973), Prajinskaya (1975), and Prajinskaya *et al.* (1976) have developed regional agricultural models with heavy emphasis on crop production. Livestock production is considered as an exogenous variable. All of these models maximize the net benefit difference between gross costs and production costs in the respective regions.

From the studies reviewed, the following conclusions can be made:

● The methodology is available for LP modeling of agricultural production when it is considered as being static with deterministic inputs. Models can be constructed for both individual and regional activities. Aggregation from one level to the next is also possible (Miller 1966). Water demand functions can be derived from these models. If the dynamics of agricultural production and its inherent uncertainties are to be taken into account, application of LP is difficult because of computational and analytical limitations, including all the difficulties pertaining to data collection, data checking, model verification, and understanding the huge amounts of computational results.

● Many models are described in the professional literature that have still not found real-world applications. Among many reasons responsible for this situation, it seems that the difficulty in transforming actual objectives into an objective function is one of the major ones. Most of the models reviewed have as an objective function either cost minimization or maximization of net benefits. Sometimes other objectives such as maximization of foreign exchange earnings, or environmental enhancement, may have a greater impact on agricultural production decisions.

Although LP is the most widely used technique for modeling agricultural water demands by individual and regional activities, a number of other mathematical programming and simulation methods have also been applied. To mention just a few, the studies of Asopa et al. (1973), Palmer-Jones (1977), Dudley et al. (1971a,b, 1972), Windsor and Chow (1971), and Ahmed and van Bavel (1976) are representative in this respect. In various ways these methods take into account some of the nonlinear, dynamic, and stochastic aspects of irrigation systems, which are difficult to deal with in linear programming. The models are primarily concerned with scheduling the depth and timing of irrigation in response to changing weather conditions.

The crop production functions used in these models (crop yield as a function of the amount of irrigation water applied) are either estimated by statistical regression employing historical data, or simulated, using some hypothesis about the relationship between soil moisture and crop growth. The optimal timing and depth of irrigation are then estimated by dynamic programming or simulation. While dynamic programming gives a more accurate solution than simulation, it is very difficult to apply this method to more than one crop and soil type at a time because of the well known "curse of dimensionality". Simulation is less limited and can also be extended to higher-level analysis (determination of crop areas, and total area irrigated) as Dudley et al. (1971b, 1972) have demonstrated.

Agricultural Water Demand in the Silistra Region[3]

Introduction

During 1977 a case study in the Silistra region of Bulgaria was carried out at IIASA in collaboration with the Bulgarian Ministry of Agriculture and Food Industry. The goals of the case study were:

- to provide planners and decision makers in the Silistra region with detailed information about water demands and their impact on agricultural production in the region; and
- to improve the systems analysis methodology for deriving and forecasting agricultural water demands by studying a real-world problem.

[3] The authors wish to express their appreciation for the help of Mr W. Sikorski (IIASA), and of Drs V. Genkov and S. Stoykov (Ministry of Agriculture and Food Industry, Sofia) in carrying out the case study and implementing the model in Bulgaria.

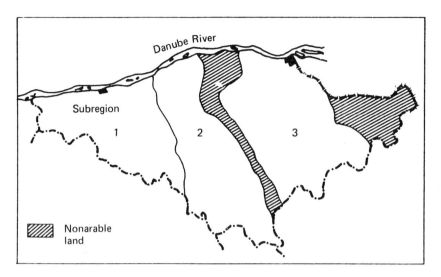

Figure 4.5. The Silistra region of Bulgaria. Numbers refer to the main irrigation areas.

The Silistra region has a population of 175 000, covers an area of about 2700 km², and is situated in the northeastern part of Bulgaria (Figure 4.5). All agricultural activities in the region are organized into a large agroindustrial complex called Drustar. In the terminology adopted in this chapter, an agroindustrial complex is an example of a regional agricultural system that consists of the following basic subsystems: crop production and processing, livestock production and processing, marketing, and the environment. One administrative body is responsible for overall planning, development, and management of the complex.

Within the complex, crops are grown and harvested, stored, and fed to livestock housed in concentrated feedlot areas. The Silistra regional planners consider self-sufficiency an important goal and as far as possible, they wish to supply all the region's needs from its own resources and export the surpluses. Because management is integrated, it is reasonable to model the agricultural production system of the Silistra region as one unit. This is in contrast to modeling it as an assembly of separate units, as would be appropriate for regions with a different management structure and different goals.

Since rapid development is occurring at present, it is essential to choose the best way of directing future agricultural activities and investments. In the list of problems to be investigated in this respect, water resources appear to play a key role, for two important reasons:

● Water resources within the region are limited to the bordering River Danube. There are no other rivers in the region. Groundwater is available only in small quantities or at depths exceeding 400 m, which makes it an unimportant resource as far as crop irrigation is concerned.

● Vast irrigation development is to take place in the coming years to meet the feed requirements of meat- and milk-producing livestock—hence, to ensure stable agricultural production, a large reliable water supply has to be made available within the region.

Climatic conditions in the region are favorable for crop and livestock production, supported by irrigation. The average monthly rainfall in the irrigation season (May–September) is 46 mm, but extremes ranging from 0 to 137 mm have been recorded. The average monthly evapotranspiration for the same period is 171 mm, so that irrigation is necessary to ensure a positive soil moisture balance over the growing season.

To overcome the difficulties associated with scarce water resources within the region and a negative soil moisture balance, intensive investigations have been carried out over the past few years. As a result, a number of alternatives for augmenting the available water supply have been proposed, including the construction of several reservoirs in various parts of the region; others combine use of pumping stations and reservoirs, the construction of long-distance canals, and so on. The common characteristic of all alternatives is that, first, they rely on the Danube and, secondly, all of the alternatives are rather costly. Obviously, one way of decreasing supply cost would be to reduce agricultural water demands for irrigation, while keeping the production targets at the desired level. However, any reduction of agricultural water demands involves additional costs. The question is: are these costs greater than the supply cost, and at what point is the water resource system in equilibrium, i.e., at what point is the incremental cost of additional supply equal to the incremental benefit that it produces?

During the course of the study, this and other relevant questions have been thoroughly examined with the aid of two LP models, SWIM 1 and SWIM 2 (Silistra water for irrigation model). The first version, SWIM 1 (Gouevsky and Maidment 1977) takes into account only crop production, processing, and marketing. It is a moderately sized LP model, comprising 56 constraints and 68 decision variables. In SWIM 2, livestock production and processing, and some environmental issues were added, thus increasing the model size to 152 constraints and 218 variables (Gouevsky et al. 1980). The following discussion summarizes the basic modeling approach and the results obtained in order to illustrate the application of LP methodology to the study of agricultural water demands.

Description of the model

The main objective of the model is to make a thorough analysis of factors that influence agricultural water demands and associated production in the

Silistra region, taking into account the major goal, which is to maximize the total net benefit from crop and livestock production with the limited regional resources. The model is intended to provide information for:

- estimating irrigation and livestock water demands and their distribution in space and time within a given year;
- forecasting the growth in these demands in response to different growth scenarios for the numbers of livestock in the region;
- determining what proportion of the arable land within the complex should be developed for irrigation; and
- evaluating the impact on water demands of various factors, including weather variability, and the availability of other input resources (e.g., fertilizers).

The Agricultural Production System

There are about $1500 \, km^2$ (150 000 ha) of arable land in the Silistra region on which crops are grown to feed the livestock in the region and to meet the needs of the local population; 11 400 ha are irrigated, all with sprinklers. In the model, the region is divided into three main irrigation areas (see Figure 4.5), all of which will utilize Danube water.

For modeling purposes, agricultural production systems may be broken down into a number of subsystems, as shown in Figure 4.6. Input resources such as land, water, and fertilizers go into producing crops whose output is processed for marketing or feeding to livestock. Crop production, supplemented by purchases from the market, is fed to livestock whose products are processed and sold. Livestock production may have substantial environmental impacts, such as those due to feedlot effluents, and these impacts may, in turn, affect crop production.

Figure 4.6 indicates all processes that are involved in crop production and the uses of the crops. The input resources are land, water, seeds, fertilizers and chemicals, labor, machinery, fuel, and capital investments. Decision makers for the Silistra region consider that land is the only fixed input resource. All others are variables.

Let us use wheat as an example. The input resources enter the crop production subsystem, which has various alternatives for producing wheat. It may be grown in any of the three subregions; it may or may not be irrigated; if it is irrigated, the usual amount of fertilizers may be supplied or these fertilizers may be reduced to 80 % of their usual amounts. Thus, there are nine alternatives; no irrigation, irrigation with 80 % fertilizers, and irrigation with 100 % fertilizers, each of which can take place in any of the three subregions. In the next subsystem wheat undergoes processing to obtain grain, straw, flour, and bran.

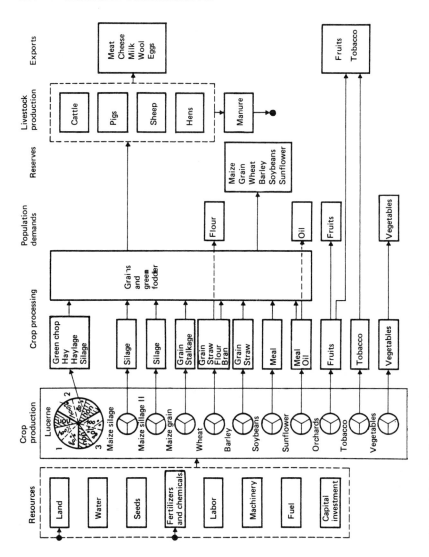

Figure 4.6. Agricultural production in the Silistra region.

The products are then distributed among different subsystems; grain goes to reserves and to livestock production, straw and bran go directly to livestock production, and flour is sent to the market to meet the demands of the population.

Crop products feed four types of livestock—cattle, pigs, sheep, and hens—all of which are housed in feedlots. Livestock products are exported from the region. The by-products of the livestock production subsystem, animal wastes from feedlots, are spread onto some of the land and partially substitute for fertilizers. However, these wastes may also have undesirable environmental impacts.

Water is one of the key parameters to be modeled in the system because it directly influences crop production, which in turn controls livestock production. The reverse also applies. If livestock numbers change, this will change the demands for crop production, and for irrigation and drinking water.

Modeling Assumptions

The decision makers for the Silistra region are considered to have a number of objectives in mind in planning the agroindustrial complex:

- *Maximum production*, to generate a high level of exports from the region and to meet the needs of the Silistra population for food and other agricultural products.
- *Efficient production*, i.e., at a minimum cost per unit of input. This implies that the flows of materials between the various subsystems in Figure 4.6 are in harmony with one another and that the least-cost combinations of inputs are used.
- *Sustainable production*. Over the short term, this involves minimizing the impact of weather variations by providing irrigation and production reserves. Over the long term, soil fertility must be maintained through proper cultivation and crop rotation.

These objectives have been substantially incorporated into SWIM 2 either in its objective function or in its constraints. It may be noted that there could be other important objectives in the region that are not explicitly included in the model, such as increasing the efficiency of agricultural labor.

In the process of modeling agricultural production and deriving water demands, four basic assumptions have been made.

(*a*) The agricultural system is modeled for one year. Depending on the coefficients included in SWIM 2, this one year can represent the conditions of any specified year. SWIM 2 does not contain year-to-year variations in its model structure, however.

(*b*) The inputs and outputs of each of the seven subsystems shown in Figure

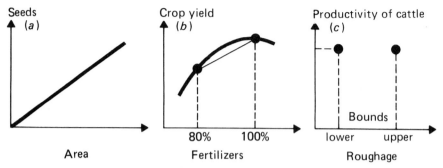

Figure 4.7. Relationships between decision variables.

4.6 represent the decision variables in the model. It is further assumed that there are three types of relationships between decision variables:

- A linear-by-nature relationship; for example, the amount of seeds for planting a given crop is a linear function of the area to be planted (see Figure 4.7a).
- A nonlinear relationship; for example, crop yield versus fertilizer applications. In this case the nonlinear function is linearized and the linear segments obtained are introduced as separate decision variables in the model (Figure 4.7b).
- A relationship where the decision maker is indifferent to a certain interval of variation of the dependent variable, or where the dependent variable is constant over a specified range of the independent variable (Figure 4.7c).

(c) All costs, prices, and technical coefficients are known; economies of scale are not explicitly included. For example, in a given subregion the cost per hectare of bringing irrigation water to the field does not depend on the number of hectares irrigated.

(d) No interest rates or investments are included in SWIM 2 because, at present, interest rates are not considered to be the only or most important indicator of the socioeconomic value of investment in Bulgaria. For each piece of equipment purchased or facility developed by means of investment, the fixed cost is included in SWIM 2 as an annual cost found from a straight-line depreciation of the investment over the useful working life of the facility. There are also other assumptions that relate to each of the subsystems described below.

Description of the Subsystems

Input resources: All input resources are introduced into SWIM 2 as rates of use of resources per hectare of land or per animal. These rates may be taken directly from crop and livestock production manuals (e.g., Lidgi *et al.* 1976) and adapted to the region's conditions, or they may involve more detailed computations such as those for irrigation water in this study.

Land: The main soil type of the complex is chernozem (black earth). It is assumed that the soil structure and productivity are uniform over the region. SWIM 2 allows for different soil types in the three regions defined in Figure 4.5, but there were no relevant data available concerning different soil types at the time of modeling. Out of 150 000 ha of arable land, about 4500 ha are reserved for seed production. The seed area is determined internally in the model solution. To allow for better land utilization, SWIM 2 takes into account the possibility of having maize silage as a second crop (maize silage II), after the midsummer harvest of wheat and barley. The model also computes the amount of irrigated or nonirrigated land planted with orchards and tobacco, as well as the irrigated area of vegetables. The areas of land planted with these three crops are fixed exogenous variables.

Water: It was assumed that the Danube is the only source of irrigation

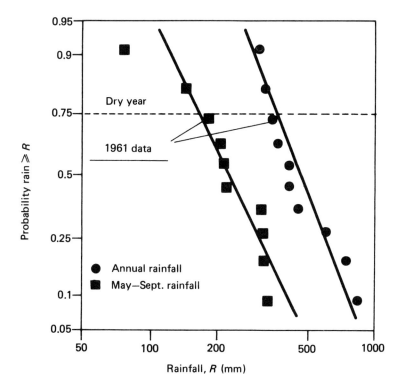

Figure 4.8. Probability analysis of rainfall.

water and because of the rolling hills and potential for erosion, sprinkler irrigation is the only application method considered. The model computes the total amount of irrigation water as well as its distribution among subregions and various crops using ten-day intervals during the irrigation season from May to September. Unit crop demands are calculated by means of a soil moisture balance model.

This model uses the rainfall and evapotranspiration in each ten-day period from March to September as input data. Calculating forward in time, 60 mm irrigation water is applied when soil moisture falls to more than 60 mm below its capacity. Drainage occurs if excess rainfall raises soil moisture beyond its capacity.

Both normal weather conditions and one-in-four dry year conditions are analyzed. Using mean monthly data recorded in Silistra for each of the years 1961–70, normal weather conditions are defined for each month by averaging the ten years of data. The conditions of 1961 are adopted as representing the one-in-four dry year by means of the probability analysis shown in Figure 4.8. Evapotranspiration is computed from data on mean monthly temperature, humidity, windspeed, and cloudiness by the Penman method (Doorenbos and Pruitt 1977). An example of the soil moisture balance calculations for maize grain is shown in Figure 4.9.

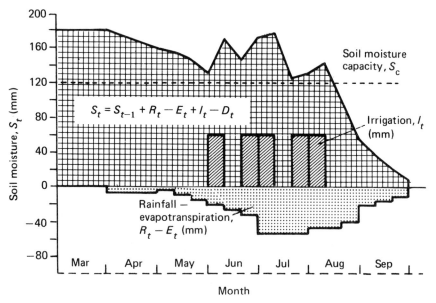

Figure 4.9. Soil moisture balance with irrigation.

A total water-use efficiency of 50 % is estimated on the basis of conveyance losses (5 %), application losses (30 %), and leaching requirements (15 %). SWIM 2 calculates the water use of each crop as the product of its unit crop water demand and the crop area. Then, to obtain the volume of water withdrawn from the Danube, SWIM 2 sums all crop water uses and divides the total by the efficiency. As in most irrigation systems, the price of irrigation water is subsidized and does not reflect the actual unit cost of supplying water. For this reason, a sensitivity analysis of water price, which is described in the analysis of the results, has been performed. SWIM 2 also computes livestock drinking water demands as the product of the unit water demand (liters/animal) for each type of animal, and the number of animals. This water is supplied from wells located near the Danube and is subsequently transferred to farms. The model does not consider treatment of wastewaters from the livestock feedlots.

Seeds: All seeds required for lucerne, maize, wheat, barley, soybeans, and sunflowers are assumed to be grown within the complex on nonirrigated land. SWIM 2 computes the area of land needed for seed growing per hectare of field crop production by dividing the seed-planting rate for each crop by its seed crop yield rate and summing the resulting seed crop areas.

Fertilizers and chemicals: Three nutrients, N, P, and K, must be supplied by fertilizers. The amount of each fertilizer needed per hectare is calculated so as to replace the nutrients removed by crop production, allowing for the natural ability of the soil to absorb or release nutrients. SWIM 2 also allows for partial substitution of fertilizers by the nutrients in animal wastes from feedlots.

As far as pesticides are concerned, there are too many individual chemicals involved to account for each one separately, as is done for fertilizers. Instead, a lumped cost per hectare is specified for each crop.

Labor, machinery, and fuel: These three inputs are interrelated in the sense that labor and fuel depend on the number of machines (the complex is considered to be fully mechanized). One type of sprinkler irrigation system, called "Blue Arrow" is considered by SWIM 2. "Blue Arrow" has fixed pipes that are towed from place to place by tractor. The number of "Blue Arrow" systems that are needed is computed by taking into account the area irrigated and the complementary relationships owing to the fact that not all crops are irrigated at the same time. To determine the number of other machines, such as tractors, that will be needed in the complex, the critical period in the schedule of field operations is taken into account when all the available machines are being used.

The fuel needed by the field machinery is computed on the basis of the fuel used for individual field operations: plowing, cultivation, planting, and harvesting. For irrigated crops, the fuel use for harvesting is higher than for nonirrigated crops because of the higher yield. For all machines and equipment two kinds of annual costs are considered: the fixed costs of depreciated capital investment over the machine life and the variable costs of operation and maintenance.

The labor needed for field operations is calculated on the basis of the number of hours each machine is in the field. The additional labor required for administration and support services is not directly computed but is assigned a cost per hectare of land. Labor costs for irrigation are included in the total cost of irrigation.

Capital Investments: SWIM 2 accounts explicitly for the capital investments required for development of the complex. Two types of capital investments are distinguished in the model: irrigation capital investments and investments for machinery, feedlots, and perennial crops (orchards). The only cost of capital investments included in SWIM 2 is their depreciation over the lifetime of the equipment.[4] The lifetime is taken from the existing standards for Bulgarian conditions.

Crop production and processing.   The key problems in modeling crop production are determining the crop production alternatives and the crop yields. Crop yields are among the most sensitive parameters of SWIM 2. The yields used in SWIM 2 under normal weather conditions are based on average yields obtained in the Silistra region. Because of lack of data, the yields are assumed to be the same regardless of the subregion in which the crops have been planted. However, the structure of SWIM 2 permits the introduction of different yields in the subregions if this is justified.

At present, some crops are not irrigated, and the expected increase in yield with irrigation can only be based on experience gained in other regions with similar conditions. The decrease in yield in response to drought, as well as the yield change in response to fertilizer application, must be similarly estimated. The yield of irrigated crops during drought is assumed not to change because the loss in rainfall is made up by irrigation water.

Crop rotation to keep the natural productivity of the soil is explicitly introduced in SWIM 2. Since SWIM 2 is a static (one-year) model, crop rotation is taken into account by constraining the ratio between the areas of field crops (lucerne, wheat, and barley) and inter-row crops (maize, soybeans, and sunflowers).

The crops harvested from the field can be processed into a number of products (see Figure 4.6). All grain crops are assumed to undergo drying before being further processed or used. No cannery processing is assumed for

---

[4] This treatment of capital costs assumes a zero rate of interest. In cases in which this assumption is inappropriate, a capital charge covering both depreciation and interest could be computed by calculating the capital recovery factor corresponding to the relevant rate of interest and investment life.

fruits and vegetables. Drying is the only processing activity for tobacco considered in SWIM 2.

Use of crop products.   Crop products can be exported, set aside as reserves for the region, fed to livestock in the region, or used by the Silistra population. All estimates of product benefits used in SWIM 2 are based on internal Bulgarian prices taken from Lidgi *et al.* (1976).

In the model, the requirements of the population for cooking oil and fruits are fixed. Vegetables are grown only for internal consumption in the region and their total production is constrained by the area planted.

The simplest way to account for the impact of dry weather on crop production is to build up reserves that can partially make up for crops lost because of bad weather; only reserves of grain crops are considered. SWIM 2 assumes normal weather conditions, but it also accounts for the additional amount of grain needed for feeding livestock if the year turns out to be a dry one. If a certain crop is grown without irrigation, the difference between the yields obtained in a normal year and in a dry year is multiplied by the crop area to give the potential amount of the crop that goes to reserves. This potential amount is further multiplied by a coefficient, which takes into account that not every year in a given sequence will be dry, to give the actual amount of reserves set aside. The reserves are assigned a benefit equivalent to the cost of purchasing an equivalent amount of grain from outside the region.

Since the complex is supposed to be a self-contained crop–livestock enterprise, the export of crops is limited only to fruits and tobacco. All excess feedstuff production is assumed to support the increase in the number of animals that provide the main export goods. The market for livestock production is assumed to be perfectly elastic. Crop imports are not allowed in SWIM 2.

The ultimate goal of the complex is to export livestock products from the region. Four types of animals are assumed to be raised in the complex: cows with associated calves and heifers, sheep, pigs, and hens. The animals are kept in feedlots, on controlled diets made up of five feedstuffs: concentrated forage from grains, green forage freshly cut from the fields, silage, hay, and roughage from the harvest residuals of grain crops. Each animal must receive certain minimum amounts of energy and protein in a balanced diet of the five feedstuffs. To do this, the weights of feedstuffs are converted into their energy equivalent in feed units, where one feed unit is the energy contained in 1 kg of oats. In SWIM 2 each animal receives a certain number of feed units and the number of feed units supplied by each of the feedstuffs is kept within a specified range to maintain a balanced diet.

Animal products are calculated on an annual basis taking into account the population structure of each animal. In certain cases where improvements in productivity beyond 1975 levels can be expected as the complex develops, perspective productivities achievable by 1985 are used. The market prices for these products are taken from Lidgi *et al.* (1976).

General Mathematical Representation

The following description formalizes the relationships between the various

Table 4.5. Aggregated matrix structure of the SWIM 2 model.

Set of constraints \ Decision vectors, x_i	Irrigated and non-irrigated crop areas x_1	Fodder products x_2	Grain products x_3	Population crop products — Grain x_4	Population crop products — Other x_5	Grain reserves x_6
Objective function	c_1	c_2	c_3	b_4	b_5	b_6
Land balance	$A_{1,1}$					
Irrigation and live-stock drinking water	$A_{1,2}$					
Irrigation equipment	$A_{1,3}$					
Fodder production	$A_{1,4}$	$-I$				
Grain production	$A_{1,5}$		$-I$			
Grain production balance			$A_{3,6}$	$-A_{4,6}$		$-A_{6,6}$
Other crop production balance	$A_{1,7}$				$-A_{5,7}$	
Livestock feedstuff requirements		$A_{2,8}$				
Livestock products						
Fertilizers	$A_{1,10}$					
Machinery	$A_{1,11}$					
Capital investments	$A_{1,12}$					
Constrained irrigation water						
Constrained fertilizers						
Constrained capital investments						
Population grain products				I		
Population other products					I	
Livestock numbers						

subsystems in the complex into an aggregated LP format. For ease in the explanation, all decision variables and constraints in the model are aggregated into 15 decision vectors and 18 sets of constraints, as shown in Table 4.5. The objective function OB, which has been adopted for the agricultural production in the region, maximizes the annual net benefits, i.e., the difference between the value of marketed livestock and crop products, and their production costs.

Export of other crop products x_7	Grain products for livestock x_8	Livestock Numbers x_9	Livestock Products x_{10}	Irrigation and drinking water demands x_{11}	Irrigation equipment x_{12}	Fertilizers x_{13}	Machinery x_{14}	Capital investments x_{15}	RHS
b_7		c_9	b_{10}	c_{11}	c_{12}	c_{13}	c_{14}	c_{15}	—
									$\leqslant l$
		$A_{9,2}$		$-I$					$= 0$
					$-I$				$= 0$
									$= 0$
									$= 0$
	$-A_{8,6}$								$= 0$
$-A_{7,7}$									$= 0$
	$A_{8,8}$	$-A_{9,8}$							$\geqslant 0$
		$A_{9,9}$	I						$= 0$
		$-A_{9,10}$				$-I$			$= 0$
							$-I$		$= 0$
		$A_{9,12}$			$A_{12,12}$		$A_{14,12}$	$-I$	$= 0$
				I					$\leqslant w$
						I			$\leqslant f$
								I	$\leqslant k$
									$\geqslant g$
									$\geqslant p$
		I							$\geqslant n$

$$OB = \max \left[\underbrace{b_4 x_4 + b_5 x_5 + b_6 x_6 + b_7 x_7 + b_{10} x_{10}}_{\substack{\text{crop and livestock production} \\ \text{benefits}}} \quad - \underbrace{c_1 x_1}_{\substack{\text{crop} \\ \text{production} \\ \text{cost}}} \quad - \underbrace{c_2 x_2 - c_3 x_3}_{\substack{\text{crop} \\ \text{processing} \\ \text{cost}}} \right.$$

$$\left. - \underbrace{c_9 x_9}_{\substack{\text{livestock} \\ \text{production} \\ \text{cost}}} \quad - \underbrace{c_{11} x_{11} - c_{12} x_{12} - c_{13} x_{13} - c_{14} x_{14} - c_{15} x_{15}}_{\text{input resources cost}} \right] \qquad (4.16)$$

where x_i is a vector of aggregated activities (see Table 4.5); c_i is a vector of costs associated with aggregated activity x_i; and b_i is a vector of benefits associated with x_i. The objective function is maximized subject to the following set of constraints. Matrices denoted by $A_{i,j}$ are located in column i and row j of the LP tableau (Table 4.5).

Land balance.   The area planted cannot exceed the available land area, both irrigated and nonirrigated:

$$A_{1,1} x_1 \leqslant l, \qquad (4.17)$$

where $A_{1,1}$ is a matrix that sums the land used in each subregion; and l is a vector of available land in the three subregions.

Demands for irrigation water and livestock drinking water, and for irrigation equipment.

$$A_{1,2} x_1 + A_{9,2} x_9 - l x_{11} = 0, \qquad (4.18)$$

where $A_{1,2}$ is a matrix of coefficients of crop water use per hectare; $A_{9,2}$ is a matrix of coefficients of livestock water use per animal; and I is the identity matrix.

$$A_{1,3} x_1 - l x_{12} = 0, \qquad (4.19)$$

where $A_{1,3}$ is a matrix of irrigation equipment requirements per hectare.

Fodder and grain production.

$$A_{1,4} x_1 - l x_2 = 0 \qquad (4.20)$$

$$A_{1,5} x_1 - l x_3 = 0, \qquad (4.21)$$

where $A_{1,4}$ and $A_{1,5}$ are matrices of yields of fodder and grain crops, respectively.

Grain production balance.   The grain produced must equal the grain used:

$$A_{3,6}x_3 - A_{4,6}x_4 - A_{6,6}x_6 - A_{8,6}x_8 = 0, \tag{4.22}$$

where $A_{3,6}$, $A_{4,6}$, $A_{6,6}$, and $A_{8,6}$ are matrices that sum up, respectively, total grain production, population requirements of grains, reserves, and grain products for livestock.

Production balance of other crops.

$$A_{1,7}x_1 - A_{5,7}x_5 - A_{7,7}x_7 = 0, \tag{4.23}$$

where $A_{1,7}$, $A_{5,7}$, and $A_{7,7}$ are matrices that sum up the production of other crops (vegetables, tobacco, and fruits), their manpower requirements, and their export, respectively.

Livestock feedstuff requirements.   Livestock feed must at least meet minimum requirements:

$$A_{2,8}x_2 + A_{8,8}x_8 - A_{9,8}x_9 \geqslant 0, \tag{4.24}$$

where $A_{2,8}$, $A_{8,8}$, and $A_{9,8}$ are matrices that sum up fodder products, grain livestock products, and animal diet requirements for these products, respectively.

Livestock products.

$$A_{9,9}x_9 - Ix_{10} = 0, \tag{4.25}$$

where $A_{9,9}$ is a matrix of livestock products generated per animal.

Fertilizers, machinery, and capital investments.   The nutrients that are needed must be supplied by fertilizer or manure.

$$A_{1,10}x_1 - A_{9,10}x_9 - Ix_{13} = 0, \tag{4.26}$$

The machines that are needed must be available:

$$A_{1,11}x_1 - Ix_{14} = 0. \tag{4.27}$$

The capital investment used is summed up:

$$A_{1,12}x_1 + A_{9,12}x_9 + A_{12,12}x_{12} + A_{14,12}x_{14} - Ix_{15} = 0, \tag{4.28}$$

where $A_{1,10}$ and $A_{9,10}$ are matrices of crop fertilizer requirements and manure generation, respectively; $A_{1,11}$ is a matrix with the numbers of each type of machine needed per hectare of crop production; and $A_{1,12}$, $A_{9,12}$, $A_{12,12}$, and $A_{14,12}$ are matrices of capital investments for developing irrigated land, livestock, farmhouses, irrigation equipment, and machinery, respectively.

Constrained input resources.   The input resources used cannot exceed those available:

$$x_{11} \leqslant w \tag{4.29}$$

$$x_{13} \leqslant f \tag{4.30}$$

$$x_{15} \leqslant k, \tag{4.31}$$

where w, f, and k are vectors of the amounts of available water, fertilizers, and capital investments, respectively.

Constrained outputs.   Some production outputs must meet target levels:

$$x_4 \geqslant g \tag{4.32}$$

$$x_5 \geqslant p \tag{4.33}$$

$$x_9 \geqslant n, \tag{4.34}$$

where g, p, and n are vectors of target levels of grain products for the Silistra population (flour and cooking oil), other products for the Silistra population (vegetables, peaches, and tobacco), and numbers of livestock (cattle, sheep, pigs, and hens).

The total dimension of the decision vectors $x_1, \ldots, x_{15}$ is 218 decision variables interrelated by 152 constraints. The LP for SWIM 2 contains 2050 data, representing about 6% of the data density in the tableau.

Analysis of results

To obtain the results of SWIM 2, the IBM 370/168 computer was used, whose LP package is contained in the SESAME mathematical programming system (National Bureau of Economic Research 1972). An optimal solution is obtained in about 280 iterations.

About 70 solutions of SWIM 2 were obtained. Each of the questions addressed has associated with it a few key variables in the model. To formulate a set of computer runs these variables are assumed to take a number of values within a certain range and the model is optimized for each of these values to obtain the required results. First, the validity of the model's representation of the conditions in the Silistra region is examined by comparing its outputs with production statistics recorded in the region in 1975. Next, the consequences of capital investment in irrigation development are analyzed and the impact of restricting the input resources is investigated.

Finally, various scenarios of future growth in water demands are determined on the basis of forecasts of the number of livestock in the region.

Validation of the Model

The goal of validation in the case of SWIM 2 is to ensure that the model adequately reflects the overall realities of the Silistra agricultural production system. It should be noted that SWIM 2 is an optimization and not a simulation model. As such, SWIM 2 possesses internal decision-making capability to maximize net benefits subject to the set of constraints. A simulation model, by contrast, possesses no internal decision-making capability; it is intended only to mirror the actual conditions so that the effects of externally specified decisions can be evaluated.

Data on actual production outputs (e.g., tons of wheat and numbers of animals) from the Silistra region in 1975 are available in the *Bulgarian Statistical Yearbook* (1976). Unfortunately, these data do not include water withdrawals from the Danube so it was not possible to check the model's computation of water withdrawals. For validation, SWIM 2 was run with an irrigated area of 11 400 ha, the amount of irrigated land in the region in 1975.

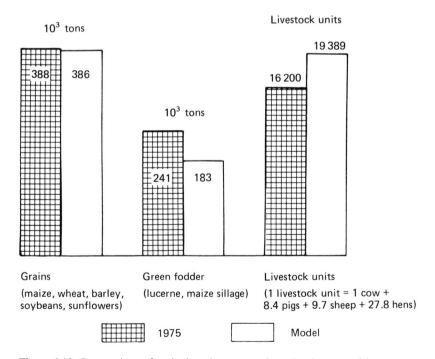

Figure 4.10. Comparison of agricultural aggregated production quantities.

Aggregated production output recorded in the region is compared with the model results in Figure 4.10. The model result shown is the sum of the optimized values of all relevant decision variables; for example, each crop has nine decision variables so the total grain production shown for five crops is the sum of 45 values. Also, in order to avoid drawing a pair of bars for each of the animals, they have all been aggregated by defining a composite livestock unit based on the ratios of the numbers of sheep, pigs, and hens, to the number of cattle in the region in 1975.

Compared with the 1975 data, SWIM 2 gives 0·6% less grain, 24% less green fodder, and 20% more livestock. This is a fairly good agreement, because some of the 1975 production may have been exported from the region and not fed to animals, as SWIM 2 assumes. It may be concluded that the model is reasonably valid at this level of aggregated production quantities.

The comparison begins to diverge, however, when details are considered. For example, Figure 4.11 compares the proportion of total grain production contributed by each crop. The model-optimal solution indicates that 13·1% of the grains should be soybeans, but soybeans were only 0·9% of production in 1975. Decision makers for Silistra have recognized the value of soybeans and progressively larger areas of it are being grown; however, no production of soybeans was recorded for 1974 (Ministry of Information and Communications 1975), so that this discrepancy between the model and the actual conditions may be attributed to the time required to introduce a new crop on a wide scale.

The model calls for more barley and less wheat than were grown in 1975. This may be due to the similar production technologies and costs of these two crops, which make it difficult for the model to choose between them. Small

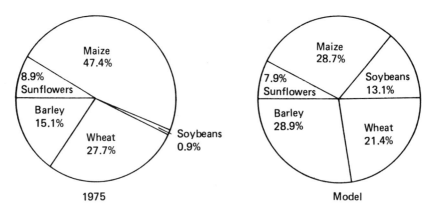

Figure 4.11. Distribution of grain production.

changes in the data can produce dramatic shifts in the balance between SWIM 2's optimal areas of wheat and barley.

The results obtained from the validation run showed that the model is relatively realistic at an aggregated level. Individual crop areas, however, should not be taken too literally—other considerations, such as traditions and methods of crop rotation, probably affect production in ways not included in the model.

Development of Irrigated Land

The most important factor in determining agricultural water demands is the area of land that is developed for irrigation. This development requires extensive capital investment to provide supply facilities at the water source, canals or pipes to bring the water to the field, and equipment to apply the water to the crops. Economic evaluation of this investment plays a central role in determining the area that will be developed.

Developing irrigation increases both the benefits and the costs of an agricultural enterprise because production is intensified. The net benefits (benefits minus costs) of irrigation development are usually positive, but normally, as additional increments of land in a region are converted from dry farming to irrigation, each additional increment in the irrigated area generates a smaller increase in the net benefits over the whole region, i.e., there are diminishing marginal returns on the investment. Before all the arable land

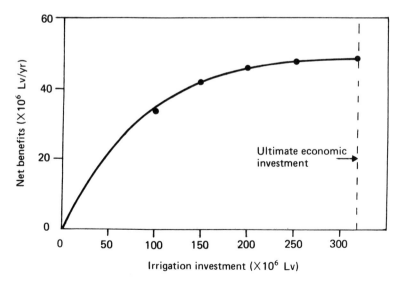

Figure 4.12. Net benefits of irrigation investment in the Silistra region.

is irrigated, a point can be reached at which the marginal cost of additional irrigation equals its marginal benefit. This point can be considered as the ultimate economical level of irrigation development.

In 1975, 11 400 ha of land were developed for irrigation in the Silistra region. Of the 150 000 ha of arable land included in SWIM 2, only 139 700 ha are considered to be potentially irrigable for physical reasons, i.e., limitations of topography, slope, and soil type. With 11 400 ha irrigated, SWIM 2 estimates the average annual net benefits as 105·6 million Lv/yr (1 Leva (Lv) ≅ 1 US$). The additional net benefits generated by investment to develop more irrigated area are shown in Figure 4.12. This figure illustrates the principle of diminishing marginal returns on investment and identifies the ultimate economical investment as approximately 320 million Lv. This is the point of maximum additional net benefits and SWIM 2 does not utilize any further investment funds made available. It should be noted that the investment shown in Figure 4.12 is just a total; it has no time dimension and could actually be provided in increments over many years. The additional net

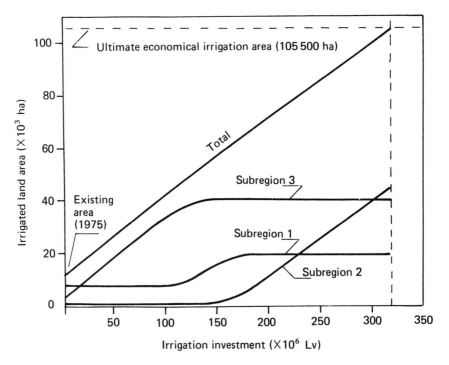

Figure 4.13. Irrigated area and investment.

benefits shown in the figure are those that would accrue on average each year after such an investment program had been completed.

The spatial distribution of future water demands depends on which subregion is chosen first for the development in irrigation. The investment to bring water to the field, expressed in Lv per hectare irrigated, is different for each of the three subregions. It is to be expected that as more investment funds are provided the subregions in which irrigation is relatively cheap will be developed first, as demonstrated in Figure 4.13. Subregion 3 (2750 Lv/ha) is developed first to the limit of its potentially irrigable area, followed by subregions 1 (2850 Lv/ha) and 2 (3170 Lv/ha). The ultimate economical investment is reached before subregion 2 is developed to its limit. The

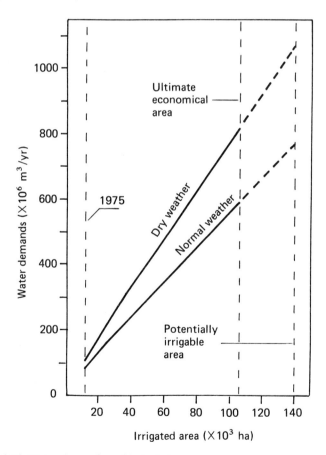

Figure 4.14. Water demands and irrigated area.

corresponding ultimate economical irrigation area is 105 500 ha, which is 70% of the arable land or 75% of the land considered to be potentially irrigable.

The demands for Danube water that result from developing the irrigated area are shown in Figure 4.14 for average weather and dry weather. (The dry-weather condition is representative of a one-in-four year, as explained previously.) The extra water demanded during dry weather is that needed for a fixed irrigation area, i.e., SWIM 2 assumes that in dry weather extra water is applied by longer sprinkling times to the area that would normally be irrigated under average weather conditions.

Under these assumptions, water demands for the 11 400 ha irrigated area are $78 \times 10^6 \, \text{m}^3/\text{yr}$ and $103 \times 10^6 \, \text{m}^3/\text{yr}$ for normal and dry weather, respectively. These demands increase approximately linearly with increasing irrigated area to ultimate economical levels of $585 \times 10^6 \, \text{m}^3/\text{yr}$ (normal) and $820 \times 10^6 \, \text{m}^3/\text{yr}$ (dry). The corresponding water withdrawal coefficients are $5500 \, \text{m}^3/\text{ha}$ (550 mm) for normal weather and $7750 \, \text{m}^3/\text{ha}$ (775 mm) for dry weather. Since an irrigation efficiency of 50% is assumed, these coefficients correspond respectively to 275 mm and 387 mm of consumptive use of irrigation water by the crops over the irrigation season.

If the results obtained from SWIM 2 are extrapolated linearly to estimate water demands for the potentially irrigable area (139 700 ha), total withdrawals of $770 \times 10^6 \, \text{m}^3/\text{yr}$ and $1080 \, \text{m}^3/\text{yr}$ are found. These demands are 32% higher than those for the ultimate economical area. From this it may be concluded that irrigation water demands in the Silistra region could be significantly overestimated if they are calculated from the potentially irrigable area.

The ultimate economical level of irrigation development identified previously is actually the point where the unit cost, or price, of water is equal to its marginal benefit. This is the point at which the water resource system is in equilibrium. The sensitivity of this equilibrium point is an important criterion in determining how much investment should be made in irrigation.

The demand function for water in Figure 4.15 can be derived by differentiating net benefits from Figure 4.12 with respect to water demands shown in Figure 4.14. Using SWIM 2 the demand function is obtained as the dual value (or shadow price) of the constraint on water when all other input resources, except land, are unconstrained. For a given level of demand the marginal value shown in this figure is the increase in average annual net benefits in the complex if one more m^3 of water is supplied. Hence, conceptually, the demand function is the locus of the points of equilibrium of the water system as the unit cost of water is raised.

The water price charged in the Silistra region ($0 \cdot 017 \, \text{Lv/m}^3$) is small compared with its marginal value. The actual unit cost of water, based on the

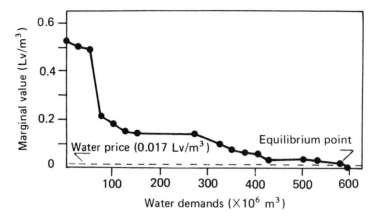

Figure 4.15. Demand function for irrigation water withdrawals in the Silistra region, with average weather conditions. Quantities shown are for one year.

costs of the supply facilities, is estimated to be approximately $0.13\,\text{Lv/m}^3$ in the Silistra region. If this were charged as the water price, the demands at SWIM 2's equilibrium point would fall to $275 \times 10^6\,\text{m}^3$, corresponding to 51 000 ha of irrigated land. The water demands of the 11 400 ha irrigated in 1975 lie in the range of very high marginal values, however, and would be unaffected even if such a price were charged.

The demand function shown in Figure 4.15 is for normal weather conditions. It could be expected that in dry weather conditions the demand for water would be larger and the price would be higher. Thus, the derived demand function for water in agriculture must be associated with a specific set of weather conditions.

It may be noted that most of the results presented from SWIM 2 are based on maximizing net benefits from a fixed area of land, i.e., land is considered as the constraining resource rather than water. This is realistic since the Danube provides an abundant water supply. However, the demand function provides a mechanism by which the effect of water as the constraining resource can be explored, and this could be very useful in regions where the available water resources are limits to development.

Forecasting Water Demands

Forecasts of water demands are the basis for the design of supply facilities. Two types of information are needed: the volume that will be demanded in future years, and the distribution of this volume within a given year to produce flow rates. In the Silistra region the growth in water demands over time is linked to the overall agricultural development of the region; the numbers of livestock are the primary decision variables. The path of agricultural development of the Silistra region will be different depending on which of the animals (cattle, pigs, sheep, or hens) predominates in the near future. The issue of which animals to concentrate on in the development of agricultural production is clearly a very complex one, involving many factors outside the scope of this study.

In order to illustrate the effect on water demands of various assumptions about the future growth in livestock, a set of scenarios has been developed. Each scenario corresponds to specified growth rates in the numbers of each type of livestock in the complex. These growth rates are all assumed to be linear from the base year 1975, i.e., a 2% growth rate means that in each subsequent year, 2% of the number of livestock in 1975 are added to the total.

Four scenarios have been formulated with equal annual growth rates for each animal of 2, 4, and 10%. Two additional scenarios favoring cattle have also been formulated, one in which cattle grow at 5%/yr and other animals at 2%/yr, and another in which cattle grow at 10%/yr, and others at 5%/yr.

For all the scenarios, the numbers of livestock in the complex in 1980, 1990, 1995, and 2000 are computed, and fed into SWIM 2 as fixed variables. SWIM 2 computes the most efficient production system needed to support these numbers of livestock.

The results for normal weather conditions are shown in Figure 4.16. For the faster-growth scenarios, the ultimate economical level of development is reached before the year 2000 so the forecast was terminated at that level. It is striking that water demands grow about four to five times faster than the

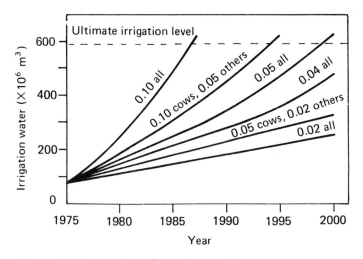

Figure 4.16. Comparison of water demand forecasts.

number of livestock. For example, in the scenario with a 5 % livestock growth rate, water demands increase from 78.1×10^6 m^3/yr in 1975 to 340×10^6 m^3/yr in 1990, an increase of 335 % or 22 %/yr. There is such a difference in the growth of water demands and livestock because the 1975 livestock numbers are almost entirely supported by nonirrigated crop production. To increase the livestock numbers, some of this must be irrigated.

Conclusions

After reviewing the technical results of the Silistra case study, it is relevant to assess the issues addressed by the study, to highlight the advantages and limitations of the model developed in addressing those issues, and to outline the lessons learned in performing this study that may aid those attempting similar studies elsewhere.

The agricultural industrial complex in the Silistra region is a vast enterprise, the largest in Bulgaria, involving about 30 000 people. Its organization resembles a vertically and horizontally integrated corporation: vertically integrated because all functions are controlled, from buying seeds to marketing animal products; and horizontally integrated because all agricultural operations within the 2700 km^2 region are centrally organized. In a market economy an equivalent activity would involve hundreds of farms and businesses.

Planning the development of such a complex is clearly a formidable task. Not only must the budget be set, specifying capital and operating expenses for each year, but also a plan must be evolved to allocate the flows of all physical resources such as water, fuel, machinery, labor, and fertilizers. The development of any sector of the complex, such as irrigation, results in a ripple effect passing through all the activities of the complex, requiring development of the crop and livestock sectors as well to accommodate the increased production from irrigation.

At the time of the study, the irrigation development of the complex was at a threshold—about 10 % of the arable land was irrigated, mostly for vegetables, tobacco and fruit, to meet the needs of the local population. It was the intention of the Bulgarian government to expand livestock production in the complex to produce export products; such an expansion requires a corresponding expansion of irrigation to produce feed crops for livestock. Yet irrigation is very expensive because the water must be pumped uphill from the Danube in pipe systems. Development of even 10 % more of the arable land for irrigation would absorb a significant proportion of the agricultural development budget for the entire country. So the major issues were to ensure that irrigation investment is economical and is in balance with the associated development of other sectors of the complex.

A number of conclusions may be drawn from the results of the SWIM 2 model. At the level of aggregated production quantities, the model compares reasonably well with data recorded in the region in 1975. When more detailed comparisons are made, there are some discrepancies between the model's results and the regional data, which is to be expected since the model optimizes rather than simulates the actual system.

An ultimate economical level of irrigation development, the level of maximum net benefit, is identified as the point where 70% of the arable land is irrigated. This area of irrigation corresponds to complete development of the potentially irrigable land in two of the three subregions within the Silistra region, and to partial development of the third subregion.

Water demands increase approximately linearly with increasing irrigated area, to ultimate economical levels of 585×10^6 m^3/yr (under normal weather conditions), and 820×10^6 m^3/yr (under dry weather conditions). The corresponding water withdrawal coefficients are 5500 m^3/ha (550 mm) under normal weather conditions and 7750 m^3/ha (775 mm) under dry weather conditions. Since an irrigation efficiency of 50% is assumed, these coefficients correspond respectively to 275 mm and 387 mm of consumptive use of irrigation water by the crops. At these levels of development, water demands are quite sensitive to the price of water. Removing the existing price subsidy on water would reduce the ultimate economical irrigation area to about 35% of the arable land.

Further development of livestock production in Silistra beyond 1975 levels would require substantial investments in irrigation because the existing livestock are almost entirely supported by nonirrigated crop production. Over a substantial range of livestock development, the associated demand for water and irrigated area varies linearly with the number of livestock. Each 1% increase in livestock from the 1975 levels requires about 650 ha of new irrigated land, or an increase of 4·5% in irrigated area. The corresponding increase in water demands amounts to $3·5 \times 10^6$ m^3/yr.

What are the advantages of using SWIM 2 rather than the conventional methods of estimating agricultural water use? The major advantage of SWIM 2 is that it integrates the regional water demands with the crop and livestock production processes that determine these demands. This allows for various substitutions to be made among the inputs to these production processes and among the production processes themselves. The integrated nature of the model is particularly important in the Silistra region because it corresponds to the centralized management structure controlling all aspects of agricultural production.

Although SWIM 2 covers only a one-year time period in each solution, it can be used to look at longer time horizons by forecasting various scenarios of the growth in livestock numbers and by running SWIM 2 for several future years to derive the corresponding forecasts of water demands. Since the numbers of livestock are the primary variables of interest to Silistra decision makers, SWIM 2 provides a means for evaluating the impact of various livestock development strategies. However, these results should be interpreted carefully, because SWIM 2 does not discount benefits or costs over time, only one set of production coefficients has been used, and no economies of scale are included.

A number of limitations of SWIM 2 may also be noted. The model is not dynamic since it does not contain internally the linkages of year-to-year evolution. Another limitation is that livestock processing is treated only in a very aggregated way. As with most models, improvement of the data on the more sensitive variables would improve the accuracy of the results. Better data on crop yields, crop production costs, prices for outputs, and water use coefficients would be especially useful.

The study was made as a cooperative endeavor between IIASA and the Bulgarian Ministry of Agriculture and Food Industry. The modelers visited Bulgaria several times during the course of the study to present successive versions of the model to officials in Sofia and Silistra, and to obtain suggestions as to how the model could be further developed to meet the needs of the region. One of the modelers is Bulgarian; the results of the work were translated into the Bulgarian language; the final model was implemented on the Ministry's computer. All of these steps are necessary to ensure that the methodology is relevant and is transferred to those whom it is meant to help. The study was probably fairly successful in this regard.

In the formulation of the study, many issues were raised for investigation—the substitution of fertilizers for water as production inputs, the choice between different types of irrigation systems, the comparison between water demands of average years and dry years, to name a few. Some of these were eliminated because of the lack of available data (e.g., types of irrigation systems), some incorporated into the model in an approximate way (e.g., average and dry year water demands), and some in considerable detail (e.g., substitution of fertilizers for water as input resources). In retrospect, it appears that because the scope of the model is so wide, covering the irrigation, crop, and livestock sectors, very detailed treatment of small variabilities in the system (e.g., fertilizer–water substitutions) should be sacrificed in the interests of ensuring that all important aspects of the system can be modeled in at least some form.

Overall, it seems that linear programming is one of the most appropriate methodologies to provide quantitative analysis of water demands for irrigation development in the region. It also has been demonstrated that a sound coverage of all the relevant aspects of the problem is more useful than detailed treatment of only some of them.

5 *Municipal Water Demands**

Introduction

In most industrialized countries more than 80 % of the population lives in cities or other urban communities. The residents of these urban areas are provided with a variety of water services, including water supply, sewage collection and treatment, and wastewater disposal. The volumes of water demanded for each of these purposes vary considerably from place to place as a consequence of the differing characteristics of the users and the uses, the physical and climatic differences between locations, and various differences in economic and social policies. Municipal water demand modeling therefore requires detailed analyses of different water uses, and the factors that affect them.

The determination of municipal demand for water is an important task for water service enterprises, and involves three interrelated activities:

(1) *Supply management:* water-use forecasts must be made so that investments in new supply facilities can be properly scaled, sequenced, and timed (Erlenkotter and Trippi 1976, Linaweaver *et al.* 1966).
(2) *Demand management:* the impact of demand management policies such as water meter installation, leak detection and control, moral persuasion, price changes, and the imposition of non-price rationing regulations (see

* This chapter was written by S. H. Hanke and L. de Maré. The authors express their appreciation to M. Dynarski and D. Koran, graduate students at Johns Hopkins University, for their assistance in computer programming and econometric analyses for the Malmö case study, and to R. W. Wentworth for his comments on an earlier draft of this chapter. The division of responsibility for the preparation of this chapter was as follows: S. H. Hanke was responsible for final editing. With the exception of the Malmö case study, C. S. Russell performed the original drafting. Russell's draft was based on materials compiled by S. H. Hanke, D. R. Maidment, J. Mülschlegel, and P. Yletyinen while they were members of the IIASA Resources and Environment Area. The case study of Malmö was the sole responsibility of S. H. Hanke and L. de Maré. Hanke was responsible for the econometric modeling and analysis, as well as the original drafting of this section; de Maré was responsible for the data collection and organization; and both authors participated in the interpretation of results.

Hanke 1970, 1980a,b, Wenders 1982, Howe and Linaweaver 1967, and Hanke and Mehrez 1979a, respectively), on water use must be estimated in such a way that the benefits and costs of changes in these policies can be evaluated (Hanke 1980a, 1981, 1982).

(3) *Demand–supply management:* water-use forecasts must be made so that supply and demand management policies can be integrated and coordinated (Hanke 1978).

It is important to re-emphasize the distinction made elsewhere in this book between water use and water demand. Water use refers to the volumes of water applied to achieve various ends; it is a descriptive concept. Demand, as pointed out in Chapter 1, refers to the schedule of quantities that consumers would use per unit of time at particular prices per unit of water used. This is an analytical concept, and can therefore provide water service enterprises with information relevant for supply, demand, and demand–supply management decisions. This is the case when water demand models explicitly contain demand management policy variables.

The discussion in the initial part of this chapter concentrates on water use. Later, prices are specifically taken into account in the case of a water demand model for Malmö, Sweden, developed within the framework of a study on water resources management in the southwestern Skåne region carried out jointly by IIASA and the Lund Institute of Technology.

An Overview of Municipal Water Use

Municipal water uses cover a wide range of activities, but for convenience these may be grouped into six categories, as set out in Table 5.1. The volumes of water and wastewater involved, and the timing of their use vary considerably within and between the different categories.

Residential water use covers all uses of water by households, both within and immediately outside the confines of a residence. Thus it includes requirements for food preparation, toilet, laundry, and bathing within a house or apartment, and needs for car washing and lawn sprinkling outside. The volume of water use varies considerably according to the nature of the residence (the stock of its water-using capital), family composition, occupation of the residents, whether use is metered or unmetered, and so on.

Industrial water used in a city may be supplied by a water supply enterprise, it may be self-supplied from nearby surface or groundwater, or both. Water for drinking, boiler feeding, and process use is often supplied by a water supply enterprise, and cooling water is obtained by the plant's own system from surface or groundwater. In some instances industrial users have

Table 5.1. Components of municipal water use. Note that some types of activity appear more than once because they occur in more than one sector.

Sector	Activity
Residential	Washing and cooking, including food preparation and waste disposal Toilet Bath and/or shower Laundry House cleaning Yard and/or garden watering Car washing Other personal uses
Industrial	Construction and demolition Light industrial activities, e.g., assembly operations Small heavy-water uses and/or water polluting industrial activities, e.g., waste paper mills, electroplating operations, textile dyeing and finishing
Commercial	Trade in goods in shops Office conducted commerce Food and beverage services Accommodation services Warehouses
Transportation	Railways Buses, taxis, and other road vehicle servicing facilities, such as stations and garages Ports and airports
Public	National, state, and local government offices Fire fighting Irrigation and care of public parks and swimming pools Street cleaning and sewer flushing Solid residuals disposal Water department uses Educational services Health services Welfare services Public toilets and public baths Other public services
Lost and unaccounted for water	Leakage in supply and distribution systems Unmetered users and non- or under-registering metered users Evaporation from open reservoirs

their own water supplies but discharge wastewater into municipal sewers. In certain cases intake water demands from the municipal system are very large, amounting to millions of liters per day. In other cases, intake water demand is small, but the wastewater contains large quantities of residuals or quantities of difficult-to-treat residuals, such as chemicals from electroplating operations.[1]

Commercial services include such diverse activities as banking, the retail trade, hotel accommodation, and catering services. The ways in which water is used in these activities, the qualities required, the quantities and types of liquid residuals generated, and the magnitudes and time patterns of use vary widely within the sector and even within a given type of activity, as identified in Table 5.1.

Transportation services make some demands on water supply and waste disposal services, including water for washing locomotives, vehicles, or aircraft; water supply for trains, buses, and aircraft; and means of discharging wastes from these activities.

Public services also include a wide range of activities, such as government offices, fire fighting, hospitals, street cleaning, solid residuals collection/handling/disposal. In some instances these uses account for a significant portion of the total municipal water demand, especially in communities that have little manufacturing industry or in which a strong emphasis is placed on the maintenance of parks and similar facilities.

Lost and unaccounted for water includes leaks in the water distribution system, evaporation from reservoirs, and/or improperly registered (metered) use, sometimes amounting to as much as half the water supplied to a community (Howe 1970). *~ mars well ats l sustainability*

Residential water use[2]

Residential water use may constitute well over half of the total municipal use in many communities. This conclusion is supported by information compiled in the USA (Howe and Linaweaver 1967), in the Netherlands (Mülschlegel 1979), and in Australia (Hanke and Smart 1979).

Because residential water use is generally the most important component of municipal water use it is worth examining in detail the set of residential water use unit processes, using data collected from residences in various locations in the US, Sweden, and the Netherlands. Consider the summary material in Table 5.2, and note the substantial differences between certain

[1] Note that this category is dealt with elsewhere in this volume and so is not discussed further in this chapter.

[2] A few definitions will help keep things straight in the subsequent discussion. A *household* can consist of a single individual or a group of individuals living together. The physical area in which they live, comprising rooms and any associated garden or lawn, is the *residence*. The living area inside a building is termed a *dwelling unit*. Total residential water use is made up of two major components: *in-house* or so-called domestic uses are those that take place inside the dwelling unit; and *outdoor* uses are those such as lawn sprinkling that take place outside the dwelling unit.

Table 5.2. Residential water use in selected countries.

(*a*) Mean residential water use (in l/person/day).

Type of activity	Netherlands[a]	Sweden[b]	USA[c]
Kitchen	17	50	45
Bathroom	27	70	60
Toilet	39	40	70
Laundry	17	30	45
Other (incl. outdoor use)	4	25	75
Total	104	215	295

[a] Mülschlegel (1976).
[b] VAV (1975).
[c] Meta Systems (1977).

(*b*) Water use in various types of residence (in l/household/day) (from Liimatainen and Virta 1975).

Type of residence	Water use
German Democratic Republic	
Single-family house	
without bath or shower	25
with bath, without shower	50
without bath, with shower	60
with bath and shower	100
Multi-family house	
without bath or hot water	60
with bath, without hot water	80
with bath and hot water	100
Row house, with bath, hot water,	
and district heating	200
Farmhouse	150
Modern single-family house, with all appliances, garden, and car	250
Soviet Union	
Residence	
with shower, without bath	125–150
with shower, without bath, with gas	130–160
with shower and bath, central heating with solid fuel	150–180
with shower and bath, central heating with gas	180–230
with shower and bath, and district heating	275–400
without water pipe or shower	30–50

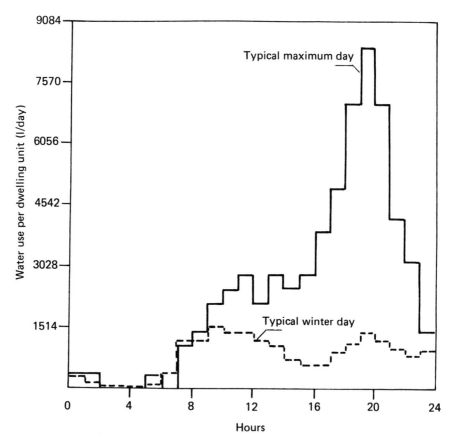

Figure 5.1. Diurnal pattern of water use in a single-family residential section in Baltimore, Maryland, USA (from Wolff *et al.* 1966).

categories, particularly those for outdoor uses. However, the total household uses in Sweden and the US are rather similar, and the similarity is even more pronounced when outdoor use is subtracted, and we focus on total indoor use.[3] Determining the variables that explain both these similarities and differences is an important aspect of water demand modeling.

Significant variations in residential water use occur according to the time of day and the season. Figure 5.1 shows the diurnal pattern of water use in a

---

[3] One complication not reflected in Table 5.2 is created by heating systems based on centralized provision of hot water, such as from a district utility. If the water that enters the house's heating system is counted in "use" the figures in the table would be substantially increased—perhaps by 100–170l/day per household (based on data from Liimatainen and Virta 1975).

single-family residential section of Baltimore, Maryland, USA, which reflects the variations in activities in residences throughout the day. Seasonal variations in residential water use depend particularly on climate, culture, and economic circumstances. For example, in some arid regions of the US, peak residential water use in summer is several times greater than peak use in winter, reflecting the use of water for lawn sprinkling, air conditioning, and swimming pools.

Variations in residential water use within the same type of dwelling unit and with the same size of household are primarily reflections of differences in economic circumstances, available technology, behavioral patterns, and the impact of various external factors such as public policy with respect to water pricing, water allocation programs, and water quality standards. A household's choice of water-use technologies is determined by these factors. For example, in the long term, the consumer can choose between various toilet tank sizes, going from as low as 6 liters (typical in Finland) to as high as 20 liters (typical in the US). Further, low-water-use washing machines, dishwashers, and shower heads are widely available (Howe 1970). There are also technological innovations that *indirectly* affect residential water use; for example, the shift from fresh to processed fruits and vegetables and to the preparation of vegetables in stores (e.g., removing tops of vegetables, wash-

Table 5.3. Water use in ten metered and eight flat-rate (unmetered) areas in the US, October 1963 to September 1965 (Howe and Linaweaver 1967).

	Metered areas (10)	Flat-rate areas (8)
Annual average (l/day/dwelling unit)		
Leakage and waste	95	137
Household	935	894
Sprinkling	705	1590
Total	1735	2621
Maximum day	3706	8910
Peak hour	9391	19569
Annual (cm of water)		
Sprinkling	31	99
Potential evapotranspiration	76	66
Summer		
Sprinkling	19	70
Potential evapotranspiration	30	39
Precipitation	1	11

ing, and packaging) has resulted in reduced residential water use in food preparation.

An important factor that influences consumer choices of alternative water-use technologies and their utilization rates is the price charged for a unit of water. When prices per unit are relatively high, consumers will choose relatively low utilization rates or will use water-conserving technologies. At one extreme, unmetered households face a unit price of water that is zero because the decision to use one more or less liter of water will not affect the payment made to the supplying enterprise. Metered use and a charge per unit used, on the other hand, implies that a decision to use one more (less) unit raises (lowers) the water bill by the amount of the unit charge. Not surprisingly, studies have shown that water use is significantly lower in situations where metering has been introduced. For example, Howe and Linaweaver (1967) showed that water demand in the US was almost 20% lower in metered residences than in unmetered ones (Table 5.3); an investigation in Israel showed that water use in metered apartment units was 25% lower than in unmetered ones (Kamen and Dar 1973); and Hanke's (1970) investigation concluded that residential use in Boulder, Colorado, fell by 36% after meters were installed.

Water use by commercial activities

Commercial water-use categories include such activities as the retail and wholesale trades, restaurants and buffets, hotels and related activities, barber shops and beauty parlors, cinemas and theaters, and various types of offices. Although much less effort has been devoted to the study of water uses in such activities than to that in residences, the results of the research undertaken indicate that there are significant variations in water use both within and across activity groups.

For many of these activities it is appropriate to measure water use in units of litres per day per employee (l/emp-d), although in other cases more specialized units relating to the particular activities are appropriate (Wolff et al. 1966). As shown in Table 5.4, for normal activities where water is used primarily for personal use by employees and for keeping working areas clean, water use appears to average about 30 l/emp-d. This may increase to 100 l/emp-d if conditions are dirty, and be even higher where an activity uses water in its operations, as do laundries and restaurants.

Water use in commercial activities is affected by some of the same general factors that influence residential water use. Thus, use in offices is likely to be conditioned not only by the specific technologies available, such as the size of toilet tanks, but also by the behavioral patterns of workers, notably the times they arrive for and leave work, the frequency with which they take breaks,

Table 5.4. Water use in selected commercial service activities.

Type of facility	Water use	Source
Offices	20–25 l/emp-d[a]	2
Offices	40–55 l/emp-d	1
Shops	20–25 l/emp-d	2
Shops	200 l/day/meter frontage	1
Other businesses		
with dirty conditions	50–100 l/emp-d	2
bakery	150–450 l/emp-d	2
butcher	100–400 l/emp-d	2
hairdresser	100–300 l/emp-d	2
garage	35 l/day/car	2
garage	40 l/day/car	1
laundry	40–80 l/kg clothes	2
laundry	950–1900 l/day/machine	1
Hotels		
room without bath	50–100 l/day/room	2
room with bath	100–150 l/day/room	2
Motel (without kitchen)	380–570 l/day/unit	1
Restaurants	25–40 l/customer	1

[a] Emp = employee; emp-d = employee day.
Sources: 1. Metcalf and Eddy (1972); 2. Liimatainen and Virta (1975).

and their interest—if any—in water conservation. Water use in hotels can also vary considerably, depending on the number of baths or showers provided, whether automatic turnoff valves have been installed on basin faucets, and whether the management is conscious of and has a program for reducing water wastage.

Although no satisfactory studies have reported on the responsiveness of activities in the commercial sector to metering and water pricing, it seems reasonable to assume that there would be some response. However, since the users (often employees) do not pay the bills, the incentive to conserve is indirect, often coming from management policies and/or municipal regulations, such as those incorporated in municipal building codes. Therefore, one should expect a somewhat less marked response to metering and water pricing for commercial water-use activities than for similar residential activities.

Water use by public service activities

The public service sector includes a wide range of activities, such as government offices, hospitals, schools, fire fighting, street cleaning, and

Table 5.5. Water use in selected public service activities.

Type of facility	Water demand	Source
Hospitals (l/day/patient)		
average	570–950	1
average	400–600	2
average	630	3
psychiatric or for permanently disabled	330	3
Nursing home	300	3
Nursing home (for elderly)	100–400	2
Schools (l/day/student)		
without showers	1·5–2	2
with showers	10–15	2
with cafeteria	40–55	1
with cafeteria and showers	55–75	1
kindergarten	15	3
primary	9	3
secondary	8	3
secondary trade	15	3
slow-learner	10	3
Swimming pools		
for showers (l/customer)	40–200	2
for water changes (l/day/m³ pool)	100–150	2

Sources: 1. Metcalf and Eddy (1972); 2. Liimatainen and Virta (1975); 3. Mülschlegel (1977).

recreational services in public parks. However, there have been fewer investigations of the factors affecting water use in these activities than in residential activities. Some data on water use in hospitals, schools, and public swimming pools are shown in Table 5.5. The average water use for hospitals is about 600 l/day/patient, but less water is used in special types of hospitals such as those for the permanently disabled or the elderly. Schools display a range of water-use levels, from 1.5 to 75 l/day/student, depending on the facilities at the school.

Among other public services, fire fighting can sometimes be an important municipal water user. An equation developed by Camp and Lawler (1969) may be used to calculate the volumes required for such services:

$$Q_f = 64·6\sqrt{P}(1 - 0·01\sqrt{P}),$$

where Q_f is the water flow in l/sec needed for fire fighting for a municipal area of population P (in thousands). This flow should be sustainable for four hours for a population of 1000, six hours for 2000, eight hours for 4000, and 10 hours for 6000 or more. In the US, at least, a major influence on planning for water supply for fire protection is the set of design values established by the American Insurance Association, which are similar to those presented by Camp and Lawler (1969).

The available data on public service activities indicate that there are important diurnal, seasonal, and locational variations in water use, but there has been little empirical investigation of the factors that influence these variations. Moreover, since charges are usually not assessed by these public activities according to water intake and wastewater discharge, even where use is measured, it would not be feasible to determine the impact of price changes on use. Even if charges were assessed, it is not clear to what extent—if at all—they would affect water demand by the public authorities conducting these activities, since the public sector managers are driven by different incentives for conservation than those in the private sector (Niskanen 1971).

Lost and unaccounted for water

In all municipal systems, some water is inevitably lost between inlet meters and legitimate customer withdrawal points. Some of this leaks out underground through faulty pipes, joints, and valves, and some may be lost because of illegal, or at least unrecognized, connections. For systems in which all legitimate users may be assumed to be metered, it is possible to estimate the fraction of water lost through the combination of these causes, and, as has been pointed out above, such estimates run as high as 50% (Hanke 1981). Such figures naturally give cause for great concern, for they suggest that in all systems losses may be one of the most important "users" of water.

There are, however, reasons for treating such estimates with caution, the most important being the bias built into the measurement system. New or newly reconditioned water meters are designed to record water volumes accurately, but after some years deterioration causes them to *under*-register. Thus, depending on the age of a system's meters, a greater or smaller percentage of water introduced will appear to be lost simply due to meter performance. This under-registration can amount to a significant fraction of the "losses" calculated as the simple residual: metered input minus metered output. Unfortunately, there seems to have been no careful and comprehensive research into the extent of meter under-registration and true system losses over a range of fully metered systems of various ages and using various maintenance techniques and schedules. Such research would help in understanding observed (apparent) water-use patterns, and would begin to give a firmer foundation for dealing with analyses of aggregated demands.

Aggregation of Water Uses at the Municipal Level

The average water use for an entire city or section of a city can be estimated using data on the individual water-use activities presented above, together with knowledge of the distribution of these activities in the area

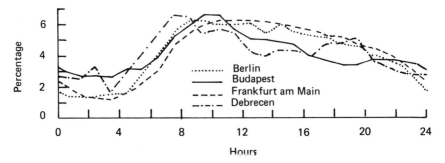

Figure 5.2. Diurnal patterns of water use in some European cities (from Csuka 1976).

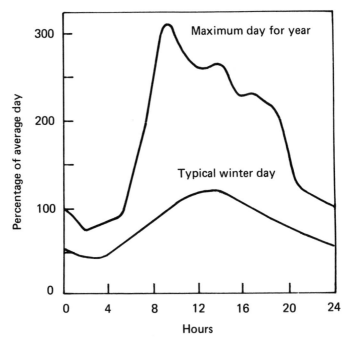

Figure 5.3. Diurnal pattern of water use in Palo Alto, California (from Linsley and Franzini 1972).

under consideration. Account must also be taken of the diurnal and seasonal variations in water use. Figure 5.2 shows the diurnal variations in demand for several European cities. In these cases water use peaks between mid-morning to mid-day and is lowest from midnight to 4 am. Considerable seasonal variations may also occur, as shown in Figure 5.3, which is based on data from Palo Alto, California, where the peak demand during the maximum day for the year is more than three times the average daily demand.

Modeling Municipal Water Demands

A variety of attempts have been made to improve understanding of municipal water demands through the development of models. Either of the two approaches discussed in Chapter 2 may be used: the statistical or engineering method. By far the greatest emphasis has been on the first approach.

The statistical approach

Statistical techniques can be very helpful in identifying factors to account for variations in municipal water use. The most commonly used statistical technique has been multiple regression analysis, in which cross-sectional data are regressed on water use. Other variations of the statistical method involve the use of time series data or pooled time series and cross-sectional data.

The statistical studies of aggregated or total municipal water demands have been most popular, since aggregated water production data are relatively easy to obtain. The most noteworthy finding is that there is an inverse relationship between the amount of water produced and the price charged per unit of water (see, for example, data reported in Hanke 1978).

Residential water demands have also been the subject of considerable statistical modeling and studies, which also display the inverse price–quantity relationship. In addition, these studies enable several other general observations to be made: (1) per capita water use is inversely correlated with household size (Morgan 1973); (2) per capita water use is positively correlated to income per capita (Danielson 1979); (3) water use per residence is inversely correlated with rainfall per unit of time (Danielson 1979); (4) water use per residence is positively correlated with average temperature (Danielson 1979); and (5) water use per residence is positively correlated with irrigable area (lot size) per residence (Linaweaver et al. 1966).

The engineering approach

Engineering or unit process models, although not often used outside the industrial category, can also be applied to analyses of water demand relationships in the municipal sector. By giving detailed consideration to costs of alternative combinations of inputs in specific settings, these models can yield useful indirect estimates of water demand. Also, aggregation of these unit processes in various user categories is conceptually, if not necessarily practically, straightforward.

An illustration of a specific application of this approach is the analysis of water conservation in residences. The approach would be to estimate the costs of different types of devices that would reduce water use for given purposes. The resulting information could then be used in an attempt to compute behavioral responses to such factors as increases in water and wastewater-disposal prices, the imposition of regulations, and combinations of these two. Such a study was conducted by Howe (1970) for the US National Water Commission, containing a very careful inventory of prices and characteristics of alternative technologies in the major household water-use areas. Using a range of household interest (discount) rates, Howe calculated, for each technology, the water price at which it would become attractive to the homeowner by balancing capital cost (purchase price) against future savings in water bills (net of additional operating expenses where these would be incurred). In this way he derived a price–quantity relationship for residential water demand.

Although the engineering approach can be used to gain valuable insights into probable changes in water-use patterns, particularly for industrial use, the statistical approach appears to be the most promising for the residential use category. It is to this statistical modeling of residential demands, the largest category of municipal water use, that we now turn our attention.

Residential Water Demand: A Statistical Case Study

In this study of residential water use, attention is focused on the estimation of water demands (rather than a description of water uses) for purposes of demand management. Hence we concentrate on the estimation of price impacts (price elasticities) on residential water demand.[4] The plan is as follows: first, an attempt to measure the price elasticity of demand for urban (municipal) water use in southwestern Sweden is described and reviewed; secondly, an analysis of the residential water demand, which includes estimates of price elasticities, for Malmö, Sweden, is presented; and thirdly, some observations are made concerning the most effective procedures for

[4] The price elasticity of demand is defined at the point P, Q as $(dQ/dP)(P/Q)$, where P is the real price, Q is the quantity of water demanded, and Q is a function of P.

collecting and analyzing water-use data so that they can be used to determine the demand for water and more specifically the price elasticities characterizing that demand.

Urban water demand in southwestern Sweden

An initial attempt to model urban water use in southwestern Sweden was made by Hashimoto and de Maré (1980) using multiple regression analysis. Their study contained several noteworthy characteristics common to many studies of urban water demand. First, water production data were utilized as proxies for the amount of water actually "used". Secondly, it was a study of aggregated water use, including all categories of total urban water use. Thirdly, the models employed cross-sectional data from 20 communities from the year 1975.

From the perspective of water demand modeling, however, this study failed to generate satisfactory results, since the real price of water was found to be positively correlated with total water produced per capita, whereas demand theory indicates that the amount of a normal commodity that consumers demand in any time period should be negatively correlated with its real price (Becker 1962). It is therefore necessary to question this approach.

The first problem associated with the Swedish study concerns the use of water production data as proxies for metered water-use data. Since water production data were a measure of all water produced in each community, they included all types of water uses, including system leakage. However, for the purpose of water demand modeling, one must employ water-use data measured by metered consumption, not production. It is this use that individuals and firms can control directly by their individual water-use decisions. Hence, this use reflects the amount of water that consumers and firms demand at various prices.

Data from water production records contain too much "noise" to be meaningful for demand modeling. Hence, the signs and magnitudes of the explanatory variables in demand models (regression equations) cannot be relied upon. Since water production data include system leakage, water demand measures based on water production per capita will exceed measures based on metered use per capita. Hence, at the extreme, it is possible to obtain a positive correlation between real price and water produced per capita. This can occur in cross-sectional studies if communities with relatively high real water prices also lose a relatively large proportion of their water production through system leakage.[5]

---

[5] If the percentage of water lost due to system leakage remains roughly the same over time, this problem will not be as serious in time series studies.

The second problem encountered in the initial study is related to the aggregation of all classes of water users. Even if the total metered water use for each community had been used, rather than total water production, however, the aggregation problem would still have been present.

The aggregation of water-use classes presents a problem in demand modeling because different classes of water users respond to price changes in different ways; i.e., they have different price elasticities for water demand. Hence, the demand elasticity obtained using aggregated water use (or production) data will be nothing more than a weighted average elasticity for the area studied. In a cross-sectional study it is dependent, in part, on the percentage of aggregated water use (or production) in each water-use class in each community. Hence, unless all communities in the population have the same percentage of water use (or production) in each user class, the elasticity derived will vary, depending on the sample of communities chosen.[6] It is even possible that aggregation itself can produce such anomalies as a positive coefficient on price, if the price structures faced by the individual user classes are different.

The last problem associated with the initial study is endemic to all cross-sectional demand studies. Price elasticities derived in this way measure how individuals (or aggregations of individuals) in different locations have responded to different real prices at the same point in time. To use these elasticities to predict changes in water use by one individual (or aggregation of individuals) at one location, over time, one must assume that the same individuals will respond to real price changes over time in a way that is equivalent to the way in which different individuals have responded to different real prices at the same point in time. This is a rather bold assumption.

Water demand models and price elasticity estimates for demand management purposes should be based on the following types of data (for a more detailed discussion of these issues, see Hanke 1970, Hanke and Mehrez 1979b):

(1) metered water-use data;
(2) data disaggregated by user class (these user classes should be defined so that they contain similar customers who are likely to have similar responses to price changes. Moreover, these data can be collected most

---

[6] If the percentage of water use (or production) by customer class remains constant over time and aggregated data are used, then the problem of variability in elasticities, depending on the sample period chosen, will not be serious in time series studies. However, even in this case, aggregated data will only yield a weighted average elasticity for the area under study.

efficiently by taking a sample of individual users within each user class; see Hanke and Mehrez 1979b); and

(3) water-use and price data collected over a relatively long time series, with a relatively large number of real price changes.

Residential water demand in Malmö, Sweden

A study of residential water demand in Malmö, Sweden, that corrects for the deficiencies of the initial attempt and related studies is now presented (Hanke and de Maré 1982). Before this study is described, it will be instructive to make a few observations about other time series studies. First, it is important to note the paucity of urban water demand studies based on time series data (see Danielson 1979, Carver and Boland 1980, Colander and Haltiwanger 1979, Hanke 1970, Hanke and Mehrez 1979a, Hogarty and MacKay 1975, Morgan 1974, Wong 1972, Young 1973), in sharp contrast with the relatively large number of studies based on cross-sectional analyses. Secondly, and more importantly, only one of these studies (Danielson 1979) is based on the type of microdata that is recommended when conducting water demand (price elasticity) studies. However, even this study should be viewed with some caution, since it is based on a relatively short time series (five years), and contains only three changes in the nominal price of water.

Characteristics of the Malmö Data

The data collected in Malmö meet the criteria outlined above, and therefore provide a unique opportunity to analyze residential water demand and to estimate price elasticities. Table 5.6 provides a summary of the data collected. Several points are particularly noteworthy. The time series data used are for 14 semi-annual time periods, starting with the last quarter of 1971 and ending with the third quarter of 1978. The cross-sectional data are from a stratified sample of 69 single-family houses in Malmö.[7] The water-use data are from semi-annual, metered water-use records. The income data are from income tax records. The number of adults and children occupying each house, and the rainfall per semi-annual period are all from records maintained by the city of Malmö. The price of water is the real (constant crowns) marginal price per m^3; a value that remains constant for each house in each billing period, regardless of the quantity of water used. During the study period the nominal (before deflation) price per m^3 was changed five times and the real price changed in 12 of the 14 semi-annual periods.

---

[7] The 69 houses were separated into two groups. One group was constructed in the period 1936–46 and the other in 1968–69.

Table 5.6. Characteristics of the Malmö data (1971–78).

Variable	Mean	Standard deviation	Type of data
Q	75·2106	36·2893	TS–CS
Inc	49497·0000	21781·0000	TS–CS
Ad	2·0500	0·7460	TS–CS
Ch	0·9260	1·0418	TS–CS
R	39·1324	7·7768	TS
Age	0·5401	0·4986	CS
P	1·7241	0·3190	TS

Notes: It is important to note that these data contain no proxies. Data represent real values for the variables studied.

Q = quantity of metered water used per house, per semi-annual period (in m^3).

Inc = real gross income per house per annum (in Swedish crowns; actual values reported per annum and interpolated values used for mid-year periods).

Ad = number of adults per house, per semi-annual period.

Ch = number of children per house, per semi-annual period.

R = rainfall per semi-annual period (in mm).

Age = a dummy variable with a value of 1 for those houses built between 1968 and 1969, and a value of 0 for those houses built between 1936 and 1946.

P = real price in Swedish crowns per m^3 of water, per semi-annual period (includes all water and sewer commodity charges that are a function of water use).

TS = time-series data (14 semi-annual periods, starting with the last quarter of 1971 through the first quarter of 1972 and ending with the second and third quarters of 1978).

CS = cross-sectional data (69 houses that have remained with the same head of household during the seven-year study period).

Model and Empirical Results

Since the data available are of both the time series and cross-sectional type, and since they meet the criteria for pooling (Pindyck and Rubinfeld 1976, pp 202–11), one is able to perform demand modeling (multiple regression analysis). This pooling approach has two advantages compared with either pure time series or pure cross-sectional analyses. First, the number of observations and, therefore, the degrees of freedom in our regression equations are increased. Instead of a time series study with 14 observations or a cross-sectional study with 69 observations, data pooling yields 959 observations.[8] Secondly, pooling allows us to include variables that vary over time (price and rainfall) or over households (age of dwelling), but that do not vary over both dimensions. For these reasons, a pooled analysis yields more efficient estimators for regression equations than either pure time series or pure cross-sectional analyses.

[8] Note that data are not reported for some variables, for some of the houses, for some of the time periods, yielding, therefore, less than the potential of 966 observations.

Table 5.7. Demand equation for Malmö.

Linear model

$Q = 64 \cdot 7 + 0 \cdot 00017\, Inc + 4 \cdot 76\, Ad + 3 \cdot 92\, Ch - 0 \cdot 406\, R + 29 \cdot 03\, Age - 6 \cdot 42\, P$

$\qquad\qquad (3 \cdot 26) \qquad (2 \cdot 98) \quad (3 \cdot 09) \qquad (3 \cdot 12) \quad (11 \cdot 54) \quad (1 \cdot 99)$

$R^2 = 0 \cdot 259$

Notes:

1. Numbers in parentheses are t-statistics.
2. For the degrees of freedom in our equation, the critical value for the t-statistics, at the 5 % level of significance, is 1·98.
3. Tests for multicollinearity, serial correlation (the Durbin–Watson test) and hetero-skedasticity (the Goldfeld–Quant test) have been made to ensure that the methodology (OLS analysis) is consistent with the assumptions required to obtain un-biased estimates of the parameters and t-statistics. The equation presented passed these tests. Hence, the price elasticities derived are efficient elasticities.
4. It is important to realize that our pooled data are dominated by cross-sectional data. Hence, the value of R^2, which would be low for a pure time-series study, is satisfactory for our pooled analysis because of the large variation across individual units of cross-sectional observation which is inherently present in the data. For purposes of estimating elasticities in this context, the t-statistics are most important and these are significant at the 5 % level for each coefficient in our model. For a discussion of these issues, see Pindyck and Rubinfeld (1976, pp36–7).

Using the pooled time series and cross-sectional data, and a static equilibrium approach, estimates of the residential water demand in Malmö are made.[9] A linear relationship between variables is taken to be the appropriate functional form. The results of applying ordinary least-squares analysis (OLS) are given in Table 5.7. The equation and parameter estimates are

[9] It is therefore assumed that there is an instantaneous adjustment by consumers to new prices. That is, it is assumed that consumers do not adjust their stock of water using capital; they only adjust the rates at which they use their capital stock. Hence, the static equilibrium model generates a short-term price elasticity estimate, rather than both short- and long-term elasticities.

In this case, it is reasonable to assume that residential consumers will not change their stock of water using capital over the period studied, since users are spending a small fraction of their incomes (approximately 1 %) on water and the costs of water account for a small fraction of the life cycle costs of using residential water using capital.

If a longer time period and larger price increases had been the case, it would have been more reasonable to assume that consumers would change both their stock of water using capital and the utilization rates for their "old" capital. Under these conditions, it would have been appropriate to use either dynamic, partial adjustment or dynamic, multi-equation models. These dynamic models would have generated both short- and long-term price elasticities. For an excellent treatment of the desirability of various types of demand models, see Hartman (1979).

Table 5.8. Elasticities for Malmö.

Variable	Elasticity
Inc	+0·11
Ad	+0·13
Ch	+0·05
R	−0·21
P	−0·15

Notes:
1. We define the general concept of elasticity as follows: elasticity = $(dD/dI)(I/D)$, where D is the dependent variable and I is the independent variable. A linear demand function has a different elasticity at each point. We suggest that the mean values of D and I be used to determine a single elasticity for linear equations. For example, the price elasticity for our model is computed as follows:

$$-6·42\,(1·724/75·2) = -0·15.$$

2. A price elasticity of $-0·15$ means that water use in Malmö can be expected to decrease by 1·5% for each 10% increase in the real price per m³. Since a price increase generates a less than proportional decrease in water use, price increases will also generate increases in revenues from the sale of water on a m³ basis.

statistically significant. Furthermore, the signs of the independent variables are as one would expect.

With the results obtained, elasticity information can be presented. Information on price elasticities is required to estimate the impact of price changes on water use, and also the revenues that will be derived from the sale of water on a per m³ basis. This elasticity information is summarized in Table 5.8.

Conclusions

This chapter has provided a brief survey of the components of municipal water use and the techniques that can be used to construct municipal water demand models for each component. A model for residential water demand, perhaps the most important component, was developed for Malmö, Sweden. The modeling effort for Malmö relied exclusively on the statistical approach, since this is the most appropriate for the residential category of municipal use.

The other components of municipal use were not subject to demand modeling. A complete modeling of water demands in Malmö, similar to the regional analyses of agricultural and industrial demands presented in

Chapters 3 and 4, would have required the development of demand models for other components of municipal water use.

A demand model and a price elasticity estimate have been based on an analysis of pooled time series and cross-sectional data,[10] and some lessons concerning data collection and analysis have been derived. These will be of use in the design of future demand studies that have as their objective the estimation of price elasticities. These can be summarized by the following rules-of-thumb:

(1) collect metered water-use data;
(2) collect data that are disaggregated by user class by taking a stratified random sample of individual users within each class (a sample of 20 within each user class should be adequate);
(3) collect data (price and water use in particular) over a time series (20 time periods and 20 changes in real price should be adequate); and
(4) pool these time series and cross-sectional data for purposes of analysis.

---

[10] It is important to recognize that the price elasticity estimate can be used to predict the impact on Malmö (at one location over time) of changing real prices on residential water use and revenues from the sale of water. In addition, when coupled with information on the marginal cost of water, the elasticity estimate would make it possible to compute the changes in economic efficiency that accompany price changes (Hanke 1982).

6 Programming Models for Regional Water Demand Analysis*

Introduction

Previous chapters have discussed the construction of models of the water demand relationships for individual and aggregated water users. Each of these models is of value, in itself, to the institution or person responsible for the activity, such as the plant or farm manager, or the municipal water supply utility. But the models have another, wider utility as well, for these individual users interact in the regional setting to the extent that they share sources of water or sinks for residuals discharges. Because, even in market economies, these interactions are usually not mediated by the price system, and because they often imply conflicts among users and between users and other socially valued roles for water, it is frequently the case that decisions about the allocation of water resources must be made by public bodies at the regional level. In this chapter, the problems requiring regional decisions are briefly discussed, with special emphasis on the links between the mathematical programming models of individual water-use activities through the water resource. Then, a very simple regional modeling framework is described to make the discussion of linkage more concrete. Some attention is given to possible elaborations of this simple framework designed to carry the analysis beyond instream quantity alone. Finally, some of the central points are illustrated with a regional environmental quality model of a highly industrialized region of the United States.

The Regional Setting

A region, for purposes of this chapter, is a geographic area containing a collection of separate water-use activities. The region may be defined by

* This chapter was written by C. S. Russell.

MODELING WATER DEMANDS
ISBN 0-12-407380-8

hydrologic features—in particular, as a river basin—or, as will more often be the case, by political boundaries. The less well the region corresponds with discrete hydrologic features, the more complicated the potential political problems of coordinating separate regional policies and the more difficult it will be for the modelers to determine what conditions (for example, available flow in a river) may be taken as given. But the basic points to be discussed in this chapter will remain relevant so long as there are water resources to be shared among alternative uses and some mechanism for using the analysis, deciding on a sharing policy, and putting it into practice.[1]

It is the necessity for sharing scarce water resources that is at the heart of water resources management. Another way of putting this central condition is that not all water users can have all the water they could conceivably use. Individual demands on the resource must be balanced against each other within the restrictions of the given supply system or of the expanded system possibilities defined by the development potential within and outside the region and by the government's budget for water resource investment.[2]

The kinds of conflicts that give rise to the necessity for sharing or balancing include:

- the sum of potential individual demands for water for consumptive use may be large enough to produce no flow in a stream under certain rainfall conditions, or to result in salt water intrusion or rapidly falling water levels in underground aquifers;

- the total of potential individual withdrawals, taken from above some point on a stream and not returned (discharged) to the stream until some distance below the point, may be so large as to threaten periodic drying out of the intervening watercourse;

- either consumptive use or withdrawals significantly separated from discharges may, without actually drying out a stream, threaten to reduce flow to levels too low to support desired instream uses such as a fishery or navigation;

- the quantity of waterborne residuals potentially to be discharged by up-

---

[1] In fact, the discussion is not entirely pointless even when the last three conditions do not apply. Studies of regional solutions which are improvements on the results of an uncoordinated free-for-all may help to point the way to better institutional arrangements.

[2] It is worth noting in passing that in a market economy it could be the case that the sharing of scarce water *quantity* was accomplished through prices just as is the sharing of wheat or copper or electricity. The problem of sharing the waste assimilation capacity of natural watercourses might still be a problem requiring public intervention.

stream users may be sufficient to destroy or seriously damage instream use possibilities (as for fishing and swimming), or the pollution may significantly raise the costs of downstream industrial, agricultural or municipal users;

● the timing of potential users may be in conflict, such as when a proposed flood skimming project would interfere with an anadromous fish run or peak residuals discharges coincide with seasonal low flows.

It is not necessary to set out an exhaustive catalog to illustrate the point. The idea behind regional water planning exercises is to make the "best possible" use of scarce water resources by determining how they should be allocated rather than by waiting for first-come-first-served, or some other arbitrary rule to accomplish the allocation. The quotation marks around "best possible" stress that this phrase does not have a universally accepted and unambiguous meaning. In this chapter, it shall be taken to mean "most efficient" in the sense that the economic benefits attributable to the resource, less the costs of using and sharing it, are a maximum. But it is perfectly possible for regional planning to proceed with the aim of maximizing employment, or the physical quantity of agricultural output, or even the recreational possibilities for local residents and tourists.[3] The point to be remembered here is that the analysis should show the effects of pursuing one set of objectives as against others.

Where do the benefits and costs just referred to come from? For the most part these are to be found in the water demand models of individual and aggregated water-use activities. Thus, to simplify greatly and to concentrate on water withdrawals in the longer term, there is implicit in each individual water demand model a relation of the sort shown in Figure 6.1. This relation, for a particular water user, is essentially a derived demand function for water withdrawals. It reflects the value of the water as an input to a production or service process (industrial, agricultural, municipal) or as a final consumption good for the individual users making up an aggregate user such as a municipal utility. The net value of the last unit of withdrawal will in general be greater the smaller the volume withdrawn because it requires additional

---

[3] "Best possible", in the sense used here, is a technocratic criterion. In reality, political considerations, especially the distribution of benefits and costs to particular groups, will be important in choosing regional plans and specific project designs. That realization does not vitiate the discussion here, for efficiency-based models are still useful (though perhaps not always welcome) in giving a benchmark from which to measure the costs of particular political modifications. It is also possible, as discussed later in this chapter, to structure the regional model to take explicit account of some political considerations, such as the distribution of benefits and costs by subregional areas.

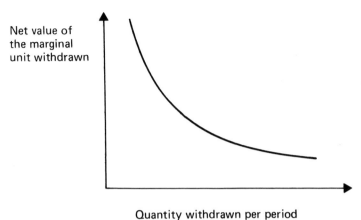

Figure 6.1. Derived demand function for water withdrawal.

inputs of other factors (additional expenses) to substitute for water with-drawals as the quantity of this factor declines.[4]

In the simplest possible regional planning situation the question would be how optimally to share out a given quantity $\hat{Q}$, available over some period, among a set of activities. To make it really simple, withdrawals and dis-charges may be collapsed into net consumptive use. Such use is shown schematically in Figure 6.2, where c_i is the quantity consumed per period at the ith activity. For the problem to be "real" for policy makers, and interest-ing mathematically, it would of course have to be true that the sum over all the users of the consumption at which net marginal values were zero was greater than $\hat{Q}$. Then, the problem could be written symbolically as

$$\max_{c_1,\dots,c_n} F(c) = \left[\int_0^{c_1} f_1(c_1)\,dc_1 + \int_0^{c_2} f_2(c_2)\,dc_2 + \dots + \int_0^{c_n} f_n(c_n)\,dc_n \right] \Bigg\}$$

$$\text{subject to } c_1 + \dots + c_n \leqslant \hat{Q},$$

$$(6.1)$$

where $f_i(c_i)$ is the function giving the net marginal value of consumption, c_i to the ith user.

It is easy to show that in this simple situation, the optimal regional policy would be to divide up the available water so that the value of the last unit

---

[4] In the very short term it may not be possible to substitute any one or several other factors for water in an industrial plant because of the nature of the capital in place. For all users, including aggregates of households, the curve will be less elastic in the short than in the long term.

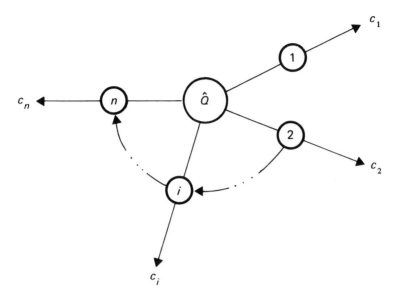

Figure 6.2. A simple regional sharing problem.

withdrawn per period is equal for every user. Thus

$$f_1(\hat{c}_1) = f_2(\hat{c}_2) = \ldots = f_n(\hat{c}_n).$$

One way of achieving this would be for the regional planning authority to charge each user a fee for the consumption privilege equal to the common net marginal value.[5]

But this situation is so drastically simplified that it lacks even the rudiments of the water modeling problems that face regional authorities in the real world. Without attempting to recreate or even review the large and sophisticated literature existing in this field, it is possible to give the flavor of these complications by including:

● spatial distribution of withdrawals and discharges; and
● consideration of instream uses.[6]

---

[5] The question of what kind of institution is undertaking this planning operation, and in particular what actions it can take and what policy instruments it can use is of course worthy of an entire book in its own right (see, for example, Kneese and Bower 1968, Ackerman *et al.* 1974, Derthick 1974, Okun 1977 for such discussions). Here it is simply assumed that there is some regional institution able to act to implement the efficiency solutions to modeling problems.

[6] A useful compendium of papers covering much of this literature is to be found in the volume edited by Biswas (1976). A simpler approach, concentrating on economics will be found in Howe (1971). An earlier classic in the field is Maass *et al.* (1962); and a later volume from roughly the same group at Harvard is Dorfman *et al.* (1972).

In addition, it is necessary to discuss the difficulties raised by flow and activity variability over time—both roughly predictable cyclical variability and stochastic elements of rainfall, runoff, and hence, streamflow. These topics will be dealt with in the next section.

Another natural candidate for inclusion in a more realistic though still schematic model is the supply side of the regional water regime. That is, if the overall flow constraint, $\hat{Q}$, can be relaxed by spending money on impoundments, interbasin transfers, pumping of deep ground water, or on any of a number of other schemes, the balancing act for regional planners will in principle involve maximizing the benefits from withdrawals less the costs spent on flow enhancement.[7] In fact, for political reasons, the opportunities for flow enhancement may be very limited, and smooth cost functions symmetric with the net benefit functions may hardly exist. But beyond this, it is again true that this question merits another entire book—both in its political and its modeling aspects.

For the purposes of the demand analysis being stressed here, the possibility of relaxing the fundamental flow constraints are for the most part ignored. The reader is, however, invited to think about the expanded problem as one of informal iteration between supply and demand planners, with the demand models discussed here providing estimates of "shadow prices" for additional flows at various points (Hanke 1978). These shadow prices could be communicated to the supply division of the authority which could determine whether any of its available projects would be worthwhile if valued at these prices.[8]

Topics of Special Interest in Aggregating Mathematical Programming Models of Individual Water-use Activities

Regional water demand modeling was introduced above in the simplest possible context: where the only policy concern was sharing a common point source of water for consumptive use by a number of would-be consumers. To

---

[7] Even this list demonstrates that the problem very quickly must involve flow variability. In most cases, flows are scarce, in relation to demands for withdrawals or consumption, only during dry periods. During high flows all sources can have all they want—perhaps even all they want at zero price. The supply options, then, will involve increasing the flow available in the watercourse in the dry periods. See, for example, Russell et al. (1970) for a discussion of this problem in the municipal context.

[8] Another qualification: if, as is likely, supply projects involve very "lumpy" investments, the addition of one to the regional system may change flows significantly. In such a case, a single shadow price will not apply, and the situations with and without the project will have to be compared using areas under the users' net benefit curves (see Maass et al. 1962).

make the picture more realistic, it is necessary to add complications. First, there are other important connections between individual water use activities and regional water resources in addition to the volume of their consumptive use. Secondly, there also exist links *between* the activities implied by the resource that go beyond simple depletion of a fixed point source. Finally, there are links between the water demands of the individual activities and the character of other shared regional resources—for example, air quality.

Links between water-use activities and regional water resources

Chapter 2 noted that there are five important dimensions of water demand: gross water applied, withdrawals, consumptive use, wastewater discharge (both quantity and quality), and timing. It is necessary to consider the last four of these in attempting to characterize "the" regional water demand problem to be analyzed, although of course it may well turn out that only some subset really is part of this problem. Whatever the problem dimensions, they should be reflected in the regional demand model if that model is to be useful. In addition, in this context, the dimensions generally show up as links between individual water users and regional water resources.

Thus, water *withdrawals*, viewed independently of consumptive use and of wastewater discharge, may be a problem if:

(1) withdrawals are large relative to stream flow or reservoir volume under certain conditions, and are widely separated spatially (or in time) from the wastewater discharges, so that a section of stream may from time to time be dried out; and

(2) the withdrawals are large and the uses are such that aquatic life in the withdrawn water is destroyed. (Such destruction could result from simple mechanical screening or agitation and does not require chemical or thermal pollution.)

The qualifier here, "under certain conditions", is very important. Because natural runoff, stream flows, and aquifer yields will in general vary both in a largely predictable seasonal component and stochastically with the weather, most "problems" discussed here are problems only some fraction of the time. A central decision in the regional analysis is how to acknowledge and allow for this. At this point, it is simply assumed that some conditions have been taken to be of special interest—for example, seven-day, ten-year low stream flows. Problems are defined relative to these conditions. At other times there may be no problem. Analysis in these circumstances may appear to make the timing dimension disappear by using a chosen base situation such as an event of particular probability. Policy may then seem to be timeless if it takes the form—reduce regional consumptive use to less than the flow available during some low flow period; for example, that expected only $X \%$ of the time. But even in this circumstance, and even ignoring supply side options involving time, there are in principle several facets of water demand timing to be analyzed. For example, water storage by individual users after withdrawal; postponement of user demand by temporary shutdowns; or changes in internal procedures.[9]

Timing may, however, enter the regional problem in other ways than the variability of the water resource. As an obvious example the water-use activity may itself have a significant time variability. Thus, irrigation may be necessary at certain stages of a crop's growth cycle; a food processing plant is often tied to the harvest rhythm; and another industrial plant may have to react to peaks in the demand for its product. If these variations in water demand lead to problems of the sort described above (low flows, unsatisfactory quality, salt water intrusion) then one can say "timing" is part of the regional water problem. To oversimplify a bit, for purposes of discussion, reference is made to problems as being those of withdrawal, consumption, or discharge quality when they arise from a roughly constant demand side interacting with the naturally variable supply of water in the regional system. The timing label is reserved for problems related to variable uses.[10]

Links between water-use activities

A regional water problem might arise simply because an individual water-use activity was (or was capable of) reducing the quality of nearby water bodies to unacceptable levels. More realistically, however, there will be many such activities, and they will interact through the water resource. This linkage will almost always be more complex than that reflected in the simple summation of consumptive uses that characterized the initial illustration in this chapter. In particular:

(1) Upstream and downstream will often be important distinctions. This immediately destroys the symmetry of the simple example, for if activity A is upstream of B, "saving" a million liters per day at B does not make another million liters available in the stream between A and B. Only A

[9] These strategies are the substance of "water deficit planning", which is to say, finding the optimal expected shortage for the regional system, determining when supply conditions warrant demand reduction measures, and choosing in advance what these measures should be (see Russell 1978).

[10] One "variable use" not mentioned in the catalog above is the support of anadromous fish runs. These may require more instream flow than would be expected on average from natural meteorological variability and planned water withdrawals and consumption, and may occur in relatively low flow seasons.

can increase stream flow between A and B by decreasing consumptive use, the possibility of pumping aside. (Analogous comments apply in the case of several activities sharing a regional aquifer, though here the relations are much less constrained to "upstream" and "downstream".)

(2) Chemical and biological processes take time to work themselves out. This means, for example, that in general, two activities, each discharging the same amount of the same residual (say biochemical oxygen demand) but located at different places along the course of a river, will have different effects on the quality of the stream at any point below them both.

For the construction of regional models these complications imply that the structure of constraints must be expanded to include the necessary book-keeping for withdrawals, wastewater discharges and resulting stream flows; and, where quality is a problem, a representation of the biological and chemical processes as they proceed with time, and hence with flow. Furthermore, this means that, where intake water quality is significant for the user — as, for example, it clearly is for municipal water supply — a single, two-dimensional derived demand function. will not suffice. The model of water-use activity must contain information on the costs of dealing with a range of intake qualities, e.g., through sand and carbon filtration of drinking water to remove suspended solids, microorganisms, and trace organic chemicals (see Sontheimer 1978). The expanded models then must reflect value–quantity relations for every quality of intake water.

Links to other environmental concerns

Because mass and energy are conserved in human production and consumption activities, one may make *a priori* the argument that a single-minded concern with a regional water problem may lead to unacceptable, though unintended, changes in other indicators of environmental quality such as concentrations of airborne residuals or acres of wetlands destroyed by dredge spoil or sludge dumping. Thus, as an obvious example, consider the possibility that a water quality problem arising from an excessive organic load will be attacked by the installation of activated sludge sewage treatment plants (and perhaps activated carbon filtration as well, if the problem is sufficiently serious or the desired instream quality sufficiently high). Then, if the sludge from the activated sludge plant is incinerated and the carbon is regenerated within the region, the result will be an increase in regional particulate concentrations.[11]

---

[11] The energy required for operation of the plants will also imply, in general, added pollution loads from the electric utility industry. Similarly, the power used in irrigation pumps and other water-related machinery will form a link to air quality.

How great this increase will be depends on the control measures taken at the incinerator and regeneration furnace. But the need for control measures can only be determined by reference to regional standards for suspended particulates, the regional situation without incineration and regeneration, and the potential contributions to concentrations of the new facilities under various control assumptions. There is, then, an argument for linking regional water demand models to models of other facets of the regional environment—especially to air quality management.

On the other side of this issue there is another *a priori* argument, namely, that these links, while real enough, are too small as a practical matter to warrant extra modeling (or policy-making) effort. The dispute, then, is an empirical matter, and one with no general answer. In principle, the possibility of important interaction should be checked in each region. In practice, the decision to proceed in one direction rather than the other will usually be made on the basis of a rough, intuitive judgment, for otherwise all the work for the linked model would have to be done to decide that such a model was unnecessary.[12]

If it is decided to aim at including linkages to the regional air quality situation, there are essentially two ways to go about it. One is to build a complete model of both the water demand and the air quality situations. This model would have, on the air side, all the sources of air pollution with costs for additional controls, and a model translating these emissions into ambient air quality. The model solution would take into account all possibilities for meeting the desired air quality constraints, not just those connected with the water demand activities.[13] A second, somewhat simpler, method would take as given, or "background", the air quality from all existing emission sources with existing (or planned) control measures. This would leave an "increment" to ambient pollution levels that would be available for the secondary residuals of the water demand activities.[14] This model would not have to be so extensive in its coverage of sources or its inclusion of control alternatives—potentially a significant saving in information costs.

---

[12] One result that seems to be generally applicable is discussed in the last section of this chapter. Experience with the Lower Delaware Valley modeling project indicates that adding the air pollution linkages is neither especially difficult in modeling terms, nor too demanding of data.

[13] It may well be, of course, that public policy on air pollution *specifies* certain treatment devices for all sources or at least for all new sources. This greatly simplifies the modeling process. The same point is true with respect to specifications on the discharge of liquid residuals.

[14] Of course, if the increment is zero (or negative) or too small to accommodate the emissions from the water demand activities using the most stringent available control technology, this simple approach is infeasible.

Links between regional water management institutions and individual water-use activities

This chapter began with an acknowledgment that a fundamental reason for regional water demand analyses is that the sharing of such scarce regional resources as stream flows and waste assimilation capacity will usually not be done in a way that would be judged socially desirable without the intervention of some institution capable of looking beyond the narrow interest of each individual activity. For the most part the discussion has been concerned with how such an institution would model the regional water resources system and the links between that system and the water users. It is relevant, however, to ask how the institution will be linked to the users, i.e., how it will achieve the results it determines to be "best" by influencing the behavior of the individual activities. It is relevant because the decision may affect the model structure.

Most importantly, if the institution will influence individual decisions by charging some amount of money per unit of water withdrawn or consumed, or per unit of residual discharged, then the model must be set up so that the charges appropriate to the desired result are explicitly calculated from the information available in the solution. One possible scheme for such a model, described later in this chapter, involves the use of trial charges as the basis for an iterative solution of a regional programming (optimization) model. In a completely linear model it would be possible to calculate appropriate charge levels from shadow prices on the various binding constraints and the parameters indicating the size of the individual activity's contribution to the constant.[15]

Analogously, if the institution is to achieve its best plan by ordering that specific actions be taken by individual activities, then those actions must be found explicitly in the model. A generalized cost-of-withdrawal-reduction curve that does not provide the institution with the name of the specific action associated with each point or segment of the curve gives no basis for policy action to achieve a "best" solution.[16]

[15] In the simplest case, a binding streamflow constraint where the problem is consumptive use, each upstream activity would subtract from the downstream flow one gallon for each gallon consumed. If the shadow price of the constraint is P_s in the optimal solution, then each upstream user should be charged P_s per gallon consumed. The constraint shadow price will not translate one to one where natural chemical and biological processes intervene. Thus dischargers of BOD upstream of a binding dissolved oxygen constraint would appropriately be charged differently depending on how far above the point identified with the constraint they were located.

[16] It also must be recognized that, in many situations, specific discharge limitations have been imposed on individual discharges, whether or not the resulting set of actions is the least-cost set to achieve desired ambient water quality standards. Any regional model must reflect these standards, and be able to assess alternative more or less stringent standards.

Problems of Size and Complexity: Simple Illustrations

To take this discussion one step closer to the actual regional modeling exercise, the following discussion pertains to some very simple model structures that can be used to illustrate how the linkages described in the previous section may be handled. As before, the initial theme will be adding complexity to the simplest situation. But the second part of this section will deal with simplification, and in particular with size reduction.

Making the simple model more complex

Consider first, a very slight change from the initial model. Instead of a point source, assume that water is withdrawn from a river and all water withdrawn is consumed by the respective water users. Then the situation may be drawn schematically as in Figure 6.3, where Q_0 is the given input flow to the part of the regional system of interest to the modeler, and the $\hat{Q}_i$ are the minimum instream flows that the regional institution wishes to maintain. The new optimizing problem, using the earlier notation for the marginal net benefits of various quantities consumed at each activity is:

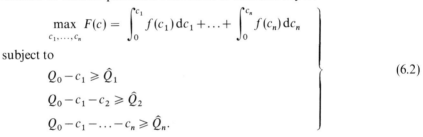

$$\max_{c_1,\ldots,c_n} F(c) = \int_0^{c_1} f(c_1)\,dc_1 + \ldots + \int_0^{c_n} f(c_n)\,dc_n$$

subject to

$$Q_0 - c_1 \geqslant \hat{Q}_1$$
$$Q_0 - c_1 - c_2 \geqslant \hat{Q}_2$$
$$Q_0 - c_1 - \ldots - c_n \geqslant \hat{Q}_n.$$

$$(6.2)$$

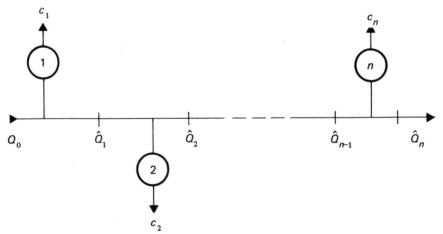

Figure 6.3. Water consumption along a river.

Instead of flow constraints, of course, the model might contain net benefit functions for instream uses. Then the problem might be written

$$\max F(c) = \left.\begin{array}{l} \int f(c_1)\,\mathrm{d}c_1 + \ldots + \int f(c_n)\,\mathrm{d}c_n + B_1(Q_1) + B_2(Q_2) \\[1em] \qquad + \ldots + B_n(Q_n) \\[1em] \text{subject to} \\[1em] \qquad Q_1 = Q_0 - c_1, \text{ etc.,} \end{array}\right\} \qquad (6.3)$$

where Q_1 no longer are set as targets, and the $B_i(Q_i)$ are functions that tell us the benefits of having a flow Q_i at point i over the period of interest.

To translate the problem into a linear framework it is only necessary to use linear approximations of the integrals of the marginal net benefit functions associated with water consumption by each water user (see Figure 6.4). Thus, for example,

$$\int_0^{c_1} f(c_1)\,\mathrm{d}c_1 \cong b_1 c_{11} + b_2 c_{12} + b_3 c_{13}, \qquad (6.4)$$

where

$$c_{11} + c_{12} + c_{13} = c_1$$

and

$$c_{11} \leqslant \hat{c}_{11}; \qquad c_{12} \leqslant \hat{c}_{12} - \hat{c}_{11}; \qquad c_{13} \leqslant \hat{c}_{13} - \hat{c}_{12};$$

and the b's are the slopes of the approximating linear segments. For the most part this discussion will concentrate on the constraint sets, but the reader should thus be able to visualize the function to be maximized.

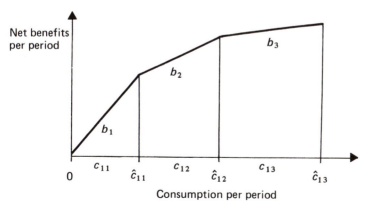

Figure 6.4. Linearizing a net benefit function.

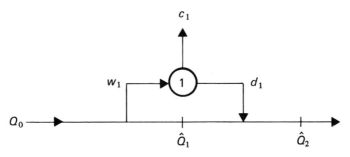

Figure 6.5. Spatial separation of withdrawal and discharge.

To complicate the situation a little more, some spatially separated withdrawals and wastewater discharges may be considered, as shown in Figure 6.5. If the net benefit relation is an unspecified function G of c_1, w_1, Q_1 and Q_2, the problem may be written for this little subregion:

$$\max G(w_1, c_1, Q_1, Q_2)$$

subject to

$$w_1 - d_1 = c_1 \qquad Q_0 - w_1 = Q_1 \qquad Q_0 - c_1 = Q_2$$

$$(6.5)$$

where, again, Q_0 is a given inflow into the subregion, and Q_1 and Q_2 are the instream flows.

If there are a number of activities in different locations and with different characteristics the constraint set can begin to look rather complicated very quickly. For example, consider the next schematic, presented in Figure 6.6; both Q_0 and Q_1 are given input flows, and the remaining Q_i are minimum flow standards. Now the problem of maximizing the net value of water use is subject to the following constraints:

$$w_1 - c_1 = d_1$$

$$\vdots$$

$$w_5 - c_5 = d_5$$

$$Q_0 - c_1 - w_2 \geqslant \hat{Q}_2$$

$$Q_0 - c_1 - c_2 \geqslant \hat{Q}_4$$

$$Q_1 - w_4 - c_3 \geqslant \hat{Q}_3$$

$$Q_1 - c_3 - c_4 \geqslant \hat{Q}_5$$

$$Q_0 - c_1 - c_2 + Q_1 - c_3 - c_4 \geqslant \hat{Q}_6$$

$$Q_0 - c_1 - c_2 + Q_1 - c_3 - c_4 - c_5 \geqslant \hat{Q}_7$$

$$(6.6)$$

So far discharges have been treated only as volumes of water. What if regional water quality is one of the problems to be addressed? Then it is

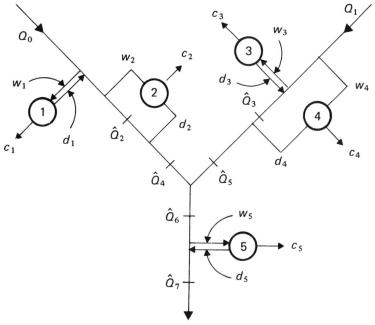

Figure 6.6. A "simple" regional flow problem.

necessary to relate wastewater discharges to the resulting quality of the regional watercourses. The models doing this are usually called "water quality models". To do justice to the theories behind and the structures of

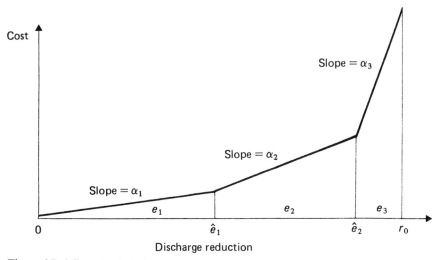

Figure 6.7. A linearized discharge reduction cost function.

such models would require a much longer explanation of water quality models than is possible here (for such an introductory discussion, see Spofford 1975). However, it will at least be possible to show how alternative levels of residuals discharge can be obtained and how these would enter a linear constraint set. This will be demonstrated by looking at one discharger of one residual. Assume that residuals discharge in the absence of control is r_0 and that the cost of reducing that discharge is approximated by the piecewise linear function shown in Figure 6.7.

Then the cost function for reduction of residuals discharge (to be incorporated in the overall objective function of the regional linear programming—LP—model) is:

$$C(r) = \alpha_1 e_1 + \alpha_2 e_2 + \alpha_3 e_3, \tag{6.7}$$

where the actual discharge, r, is produced in the LP model by a constraint

$$r_0 - e_1 - e_2 - e_3 - r \leqslant 0, \tag{6.8}$$

and

$$e_1 \leqslant \hat{e}_1 \qquad e_2 \leqslant \hat{e}_2 - \hat{e}_1 \qquad e_3 \leqslant r_0 - \hat{e}_2. \tag{6.9}$$

The instream quality constraint might have the form: the concentration of the residual at some point downstream must be less than or equal to R. Then, for the linear model, a water quality model would be used to produce a constant, γ, that related discharge "r" to downstream concentration, taking account of dilution and any processes that change the residual chemically. The resulting constraint on quality would be simply

$$\gamma r \leqslant R. \tag{6.10}$$

When there are m residuals in the wastewater stream, and n alternatives for treating that stream, the model of a water-use activity could contain a treatment section, defining discharges $r_1, \ldots, r_m$ of each residual. Thus,

wastewater treatment alternatives $\quad T_1 \ldots T_n$

removal per unit $\quad\quad\quad\quad\quad\quad\quad e_{11} \ldots e_{n1}$

treatment[17] of each r $\quad\quad\quad\quad\quad e_{12} \ldots e_{n2}$

$$\vdots \qquad \vdots \tag{6.11}$$

$\quad\quad\quad\quad\quad\quad\quad\quad\quad\quad\quad\quad e_{1m} \ldots e_{nm}$

unit costs of wastewater treatment[18] $\quad c_1 \quad c_n$

[17] It is useful to think of the unit of treatment as an amount of wastewater, say $10\,\mathrm{m}^3$, entering the treatment plant. Because inlet concentrations are known, this is a summary number for the amounts of residuals in that volume of the wastewater.
[18] Linear models deal with the portion of the cost curve over which the slope is relatively constant.

Then the objective function costs will include

$$c_1 T_1 + \ldots + c_n T_n, \tag{6.12}$$

and the constraint set will include:

$$\left.\begin{array}{l} r_1 - T_1 e_{11} - \ldots - T_n e_{n1} - D_1 \leqslant 0 \\ \quad \vdots \\ r_m - T_1 e_{1m} - \ldots - T_n e_{nm} - D_m \leqslant 0 \end{array}\right\} \tag{6.13}$$

where the D_i are the actual discharges.

This scheme can be further complicated to show that certain treatment processes are alternatives and that others must occur in sequence. This is accomplished by using the flow variable for the wastewater stream explicitly. Consider, for example, three wastewater treatment processes, the first two of which can only be used in sequence and the third of which is an alternative to the first two. In matrix form:

	Treatment alternatives			Residual discharge alternatives			
	T_1	T_2	T_3	D_1	D_2	D_3	D_4
raw wastewater flow, Q_w	-1		-1	-1			
flow out of first stage	$+1$	-1			-1		
flow out of second stage		$+1$				-1	
flow out of alternative unit			$+1$				-1
residuals in wastewater streams at each stage (kg/l)				$\begin{array}{c} r_{11} \\ r_{12} \\ \vdots \\ r_{1m} \end{array}$	$\begin{array}{c} r_{21} \\ r_{22} \\ \\ r_{2m} \end{array}$	$\begin{array}{c} r_{31} \\ r_{32} \\ \\ r_{3m} \end{array}$	$\begin{array}{c} r_{41} \\ r_{42} \\ \\ r_{4m} \end{array}$
unit costs of wastewater treatment	c_1	c_2	c_3				

Now, the constraint set includes the following relations:

$$Q_w - T_1 - T_3 - D_1 \leqslant 0, \tag{6.14}$$

which says that all the raw wastewater must either be treated in process 1, or process 3, or discharged;

$$T_1 - T_2 - D_2 \leqslant 0, \tag{6.15}$$

which says that all the effluent from process 1 must either go into process 2 or be discharged;

$$T_2 - D_3 \leqslant 0, \tag{6.16}$$

which says that any effluent from process 2 must be accounted for by discharge; and

$$T_3 - D_4 \leqslant 0, \tag{6.17}$$

which says the same thing for process 3. Attached to each of the discharge activities are concentrations of residuals in the wastewater in question (these are shown below the flow variables in the matrix section displayed above): D_1 is the raw stream; the D_2 loadings reflect the removal levels achieved in process 1; the D_3 loadings reflect the additional removal in process 2; and the D_4 loadings reflect the removal achieved in process 3.[19] It is simple to add individual accounting variables for each residual discharged in order to have explicit variables with which to enter the water quality model, assuming linearity and no joint effects.

Complexity, size, and size reduction

The model descriptions in Chapters 2–5, reinforced by the above brief discussion of how the regional context can complicate matters, should suggest that models for regional water demand analysis can become very large and complicated. But size itself can be a problem for the modeler and his or her employers. This is partly for reasons of presentation and acceptability of results and partly because of computational limitations.[20] It seems to be true that the more complex the model—either component by component or viewed as a set of components—the less likely are practical people to take it seriously. One has to admit that there is only anecdotal evidence for this assertion, and size is surely not the only significant consideration here.[21] At a guess, the acid test may be whether or not counter-intuitive results from the model can be explained in reasonable ways. It is not, of course, claimed that simple models are "better" models—for example, that they predict with more accuracy, if x then y. But, it is far from clear that bigger and more complex models are better either, and one may never know *how* the two com-

---

[19] The amount of residual i to be discharged is then

$$D_1 r_{1i} + D_2 r_{2i} + D_3 r_{3i} + D_4 r_{4i},$$

where the D_i units are $10 \, m^3$ and the r_{+i} are $kg/10 \, m^3$, for example.

[20] There also may be an insufficiency of analytical resources, e.g., combination of knowledgeable personnel, available data, and computer facilities to develop a regional model and produce outputs therefrom within the time available.

[21] Compare, for example, the public interest in US EPA's Strategic Environmental Assessment System (SEAS), which is enormously complex, and in the Meadows *et al.* (1972) *Limits to Growth* model. It will take decades of real experience to tell which model is the better predictor, but there is no contest on the interest front, and it is difficult to influence policy, for good or ill, if there is no interest.

pare if, given the choice, decision-makers prefer to rely on the simpler varieties.

Computationally, simplicity has its advantages as well, whether one takes the word to refer to size or structure or a combination of the two. This is less of a problem for simulation than for optimization models, although some of the same generic difficulties haunt both varieties. With optimization models, the limitations can really produce problems long before even a modest amount of regional detail has been included. If the form of the model is kept linear, then the powerful and reliable technique of linear programming is available for solution. Even this method has its practical size limits, however, related to matrix inversion and rounding error. These limits change as new machines and algorithms are developed, but are, at any time, below the limits of imagination of regional modelers with a thirst for completeness. The addition of integer (yes–no) variables further reduces the size of the model that is computationally practical. And once the problem is allowed to escape from the linear world, computational difficulties seem to become overwhelming. Nonlinear solution techniques, while reasonably well developed in theory, and proved workable with problems on the order of 100 variables, cannot be pushed to the sizes required for representation of any large fraction of the options for managing regional water resources. The desire to include dynamic decision elements forces the modeler into even more restrictive methods.

What alternatives are available for trying to keep regional water demand models simple? One possible line is to limit the number of actual decision variables by including many activities in what is commonly called "background". Thus, for example, if a region has a few major users of water or dischargers of residuals and a number of much smaller ones, it may well be that the total effect of even a large change in the activity levels of the smaller activities will be unnoticeable (or nearly so) on the regional level. In such a case very little is lost and considerable simplicity may be gained by treating the small activities as fixed, exogenous inputs to the model, and reserving the decision variables for the large water users.[22]

A second method of simplification involves taking an aggregate view of a particular water-use activity rather than attempting to include its individual units. This path differs from the first in that the resulting aggregated submodel may contain decision variables. That is, in general, aggregation will not imply that activities are relegated to background, but merely that the

---

[22] This need not imply that these small activities are left alone in whatever regional plan is eventually put into effect. In a water quality plan, for example, they might be ordered to reduce discharges by as much as the average large source. The point is only that whatever they are told to do will not affect the policy choice from the model by much.

Columns Rows	Production alternatives $X_1 \cdots X_H$	By-product production $B_1 \cdots B_J$	Raw material recovery $W_1 \cdots W_K$	Treatment and transport of residuals $T_1 \cdots T_L, V_1 \cdots V_M$	Sale of products $Y_1 \cdots Y_N$	Discharges of residuals $D_1 \cdots D_g \cdots D_G$		RHS
Production and sale	$+\tilde{e}_{X_1} \cdots +\tilde{e}_{X_H}$				$-\tilde{e}_{Y_1} \cdots -\tilde{e}_{Y_N}$		$\leq$	0
Input availability	$-\tilde{p}_{X_1} \cdots -\tilde{p}_{X_H}$		$+\tilde{w}_1 \cdots +\tilde{w}_K$				$\leq$	$-P$
Output quality	$+\tilde{q}_{X_1} \cdots +\tilde{q}_{X_H}$						$\geq$	Q
Primary residuals		$+\tilde{e}_{B_1} \cdots +\tilde{e}_{B_J}$	$+\tilde{e}_{W_1} \cdots +\tilde{e}_{W_K}$	$+\tilde{e}_{T_1} \quad +\tilde{e}_{V_1} \cdots$		$+\tilde{e}_{D_1}$	$=$	0
Secondary residuals		$-\tilde{r}_{B_1} \cdots -\tilde{r}_{B_J}$	$-\tilde{r}_{W_1} \cdots -\tilde{r}_{W_K}$	$\tilde{r}_{T_1} \cdots +\tilde{e}_{T_L} \cdots +\tilde{e}_{V_M}$ $-\tilde{r}_{T_L}$ $-\tilde{r}_{V_1}$ $-\tilde{r}_{V_M}$ etc.		$+\tilde{e}_{D_g}$	$=$	0
								$\cdots$
						$+\tilde{e}_{D_g}$	$=$	0
Possible discharge constraints						$+1 \quad +1 \quad +1$	$\leq$	F
Objective function	Costs of production	Costs of production	Costs of recovery	Costs of treatment and transport	Price of output	Possible effluent charges		

Figure 6.8. Schematic of models of industrial residuals management (from Russell 1973). The $\tilde{e}$ are column vectors of zeroes and ones. The occurrence of ones is determined by the function of the column in which the vector appears. Thus in $\tilde{e}_{X_1}$ a one appears in the row corresponding to the output of process X_1. All other entries are zero.

number of decision or endogenous variables will be reduced. Thus, the aggregate of households within a municipal water supply system or sewer district is a common unit of study, one discussed in Chapter 5. In modeling the natural world, an analogous approach leads us to the familiar Streeter–Phelps biochemical oxygen demand/dissolved oxygen (BOD/DO) models, for these may be thought of as aggregate approximations, not only over individuals but over ecological communities. That is, Streeter–Phelps folds into a big black box the many "compartments" of the aquatic ecological system (e.g., decomposing bacteria, algae, zooplankton, herbivorous fish, carnivorous fish) and measures empirically the net total effect of this system on incoming BOD loads and on the DO measure of stream quality.

Finally, it is possible to do the detailed work on component models first and then to return to simpler versions for the overall regional model via one or another process of condensation or approximation. For example, complex, nonlinear model(s) of aquatic ecology might be constructed and tested for the regional watercourse(s). For the regional application it might well seem worthwhile to strive for linearity and hence computational ease in the optimization. To get there, it is possible to linearize the model around a point (a vector of flow, residuals discharges and other exogenous variables) and to use the linearized version in the regional model. Of course it would be valuable to have a better idea than one now does about the costs of such a strategy—especially by how much flows and discharges could be changed before the approximation became unacceptable.

Somewhat less exotic is the possibility of "condensing" large linear components of the regional model by repeated solution. Consider, for example, a petroleum refinery model designed to find the minimum cost of producing a particular output mix, while at the same time meeting constraints on residuals discharges and water consumption. The model would include the costs of water withdrawal, of applicable treatment and wastewater recirculation alternatives, as well as those of such purchased inputs as labor, electricity, and chemicals. Schematically, the model might be represented as shown in Figure 6.8. For any particular run all relevant prices may be chosen and all the constraints set at desired levels.

Such a model might, for example, be used to trace out a cost curve for BOD discharge reduction, for given values of all the other prices and constraints, simply by making successive reductions in allowed BOD discharges. If the values of other variables used in this first exercise are kept the same and another residual discharge constraint tightened, the result is a second discharge reduction cost curve compatible with the first. This process may be repeated for all residuals singly and for combinations of discharge constraints on 2, 3, up to all residuals. The costs of changing water consumption or withdrawal may be similarly investigated. Pursuing such a course produces a large amount of information that may conveniently be summarized as a set of vectors of the following form:

	Vector i
Discharge level for residual 1	r_{1i}
Discharge level for residual 2	r_{2i}
$\vdots$	$\vdots$
Discharge level for residual m	r_{mi}
Consumption of water	c_i
Cost of the chosen constraint set[a]	Z_i

[a] The cost of the constraint set is the difference between the objective function value with those constraints and the value for the base case, i.e., generally the situation with no constraints on water consumption, residuals discharge, or other matters involved in the regional problem context.

Because a refinery is usually characterized by its size in thousands of barrels of crude oil input per day, it is convenient to think of all this information in per-barrel-of-crude terms. Thus, dividing through by the refinery size, S, we get a new set of vectors:

	Vector i
Discharge of residual 1 per barrel of crude input	r_{1i}/S
Discharge of residual 2 per barrel of crude input	r_{2i}/S
$\vdots$	$\vdots$
Discharge of residual m per barrel of crude input	r_{mi}/S
Water consumption per barrel of crude input	c_i/S
Cost per barrel of crude input	Z_i/S

These may be combined into a new and very simple linear model of discharge reduction at the refinery, *given* the particular constellation of prices and products chosen for the runs described above. This model has only $m+2$ rows: one for each residual; one for water consumption; and one for a "production constraint"; that is, a requirement that the refinery operate at the size level S. Thus:

Production alternatives: A^1	$\cdots$	A_n	R_1	R_2	$\cdots$	R_m	C	RHS
Matrix:	1	1	-1					$\geqslant S$
	r_{11}/S	r_{1n}/S						$\leqq 0$
	r_{21}/S	r_{2n}/S		-1				$\leqq 0$
	$\vdots$	$\vdots$			$\cdots$			$\vdots$
	r_{m1}/S	r_{mn}/S				-1		$\leqq 0$
	c_1/S	c_n/S					-1	$\leqq 0$
Objective F_n:	Z_1/S	Z_n/S	E_1	E_2	$\cdots$	E_m	W_c	

where E_i is a unit charge on the discharge of the ith residual, and W_c is a charge per unit of water consumed. In the regional context, $R_1 \ldots R_m$, the discharges, enter the relevant water quality models, and C the relevant flow book-keeping constraints. The charges may be arbitrarily assigned as part of a simulation of a possible regional policy, or they may be chosen in some systematic way. (In one such way, described in the next section, these charge parameters are central to an iterative technique for solving a nonlinear regional model.) Thus, when, for the regional analysis, one is content to choose a single set of product requirements, input prices, and so forth, one can dispense with all of the mathematical programming model except the result summary. All the other capabilities will be wasted in any case. By making this choice to restrict the field of vision, one can reduce individual activity models in row size by factors of 30–50, reducing 300–500 rows to about 10 (for further details, see Russell 1973).

A Regional Example

To see how the ideas treated abstractly in the above sections may be applied to real problems, it would be useful to have an example of a complex, operating, regional model, one focused on water quantity and incorporating demand functions for individual water-use activities. Efforts to construct such models have been made (for an early example, see Maass *et al.* 1962). But the models that seem best to fit the other didactic requirements of this chapter involve water *quality* rather than quantity. This is because it is in the area of water pollution control that individual activity models seem to have been most fully developed. One such model is that of the Lower Delaware Valley constructed at Resources for the Future in the 1970s, and its general structure, together with some detail about its activity components, will be described below.

Even though water quantity and quality are not perfectly interchangeable problems, they do share the important characteristic of involving over-

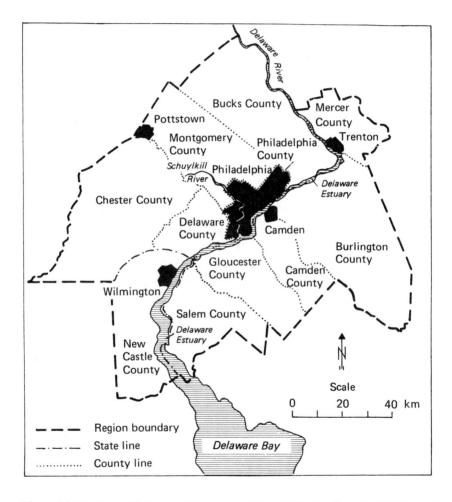

Figure 6.9. The Lower Delaware Valley region. From W. O. Spofford, Jr, C. S. Russell, and R. A. Kelly (1976) *Environmental Quality Management: An Application to the Lower Delaware Valley* (Washington, DC: Resources for the Future), Fig. 1. Reproduced with permission.

arching constraints that link the individual activities through the water-course(s) of the region. Thus their general structure is very similar, though the necessary models of the natural world are more complex in the water quality problem. At the same time, even though quantities withdrawn and discharged are not the focus of this model's activity components, the same modeling techniques described in Chapter 2 are relevant. Therefore, this example is rather more to the point than may appear from the shift in emphasis.

The basic purpose of the Delaware Estuary modeling project at Resources for the Future was to investigate the problems, and potential gains in information obtained, associated with adding certain complexities and refinements to previous approaches to regional water quality management.[23] Specifically, the intentions were to investigate the feasibility and desirability of:

● including air quality and solid waste management, together with water quality, in a single model so that nonmarket interactions among these problems were reflected in the simultaneous solution for the three problem areas;
● introducing a complex, nonlinear aquatic ecosystem model into the water quality management subsystem;
● expanding the information available from the model beyond the familiar aggregate efficiency results to include the incidence of costs and ambient quality levels on geographically defined political jurisdictions throughout the region.

These goals were pursued in the context of an intensely developed industrial region of the Lower Delaware Valley, with many very large and complex sources of residuals discharges (see Figure 6.9). The model structure involved minimization of the costs of meeting ambient environmental quality constraints. There was no explicit concern with water *quantity* in the estuary, though volumes of withdrawals and wastewater (residual) discharges for individual sources were usually known and were used in costing treatment and recirculation activities. This was a conscious decision, for it was taken as a starting point that the water management problem in the region was water quality.[24] It was further assumed that the policy targets to be chosen in this connection would be instream water quality standards, and that the instru-

----

[23] For a description of the earlier Delaware modeling work, which represents the "classic" case, see Delaware River Basin Commission (1970). The material in this section is based on two recent reports from the project: Russell and Spofford (1977), and Spofford et al. (1976).

[24] This is not strictly true, as will be discussed below.

ments used to achieve the targets would be either discharge standards or effluent charges.[25] (The two instruments are conveniently "dual" in the ambient quality optimization problem.) On the institutional side it was assumed, purely for research purposes and not because the outcome was thought likely, that the quality targets would be chosen by a regional institution in which decisions would rest with a "legislature" made up of one representative from each of 57 jurisdictions each with a population of about 100 000 (these jurisdictions were designed by the modeling team and were combinations of existing local jurisdictions). The representatives to this legislature were assumed to be particularly interested in the cost and ambient quality implications for their own jurisdictions of alternative management plans.

Because the modeling team felt that it would be causing itself plenty of problems with the complexities already identified, it chose to make the model a static rather than dynamic or stochastic one, and to confine the study to a partial view of economic equilibrium   that is, the model traces only the first round of effects from a policy and not the subsequent rounds of adjustment that are captured in, for example, an input–output model.

The model that grew out of all of these considerations is shown schematically in Figure 6.10. In the upper left-hand block is the basic driving force, an LP model of residuals generation and discharge. It is in this block that the minimum "production" constraints are found. The output of this submodel is a vector of residuals discharges, identified by substance, discharge medium, and location. The block below this represents the environmental models; in particular, the aquatic ecosystem model of the Delaware Estuary (Kelly 1976) and the regional dispersion models for gaseous emissions (TRW, Inc. 1970). These submodels accept as inputs the vectors of residuals from the production–disposal LP and produce as outputs vectors of ambient quality levels (e.g., SO_2, suspended particulates, dissolved oxygen, and fish concentrations) at numerous locations in the region. These concentrations are, in turn, treated as input to the environmental "evaluation" submodel in the lower right of the diagram. Here the ambient concentrations implied by one solution of the production–disposal submodel are compared with the environmental quality constraints (ambient standards) imposed for the model run. To the extent that specific constraints are violated, "penalties" are

---

[25] The work began in 1969 before passage of the 1972 Amendments to the Federal Water Pollution Control Act. These Amendments mandated the adoption of discharge limitations based on the capabilities of technological processes. However, the Act also specified that if the installation of such measures were insufficient to achieve the ambient water quality standards adopted under the aegis of previous legislation, additional measures would have to be taken.

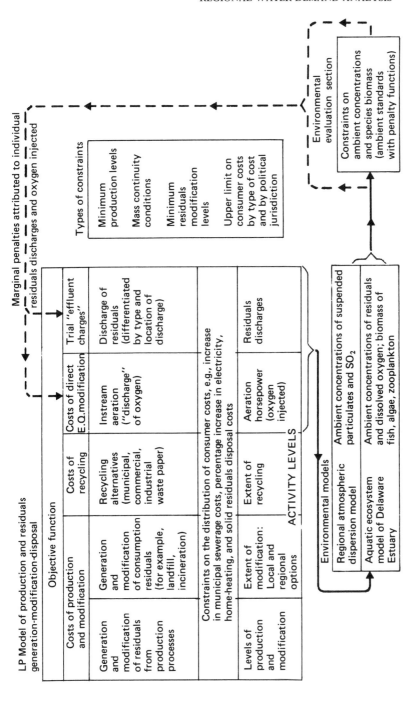

Figure 6.10. Schematic diagram of the Lower Delaware Valley residuals—environmental quality management model. From W. O. Spofford, Jr, C. S. Russell, and R. A. Kelly (1976) *Environmental Quality Management: An Application to the Lower Delaware Valley* (Washington, DC: Resources for the Future), Fig. 4. Reproduced with permission.

Table 6.1. Lower Delaware Valley model: residuals generation and discharge modules.

Module identification	Size of linear program			Description[a]	Percent extra cost constraints for the 57 political jurisdictions (except as noted)[b]
	Rows	Columns	Discharges		
MPSX 1	286	1649	130	Petroleum refineries (7) Steel mills (5) Power plants (17)	57 electricity
MPSX 2	741	1482	114	Home heat (57) Commercial heat (57)	57 fuel 57 fuel[c]
MPSX 3	564	1854	157	"Over 25 μg/m³" dischargers (75)[d]	
MPSX 4	468	570	180	Delaware Estuary sewage treatment plants (36)	46 sewage disposal ($/household/yr)[e]
MPSX 5	951	1914	88	Paper plants (10) Municipal incinerators (23) Municipal solid residuals handling and disposal activities	57 solid residuals disposal
MPSX 6	229	395	117[f]	Delaware Estuary industrial dischargers (23)[g] In-stream aeration (22)	57 in-stream aeration (absolute extra cost per day)[h]
TOTAL	3239	7864	786		

[a] Numbers in parentheses indicate the number of plants or activities that are included in the module with residuals management options.

[b] Numbers in this column indicate the number of distributional constraints of a specified type that are incorporated in the model.

[c] The commercial heating requirements in this module are based on the differences between SO_2 discharges from area sources in the US Environmental Protection Agency's Implementation Planning Program's (IPP) inventory of gaseous emissions and SO_2 emissions from the home heating model. Commercial heating requirements for eight political jurisdictions are equal to zero.

[d] Industrial plants whose gaseous discharges result in maximum annual average ground level concentrations equal to or greater than 25 $\mu g/m^3$. To determine this group, all stacks (point sources) in the IPP inventory were considered except those in MPSX 1 above (petroleum refineries, steel mills, and thermal power plants). The maximum annual average ground-level concentrations (of SO_2 and suspended particulates) were computed for each stack. For all stacks at the same x–y location (i.e., the same plant), the maximum ground-level concentrations were added together. Those plants associated with maximum ground-level concentrations—for either sulfur or suspended particulates—equal to or greater than 25 $\mu g/m^3$ were placed in this category.

[e] Only 46 of the 57 political jurisdictions discharge all their sewage directly to the Delaware Estuary.

[f] Does not include the 22 oxygen "discharges" from the in-stream aeration option.

[g] 12 of the Delaware Estuary industrial wastewater dischargers in MPSX 6 are also represented by the SO_2 and/or particulate dischargers in MPSX 3, and the gaseous discharges of another are included in MPSX 5.

[h] The model currently reports the total regional absolute extra cost per day for in-stream aeration. This cost is then allocated equally among the 57 political jurisdictions. Any other distribution is also possible.

From W. O. Spofford, Jr, C. S. Russell, and R. A. Kelly (1976) *Environmental Quality Management: An Application to the Lower Delaware Valley* (Washington, DC: Resources for the Future). Reproduced with permission.

imposed using steeply nonlinear penalty functions, so that the size of the penalty grows very rapidly as the size of the violation increases.[26]

The marginal penalties calculated in the evaluation submodel after a solution of the production–disposal submodel are then transferred back to the production–disposal block where they are applied as trial "effluent charges" to the appropriate discharges.[27] The production–disposal submodel is then solved again, subject to all the original constraints, and with the new unit costs attached to discharges. The resulting solution is used as the basis for another pass through the other parts of the model. This discussion over-simplifies the actual algorithm, but gives the reader its flavor. One additional complication should, however, be mentioned here. At each iteration, it is necessary to provide "artificial" constraints on the discharges in the production and discharge submodel since otherwise that model, being linear, would tend to oscillate between extreme solutions.

The residuals generation and discharge portion of the regional model is composed of six separate LP modules arranged as depicted in Table 6.1. As can be seen in this table, the model is a large one, with almost 8000 variables (columns) and over 3000 constraining relationships (rows). Almost 800 individual residuals discharges, from about 300 activities in the region, enter the environmental models. The fifth column of this table describes the type, and indicates the number (in parentheses), of activities in the region that are included in the model with residuals management options. An example of the kinds of management options provided in the model is shown in Table 6.2 for the petroleum refineries. The sixth, and final, column in Table 6.1 depicts the distribution constraints potentially available in each of the six LP modules. These constraints allowed the model user to specify, for example, that electric utility bills could not rise in jurisdiction j by more than $x\%$ in a particular run; or that household payments for sewage treatment could not rise by more than $y\%$. Except for the costs of sewage disposal, there is one constraint for each type of extra cost for each of the 57 political jurisdictions into which the Lower Delaware Valley was divided for modeling purposes. (There are only 46 extra costs for sewage disposal in the model because 11 jurisdictions do

---

[26] These penalty functions are simply mathematical devices designed to allow the solution of an optimization problem in which the constraints are inherently nonlinear. Their function, very briefly, is to transfer the nonlinearity from the constraint set to the objective function where it is more easily dealt with. The study was concerned with the marginal penalties attributable to specific discharges (by substance and location). These are calculated in the evaluation submodel, using information from the environmental models. This latter information consists of environmental "response coefficients", which relate small changes in specific discharges to ambient concentrations.

[27] At the optimum, the marginal penalties do represent the optimal, or efficient, effluent charge set.

Table 6.2. An example of residuals management options available to dischargers in the Lower Delaware Valley model—petroleum refineries. From W. O. Spofford, Jr, C. S. Russell, and R. A. Kelly (1976) *Environmental Quality Management: An Application to the Lower Delaware Valley* (Washington, DC: Resources for the Future), Table B-2. Reprinted with permission.

Management option available	Primary residual reduced	Secondary residual generated
Change in raw material input mix:		
1. Purchased fuel alternatives: residual fuel oil, 3 grades (sulfur contents 0·5, 1·0, and 2·0%)	SO_2	None
2. Charge of lower sulfur crude, 2 grades (sulfur contents 0·4 and 1·44%)	SO_2	None
3. Sell, rather than burn, certain high-sulfur products, e.g., sour refinery coke (3·32% sulfur), sweet coke (1·57% sulfur), desulfurized refinery gas (0·1% sulfur)	SO_2, particulates	None
Residuals modification processes:		
1. Cyclone collectors on cat-cracker catalyst regenerator (two removal efficiencies: 70 and 85%)	Particulates	Ash
2. Electrostatic precipitator on cat-cracker catalyst regenerator (removal efficiency 95%)	Particulates	Ash
3. Secondary and tertiary treatment for sour water condensate	BOD, toxics, ammonia	Sludge
4. Various re-use alternatives for treated wastewater (cooling tower water makeup, desalter water, boiler feedwater)	BOD	None
5. Cooling tower(s) for segregated noncontact cooling water	Heat	None (heat to atmosphere ignored)
6. Sludge drying and incineration	Sludge	Particulates, suspended solids

not discharge any sewage at all to the estuary and those jurisdictions were not forced to share directly the costs of the jurisdictions with estuary discharges.)

There are potentially three kinds of lessons to be drawn from the construction and use of a model of this type in water resources management:

(1) lessons about policy alternatives;
(2) lessons about model design and utility in the policy-making process;
(3) lessons about model design, cost, information loss, and conformity to the problem.

On the basis of experience with the model, something can be said about the costs and feasibility of various alternative ambient quality standards. But because the concern of this book is with general methodological issues, only a reference to that discussion is provided (Spofford *et al.* 1976). On the other hand, there has been no use of the model in policy making, so there exist no useful lessons on point two. Accordingly, the paragraphs below deal exclusively with matters falling under point (3), lessons about model design, cost, information loss, and conformity to the problem at hand.

(*a*) Even with considerable effort at simplification, regional water demand models may become very large. In the case of the Delaware, of course, size was related closely to the goal of bringing in air quality and solid waste simultaneously with water quality. But if one has a situation in which such extensions seem necessary, the possibility of a smaller, "water only" model is not a real one (as discussed below, one is inclined to think that on balance the simultaneous treatment of the three environmental quality problems is worth its costs). In the Delaware case the efforts to simplify included:

- Condensation of the major LP submodels developed for petroleum refineries and steel mills, using the technique of repeated solution for different environmental constraints described above. Thus, instead of seven refinery submodels with 300 rows each, the model incorporated seven with about ten rows each; similarly for the five steel mills modeled.
- Aggregation of individual stacks at multiple stack enterprises (such as the refineries and chemical plants) into one large "virtual stack".[28]
- Elimination of all discharge management alternatives for sources whose airborne residuals emissions of SO_2 and particulates both resulted in maximum annual average ground level concentrations less than $25\,\mu g/m^3$. These sources, numbering over 200, were made part of regional "background".

(*b*) Happily, although large size may be very difficult to avoid, it need not be a devastating problem for the modeler, particularly the modeler who confines him- or herself to linear structures. The especially trying problems encountered in the Delaware project were not the result of size so much as

---

[28] This aggregation process was based on contribution to ground level concentrations of SO_2 and suspended particulates. The virtual stack had an emission rate equal to the sum of the emission rates of the stacks it replaced, but the stack height, and gas exit velocity and temperature were chosen to produce the same maximum contribution to ground level concentration at the same direction from the stack as was the case for the combination of original stacks. (In the inventory of sources used, multiple stacks for a single plant were always listed at the same grid coordinate. The inventory was: US Environmental Protection Agency, Implementation Planning Program Air Quality Control Region Inventory of Gaseous Emissions.)

of nonlinearity and possibly nonconvexity. In particular, it was found that the model was very expensive to run and that one could not put very much stock in the exact solution values for the choice variables—most importantly, the discharges of residuals by source. The cost problem was principally accounted for by the iterative nature of the nonlinear solution algorithm. Generally runs were stopped after 30 iterations even when the exact requirements for internal stopping had not been met. At the cheapest rates available to the modeling team such a run cost about $40 per iteration or $1200 per run.

The unreliability of the solution variables has been variously interpreted: as evidence of a flat response surface; as evidence of the substantial inefficiency of the home-grown algorithm; and as evidence of nonconvexity. The author's inclination is to accept the last diagnosis, particularly in light of an

Table 6.3. The Delaware Estuary ecosystem model (for details, see Kelly 1976).

Endogenous variables (compartments, mg/l)
    Algae
    Zooplankton (herbivores, detritivores, and bacterivores)
    Bacteria
    Fish
    Dissolved oxygen (DO)
    Organic matter (as BOD)
    Nitrogen
    Phosphorus
    Toxics
    Suspended solids
    Temperature (°C)

Inputs of residuals (lb/day)	Target outputs[a] (mg/l)
Organic material (as BOD)	Algae
Nitrogen	Fish
Phosphorus	Dissolved oxygen
Toxics	
Suspended solids	
Heat (Btu)	

Model
    Type: materials balance—trophic level
    Characteristics: deterministic, nonsteady state
    Calibration: based on September 1970 flow at Trenton, NJ, of 4146 cfs

Reaches
    Number: 22

[a] Management model operated for relevant minimum, or maximum, allowable ambient concentrations ("standards").

informal comment by an authority in the field to the effect that 90% of all applied nonlinear models will be nonconvex. Recently, a fully linear model of the same system has been completed and run on a very preliminary test basis. Indications are that the cost problem is considerably mitigated, though per run costs are still far from negligible because decomposition is necessary, and so iteration is not avoided.

(c) Whatever the reason for the unreliability of model output, the existence of the problem severely curtailed the model's usefulness in addressing the range of questions for which it was designed. While no inconsistencies were observed in solving for the costs of various alternative quality standards, it was found that when constraints on the distribution of costs were added, things broke down. Specifically, adding such constraints would sometimes make the overall cost of the ambient quality standard lower—clearly a nonsense result. If such unreliability is related to nonlinearity and nonconvexity, and if nonconvexity is indeed pervasive in applied modeling, this seems a powerful argument against the use of nonlinear optimization models for complex water management problems (or for any problem for that matter).

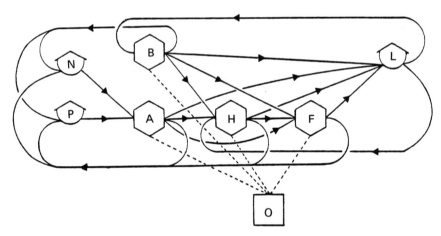

Figure 6.11. Diagram of material flows among compartments within a single reach, Delaware Estuary ecosystem model. Notation: N, nitrogen; P, phosphorus; A, algae; B, bacteria; H, zooplankton; F, fish; L, organic matter (as BOD); O, dissolved oxygen. Note: the three remaining variables—heat (temperature), toxics, and suspended solids—are assumed to affect the rates of material transfers among the ecosystem components (compartments). From W. O. Spofford, Jr, C. S. Russell, and R. A. Kelly (1975) Operational problems in large-scale residuals management models, in E. S. Mills (ed) *Economic Analysis of Environmental Problems* (New York: National Bureau of Economic Research). Reproduced with permission.

To give the reader a taste of the ecological model included in the Delaware model, Table 6.3 shows a summary of the variables it contained, the inputs accepted, and the outputs generated. Figure 6.11 is a schematic of the material flows linking the several compartments. It is only fair, however, to note the assertion often made by ecologists that only such nonlinear models as this one, or preferably an even more complex version, can do justice to the ecological system—the food web—and that while linear models may be constructed to do well in the neighborhood of the flow and discharge levels of the initial conditions, significant changes in any of these will have serious detrimental effects on their accuracy.

(d) The inclusion of air quality and solid waste management simultaneously with water management narrowly defined is probably, in many situations, worth the costs. These costs are not overwhelming. Data are no worse (and no better) for air pollution generation and control costs than for water, and no nonlinearities need be introduced simply because a decision is made to cut across the media. On the other hand, there was evidence in the Delaware model runs of significant interconnections among the ambient environmental quality standards, with the marginal costs of meeting increasingly tougher water quality standards being higher the stricter the air quality standards applying at the time. This kind of effect, if ignored, in the process of choosing water quality standards, could lead to political problems in implementation, for actual costs could be significantly higher than estimated costs. With full knowledge of the implications of interactions, a different (lower) quality standard might be chosen.

(e) Finally, the Delaware modeling experience makes it likely that a serious attempt at water management modeling will outstrip the available data without much effort. To the extent data are available at all, they have probably been collected disjointedly, by researchers from different disciplines and institutions with distinct research interests. Because water management models will generally involve integration of various parts of the system—especially human economic activities and natural processes—they will demand integrated data for fitting *and* for verification of predictive ability. For the Delaware, for example, it would have been extremely useful to have had several sets of related data on streamflows, ambient water quality and charges. Here "related" means that the timing of the discharge data was such that it would be reasonable to see them as a *cause* of the water quality readings. In fact, there were no such data, but only one set of baseline discharge quantities and a few completely unrelated sets of water quality readings. In such circumstances, it is impossible to have even the roughest assurance that the overall model approximately describes the real world, and one is flying on faith. Such a situation would make it nearly impossible to sell the model as a useful basis for choosing between alternative policies, even if policy makers were inclined to seek such bases for their decisions.

Conclusions

This chapter represents an attempt to bring together some of the key issues involved in the design and construction of models for the analysis of *regional* water demand problems. The approach taken has been to concentrate on how mathematical programming models of individual water use activities, such as those described in Chapters 3–5, can be linked in the regional context and how those links can be translated into model variables. The points made about these links were illustrated using a few simple, schematic, "regional" situations. Even in these very simple contexts, it became evident that regional models might easily become enormous and complicated, so some time was spent discussing techniques for size reduction and simplification, particularly as applied to large programming models for individual water-use activities. In the last section of the chapter a regional modeling project conducted at Resources for the Future was described. While the resulting model dealt only with water quality and not quantity, it served to emphasize many of the points made in the other sections, for problems of design and of model size reduction were important in the project.

In the final analysis, however, every regional model will be to some extent custom-built, for the policy problems, data resources, and institutional situations encountered make each region unique. The principles and tricks described here may be useful, but it does not seem possible to produce a thorough "handbook" of regional modeling that will reduce the job to a mechanical combining of standardized parts. This means there are still many challenges for ingenious modelers, but it also means that the creation of models in real situations will remain expensive undertakings.

7 The National Perspective in Water Demand Modeling*

Introduction

The structure chosen for this book leads at this point to a consideration of the next level of demand aggregation: that of the nation. That is, whether one views a nation as a collection of geographic regions or of economic sectors— each subunit in turn made up of individual water-use activities—a national water demand model ought in principle to be producible from the building blocks described in Chapters 3–6. Indeed, there is no reason at this level of abstraction to stop at the national level. A multi-country model might in some circumstances be a useful analytical tool. Even a continental model could be considered (and has been, at least as far as water use rather than demand is concerned. Reid and Muiga (1976) describe the first steps in developing models based on water-use coefficients per capita in Asia, Africa, and Latin America). The grandest design of all would be a global water demand model; and Batisse (1976) has attempted an informal and highly aggregated analysis along these lines.

This chapter deals only with national models, however; and, in fact, almost all the works referred to are national water *use* rather than national water *demand* studies. Why there should be this rather large gap between analytical possibilities and realizations is not an easy question to answer in a complete and convincing way. Some partial but persuasive reasons may, however, be suggested here. First, the concept and practical meaning of the price (or even of user cost) of water are altogether unclear at such an aggregated level. Water markets, even where they exist, are segmented both by institutional and by physical realities. Administered prices differ for many reasons between water supply organizations, and most large withdrawers, especially industry and power generation, often face only internally defined user costs since in most countries there are still no organizations that have the power to charge them for the withdrawn volumes. Predicting, say, withdrawal volumes across

* This chapter was written by J. Kindler and C. S. Russell.

MODELING WATER DEMANDS
ISBN 0-12-407380-8

a nation therefore involves considerable difficulty since in most countries there is no such thing as a uniform nationwide "price" per cubic meter of water. In addition, there are the problems of aggregation and the distinction between net and gross withdrawals which, as is discussed below, can wreak havoc with the interpretation of national, sectoral, or even regional totals. Finally, it is undoubtedly of some importance that this area has traditionally been the province of engineers, and particularly engineers attached to government agencies with responsibility for supply project evaluation and planning. This orientation, naturally enough, has encouraged concentration on use requirements that should be met, rather than on schedules of demand that would be relevant only to agencies with price-setting authority.

Within this limited approach, however, there exists a large number of exercises aimed at one or another of the model purposes identified in Chapter 1: baseline forecasting; the analysis of the impact of government policies; or the balancing of water use and supply. In the sections that follow, each of these purposes is discussed in turn, with reference where appropriate to a sample of studies from a variety of countries. The purpose here is not only to describe, however; we also attempt to offer observations and critical comment on the utility of national level studies generally.

Baseline Forecasting

Because this purpose, by definition, involves projections in which baseline conditions, including relative prices and unit costs, are held constant, as well as those in which no changes in base-line public policies are allowed to enter, the distinction between demand and use is not an especially useful one in this context. While it may seem most unlikely that such a condition of constancy would ever be observed over any significant period in the future, there is no reason to think it any less likely than the occurrence of any other highly specific prediction. There is therefore no reason to assume that baseline water-use forecasts are *a priori* invalid or ridiculous. This section includes a few remarks on the goals asserted for these studies, a brief description of some typical methodologies, and, finally, comments addressing issues other than those raised by ignoring price sensitivity and future government policy options.

Baseline water-use forecasting, as one might imagine, is usually undertaken with the idea of identifying "problems" before they become crises; or, said in a more positive way, of providing lead times for planning and consequent management actions for dealing with anticipated problems (see, for example, the two water resources assessments carried out by the US Water Resources Council 1968, 1978). In these studies, a "problem" is usually taken to exist when projected water use exceeds some (probabilistically) assured level of supply availability. Sometimes this goal is stated explicitly (as in Reid and Muiga 1976); in other studies it is implicit in the presentation of results and the tone of the discussion (e.g., Institute for Futures Research, University of Stellenbosch, South Africa, 1978, p5: "It is therefore reasonable to assume that the South African water situation is not as depressing as has been previously stated, but it is nevertheless serious. The demand for water is likely to exceed the supply by the year 2025...").

In the pursuit of the goal of problem identification, baseline water-use forecasting studies employ methods that are roughly analogous to the statistical and engineering approaches to generating water demand relations discussed at some length in Chapter 2. One statistical technique is the fitting of trend lines to existing data at the national level.

Another use of statistical methods is the estimation of equations for predicting national average water-use coefficients for different sectors as functions of exogenous variables such as income, production levels, climate, etc., as appropriate to the sector. Reid and Muiga (1976), for example, predict municipal water use per capita for inhabitants of cities in developing countries in Asia, Africa, and Latin America, as linear functions of community population, percentage of homes connected to public water supply in the community, and average annual per capita income—whether national or by city is not clear. (Because price is not included in these equations they are effectively, if not by design, the reduced form equations for quantity from the demand–supply system of equations.)

The South African report referred to above reflects a methodology with conceptual similarities to the engineering method of demand analysis. Here "detailed sectoral and regional analysis", which includes consideration of such factors as cropping patterns, power plant cooling technologies, and industrial water recycling, is ultimately translated into rates of growth of water withdrawals by economic sector. These summary measures are then simply applied to the time span of interest.[1] The engineering approach to forecasting appears again in the description of some of the studies mentioned in the next section on policy analysis. The difference is that the applications listed here do not include possible government policies as exogenous variables or explicit influences that either directly or indirectly influence water use (for further examples, see Tsachev and Tsenova 1976, Csermak 1976, Predescu and Duna 1976, Weiss 1976, Parsons 1976).

Even if these baseline forecasting studies are accepted largely on their own

[1] It is of special interest in light of one of the comments made below that this study attempts to allow for the recycling, via rivers, of return flows from agriculture, industry, and households. It does this by assuming percentages of withdrawals for each sector returned for re-use.

terms—as embodying a very simple set of assumptions in order to minimize the costs of carrying out what is in any event an extremely uncertain under-taking—there are still some problems that deserve mention. First, even if market mechanisms for sharing water resources are entirely absent, there may still be other automatic, or nearly automatic, equilibrating mechanisms built into government rules and procedures. Thus, for example, there may be rules for sharing the available flow in a river between competing activities or jurisdictions. In the base period, these rules may be effectively inoperative because the capacity of one or more competitors is below their allocation. As their use grows, the rules will require that use by their competitors decrease, and available flow need not be exceeded, though simple extrapolation might suggest that it would. (A situation very like the one described here exists in the Colorado River basin in the Western US.) More difficult to detect and allow for will be situations in which competition for a given resource will raise unit costs of the competitors and, as though there were a market, stimulate action to reduce demand (use). This might happen along a river, though most of the examples documented in the literature involve ground-water aquifers[2] (see, for example, Ingram *et al.* 1980). In either event, if it is assumed that in the future applicable policies or relative prices (costs) will remain the same as in the base period, water-use projections will be inaccurate, and in general, the error will be such as to exaggerate the potential for problems.

National aggregation of water uses can also lead to projection errors, and again something can be said *a priori* about the biases thus introduced. National totals of water withdrawals, unless account is explicitly taken of hydrologic reality in the form of the availability of upstream water discharges to downstream withdrawers, will be overstatements of the stress to be placed on the available resource (recall that the South African forecasts did try to take such re-use into account by applying a single withdrawal-reducing factor to the national forecasts for each sector). If the forecasts are done without reference to the regions, but as national aggregates by sectors, there will be two, roughly opposite, biases introduced. The aggregation along rivers will still be implicit in the totals, and thus the total net withdrawals will be overestimated. On the other hand, aggregation across regions will tend to wash out possible regional problems. It is impossible to say how, on the whole, the simple forecasting approach will have affected the probability of correctly identifying possible future problems.

As a final caution, it should be noted that the supply reliability require-

[2] Notice that even though competition for a common property resource will tend to increase costs and decrease use, no individual user will take into account his real effect on the costs of others and thus the "solution" obtained without outside intervention will in general be suboptimal.

ments, which differ substantially from one type of water use to another, are intractable at the national level of data aggregation.

These are criticisms not so much of baseline forecasting as of national water studies in a broader sense. At a minimum it seems clear that in order to avoid the worst problems, national forecasts should be done by region, and beyond that some attempt should be made to allow for upstream/downstream relations. In short, the vision of a relatively cheap and easy way to search for future water problems via baseline forecasting may be largely an illusion.

National Development Policies and their Implications for Water Use

All countries engage in planning efforts concerning their long-term economic and social development policies. In this context, policy refers to a chosen development path, such as an export promotion or import substitution orientation, and the chosen policies vary greatly among countries according to size, relation with the world economy, natural resources, level of development, and social and environmental quality objectives.

Among the many countries that have carried out national water studies, Poland provides an interesting example because of a specially long tradition of such enquiries (Łaski and Kindler 1976). The first long-term national water resources development plan was drafted by the Polish Academy of Sciences in the years 1953–1956 (time horizon of 1975). The plan was then twice revised in the early 1960s by the National Water Authority, and the time horizon was extended to 1985. In the late 1960s it became clear that the water situation, particularly in the Vistula Basin, which covers about 54% of the area of Poland, required special attention. Preliminary long-term projections developed by the Planning Commission and the Academy of Sciences indicated that the state of water availability in the basin is not compatible with future requirements. In 1968, comprehensive studies were initiated with the assistance of the United Nations Development Program, under the name of "Planning Comprehensive Development of the Vistula River System". Within the framework of these studies, alternative projections of future water use have been developed by specialized governmental agencies (14 ministries in collaboration) for two levels of development, 1985 and 2000. The common basis for all projections has been the national long-term development plan and its alternative projections of the principal macroeconomic categories such as GNP, national income, level of foreign trade, individual and collective consumption, and output of the basic economic sectors. In Figure 7.1 aggregated results of water-use projections carried out for the Vistula River

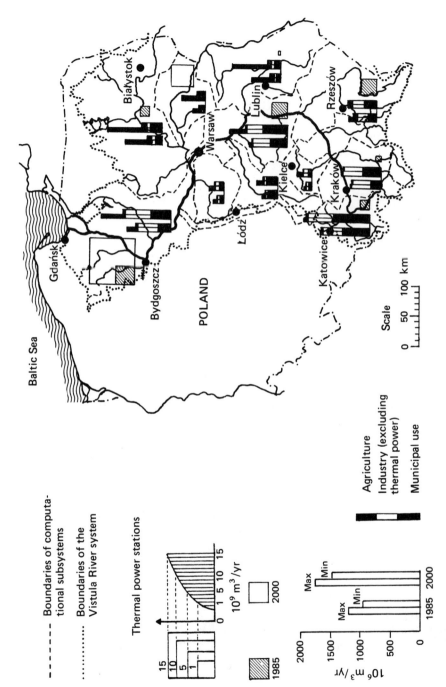

Figure 7.1. Water-use projections for the Vistula River system, Poland.

system at different points in time are presented. For the purpose of the study initiated in the late 1960s, the system was decomposed spatially into 12 sub-systems, with the water-use requirements estimated sector by sector for each subsystem.

It is not, of course, the function of the national water agency (provided such an agency exists in a given country), to decide what the country's economic and social development policies should be. This is the job of the parliament, the national planning agency interacting with sectoral agencies (e.g., ministries), and the regional authorities, working together under what-ever form of government exists. But the national water agency certainly does have a role in this process. Usually, there is a legal requirement that such an agency provide information to other agencies and to higher-level units engaged in the strategic planning, or water-related implications of the national development strategies. This does not generally mean that recom-mendations are made concerning specific water projects; rather, it is a question of looking at the different water problems arising under different national development policies affecting water use, which in turn could result in the justification for considering alternative methods of supply such as interbasin transfers, desalinization of sea water, re-use of treated water, or

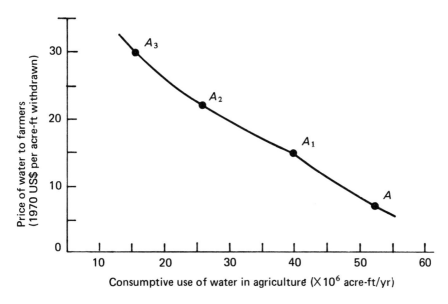

Figure 7.2. Projected agricultural water demand in the 17 Western US states (from Heady *et al.* 1972).

weather modification. This is the setting within which the examples of national policy analysis studies described here should be understood.

An outstanding example of a national sectoral study is that of Heady *et al.* (1972), who developed a macro interregional linear programming model of US agriculture (applying the engineering/programming approach introduced in Chapter 2). The model yields the least-cost distribution of agricultural production by crop type and geographic region, under assumptions regarding resource availabilities and their costs (including the price of water), farm support programs, and consumer and export demand for agricultural products. In particular, in order to evaluate the sensitivity of water use in irrigated agriculture to the price charged for water, the hypothetical price of water paid by agricultural producers was systematically increased in the model to levels above those currently charged in different regions. The resulting demand curve for consumptive use of water in agriculture in 17 Western US states (which dominate the use of irrigation water), generated by the Heady model, is shown in Figure 7.2. That the demands are quite elastic over a wide range of volumes may be seen from the figures for arc elasticities, calculated from that demand function and displayed in Table 7.1.

The above model was used, along with many others, by the US National Water Commission, which looked at the effects of changes in policy and technology on future demands for water across the US. The analysis was made not for the purpose of advocating any particular course of action, but to illustrate how significant changes in water use might occur under different "alternative futures" for the country as a whole. These involved specifying alternative future population levels, decentralization policies for urban population, food and fiber production levels, national efficiency policy, income redistribution policy, environmental quality policies, changes in lifestyles, changes in water-related institutional arrangements, and changes in the traditional ratio of financial support (for water projects) by the federal, state, local, and private sectors. It did not apparently prove possible, however, for the Commission staff, with limited time and budget, to undertake a melding of the various sector demand studies that had been commissioned

Table 7.1. Arc elasticity of demand for water for the demand curve in Figure 7.1 (from Heady *et al.* 1972).

Segment	Arc elasticity
A_3-A_2	$-1{\cdot}683$
A_2-A_1	$-1{\cdot}012$
A_1-A	$-0{\cdot}329$

(e.g., Howe *et al.* 1970). Therefore, the results of the analysis (as summarized in National Water Commission 1973) stress the range of withdrawal projections produced by varying the policy assumptions, rather than the range of demand relations that could have been produced. The flavor of the Commission's findings is captured in the following summary (National Water Commission 1973, p13):

Conclusions from the Analysis: The analysis shows that the rate of growth of the population and the economy and the alternative water policies and water use technologies that are adopted would have very significant effects on future water demands. The following more specific conclusions with respect to water use in the year 2020 were reached in the study:
1. Water withdrawals in the year 2020 may range from 570 billion gallons per day (b.g.d.) to 2,280 b.g.d. depending on the combination of variables that are assumed. In comparison, the Water Resources Council projected the total withdrawals at 1,368 b.g.d. under a continuation of policies and trends in effect in 1968.
2. Water consumption in the year 2020 may range from 150 to 250 b.g.d. in comparison to the Water Resources Council's projection of 157 b.g.d.
3. Greater recycling of industrial process water and recirculation of water used for cooling would significantly reduce water withdrawals in the nation without any substantial total increase in water consumption. This would be particularly true for steam electric power generation where the studies indicate that water withdrawals would be four times greater in the year 2020 under a continuation of present technology than with substantially advanced technology which would increase consumptive use only about 1 percent.

Another example is provided by the water-use forecasting study carried out in the early 1970s in Japan by the Water Resources Bureau and the Nomura Research Institute (Japanese National Land Agency 1977). The simulation model developed for this project has five major components: a macroeconomic model and an input–output model, which are used jointly to forecast changes in the economy of Japan and its future industrial structure; and four submodels to forecast changes in municipal, household, industrial, and agricultural uses of water across the whole country. Each of the four submodels is coupled with a procedure for projecting changes in sectoral water-use coefficients.

A large number of exogenously given socioeconomic and policy variables are included in the simulation model. These include population, economic growth, the pattern of foreign trade, food self-sufficiency, lifestyles, extent of urbanization, the progress in the development of agricultural infrastructure, and water conservation attitudes, with future values specified to make up alternative scenarios. For some of the variables, extrapolation of past trends is used; for others, breaks with the past are postulated. Except for the household sector, however, the price of water is not explicitly taken into account. The results of the study include water-use estimates under different socioeconomic "alternative futures" for each of the four water-use categories

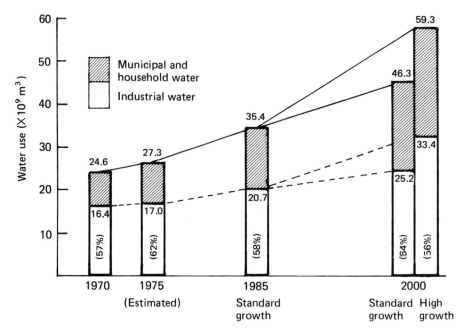

Figure 7.3. National water-use forecast for Japan (from Japanese National Land Agency and Nomura Research Institute 1979).

considered. Some indication of the nature of these results is given in Figure 7.3 and Table 7.2, which show the effect of alternative assumptions about the annual growth rate of the Japanese GNP over the period 1975–2006: high, 6·0%; standard, 4·5%; and low, 3·0%.

Balancing Projected Water Use and Supply at the National Level

The previous sections have discussed national water-use projections in the context of two purposes: simple baseline forecasting, and analysis of the implications of economic development strategies or of sectoral policies for water use. It is a natural step from such projection efforts to balance projected use with available supply, but, since the projections do not reflect the price (or cost) elasticity of water demand, the "balancing" would have to be limited to the planning of supply-increasing investments. This, indeed, has been the pattern of major regional and national-level studies that bring together water-use projections with supply alternatives (see, for example, the discussion

Table 7.2. National water use forecast for Japan (from Japanese National Land Agency and Nomura Research Institute 1977).

	1970	1975	1985 Standard growth	2000 Standard growth	2000 High growth	2000 Low growth	Annual rate of increase (%) 1970–75	1975–85	1975–2000
	10^6 m³ (%)						(%)(increase)		
Household water	5208 (21)	6750 (25)	10 040 (28)	14 650 (32)	18 250 (31)	11 680 (33)	5·3 (1·3)	4·0 (1·5)	3·1 (2·2)
Municipal water	2961 (12)	3550 (13)	4710 (13)	6410 (14)	7670 (13)	5560 (15)	3·7 (1·2)	2·9 (1·3)	2·4 (1·8)
Industrial water	16 425 (67)	17 010 (62)	20 670 (62)	25 200 (54)	33 380 (56)	18 750 (52)	0·7 (1·0)	2·0 (1·2)	1·6 (1·5)
Total	24 594(100)	27 310(100)	35 420(100)	46 260(100)	59 300(100)	35 990(100)	2·1 (1·1)	2·6 (1·3)	2·1 (1·7)
Population (thousands)	103 720	111 934	123 562	134 442	134 442	134 442	1·54(1·08)	0·99(1·10)	0·74(1·20)
GNP (10 billion yen)	72 144	91 646	165 511	380 703	399 592	202 304	4·90(1·27)	6·09(1·81)	4·58(3·06)

Notes:
1. Forecast is based on the amount of water used but does not include losses during withdrawal and other processes.
2. Direct use of groundwater is included for industrial and household use, but not for municipal use.
3. Agricultural use is estimated to increase from 57 000 × 10^6 m³ in 1971 to 65 500 × 10^6 m³ in 1985.

and citations in Howe 1967, pp 350–2 and the UK effort reported in Water Resources Board 1974).

For the most part, these studies may be distinguished on the basis of the sophistication with which they treat supply reliability, whether or not they involve general equilibrium models of the economy as inputs to the water-use projections, and whether they use methods that find least-cost supply investment alternatives or simply settle for some technically feasible set of options.

As was observed in Chapter 1, this general approach, when coupled with the recognized economies of scale in water supply projects, can and does lead to overbuilding of dams, reservoirs, and water transmission facilities. Beyond this fundamental problem of dependence on water-use projections (at any level of aggregation) in the planning of supply increments, there are certain other points that may be made with specific reference to the national level.

First, it has already been suggested that national aggregated projections of water use have certain inherent infirmities as indicators of imbalances in use and supply. On the one hand, through aggregation, they tend to eliminate possible intra-regional problems, and on the other, unless done with extreme care, they overstate net withdrawal totals by ignoring re-use via natural watercourses.

Secondly, in the context of use/supply balancing another problem may appear: the projection of use exceeding available supply at the national level may tend to focus the attention of those responsible for the balancing on very large (and hence potentially very wasteful) projects aiming at increasing water supply. It is well illustrated by Schultz (1981), who underlines that: "The allocations [of international capital aid to developing countries] are also marred by the funding of massive irrigation projects, which are as a rule a mistake". At the same time, a national system of regional use/supply balances encourages planning of interbasin transfers, and economic analyses of such proposals in the past have commonly showed that they only make economic sense to the users in the receiving region when the costs are subsidized by other regions of the nation (e.g., see Howe and Easter 1971, Ingram et al. 1980).

In short, it seems at least likely that attempts to balance available national supply with national projections of use, whether or not these projections are done by region, often encourage wastage of resources through over-investment, premature investment, or adoption of economically unjustified programs. Because the potential mistakes involve national-level aggregates they can be more magnificent than similarly motivated regional planning errors.

Conclusions

The tone of this chapter has been largely negative, not because there is anything inherently wrong with national water *demand* modeling, but because attempts to apply the concept of demand at the national level are both very difficult and of limited relevance. The results of existing national water *use* studies are subject to a fundamental bias toward exaggerating future levels of withdrawal and toward stimulating alarm and, unfortunately, action designed to provide for the projected uses.

Realistically, however, there will very likely be a growing number of national government agencies concerned with water resources and charged with identifying national problems, analyzing the effects of national plans or sectoral policies, and with suggesting and planning water resource projects. For these agencies and individuals, the message for a world of increasing scarcity (of sites for reservoirs as well as public monies for dams and pipelines) is, "Think Demand" (but, for a contrasting prescription, see Lofting and Davis 1977). Although it might once have been frivolous, the attempt to obtain and use information about the elasticity of water demand with respect to price (or cost, where appropriate) is unlikely to be so now. Indeed, an attempt to save money in the planning process by using a "requirements" approach may well be penny wise and pound foolish. And it is not necessary to pioneer. For example, the US National Water Commission prepared the groundwork for national water demand estimates reflecting estimates of responsiveness to price almost a decade ago. Studies such as those described and cited in Chapters 3–5 provide building blocks that can be assembled, even if some rough edges are left, into national demand models. Modern computational capabilities make it possible to maintain and use very large accounting frameworks such as those that would be necessary to keep track of water quantities in a national simulation model with stream location, and hence natural water re-use, built in. A model of this general type, designed to simulate the effects of alternative water pollution control policies, and performing the more difficult accounting that goes with keeping track of water pollution discharges and corresponding ambient water quality, is described in Gianessi *et al.* (1981) and Gianessi and Peskin (1981).

8 *Summary and Reflections**

An Overview

This book has presented the basic concepts and techniques of water demand modeling and has illustrated these through the reporting of case studies undertaken by IIASA in cooperation with several institutions from the IIASA National Member Organization countries. The most important idea discussed was that of *demand* itself, and more specifically, its application to water use. Thus, it has been stressed throughout that, all else being equal, farms, industrial enterprises, and individuals will choose to use less water when the price or cost per unit is high than they will when that cost is low. This amounts to saying that, while all these activities may have certain irreducible *requirements* for water, for the most part, analysis goes on and policies are made about quantities of use far above these requirements. At these higher use levels, as price or cost rises it is possible for the activities to *substitute* more of some other input or inputs for water.

This fundamental observation immediately suggests that planners at all levels should take into account the responsiveness of quantity demanded to price (as well as to other policy instruments), whether setting out to analyze the effect of new policy initiatives on water resources or deciding about the desirability of new supply and transmission capacity increments in a region. A large part of the book has been concerned with guidance on how to do that, the technique generally involving the production of water demand relations using either of two approaches: *statistical* or *engineering*. The first of these tries to infer from observations on many users at a point in time, or the same user over a period of time, or from a combination of both types of observations, the structure of the water demand relation producing the observations. The second approach attempts to construct the relation from fairly detailed engineering knowledge of the production or consumption *unit processes*, and the associated substitution possibilities, carried out by the activity.

Some of the complications and extensions relevant to these two approaches

---

* This chapter was written by J. Kindler and C. S. Russell.

were also discussed. In particular, for the statistical approach, lack of appropriate data in sufficient quantity, and the difficulties posed by simultaneous determination of prices (or costs) and quantities were stressed. In connection with the engineering approach, the potential complexity of the resulting model, seen as all possible combinations of the relevant unit processes, was mentioned; and the great practical difficulty of finding solutions to particular problems (such as finding the lowest cost reaction by an industrial plant to an increase in the cost of water withdrawals) was indicated. Into this breach was thrust *mathematical* (here linear) *programming*. This technique was shown to be a way to organize the information developed in the engineering approach in such a way that a well developed and quite efficient algorithm is available for finding optimal paths through the set of all possible unit process combinations, for different specifications of the policy instruments, such as price or waste discharge standards.

After commenting on model *verification* and the difficulties connected with that step, especially data difficulties, the general discussion concluded with remarks about *applications* of water demand relations and links between applications, levels of analysis, and choice of modeling approaches. Here again, data concerns were very important.

Following this introduction, the case studies were presented by their authors. Chapter 3 on industrial water demand modeling, by Stone and Whittington, contained examples of both major techniques: statistical and engineering/programming. The first part of the chapter was devoted to describing a small-scale attempt to develop a statistical water demand equation for Dutch paper mills using available data on water use and effective price, plant size, product, and type of technology. Along the way it was necessary for the authors to come to grips with the identification problem, and their arguments about regionally differentiated administered prices will be especially useful reading for modelers considering this method. The results of the exercise are disappointing. This disappointment should not make the examples less useful to the reader, however, for it illustrates very clearly the points made generally in Chapter 2.

The second, and much longer part of Chapter 3 on industrial water use dealt with modeling the water demand relations for a fossil-fuel, thermal power plant, the particular plant being a Polish project located on the Vistula River. In this section the authors discussed at some length the engineering realities of this production process and then showed how these realities were combined with principles of programming model design to determine the structure of the constraint matrix for the plant model. The derivation of some coefficients in that matrix was also illustrated, but since the aim of the book is not specific to power generation, the detailed submodels required for the choice of consistent combinations of temperatures and water flows, and hence for the specification of other elements of the matrix, were not described. The chapter closed with some examples of the output available from the model, showing particularly the derived demand function for cooling water withdrawals and illustrating shifts in that function due to changes in other parameter values.

The second case study (Chapter 4), by Gouevsky and Maidment, described the construction of programming models of water demand for irrigation, in the context of planning in Bulgaria. The authors took care to explain in some detail both the structure of the constraint matrix and the derivation of specific matrix coefficients (such as those giving inputs per unit output of particular crops, with and without irrigation). These pages will have reinforced for the reader the lessons presented in Chapter 3. Following this material, the authors showed how the resulting model could be used to explore the impact on agricultural choices—and hence water use—of changes in the price of water to the regional agroindustrial complex. The resulting derived demands for irrigation withdrawals were illustrated and the adjustments reflected in them discussed. As in Chapter 3, some factors that shift the derived demand function (such as changes in the availability of capital for land development and operating equipment) were explored.

Chapter 5, on municipal water demands, contained both a general discussion of what is known about the characteristics of municipal water demand functions, and a case study in which the demand function for one component of that demand, residential water demand, was estimated. The case study was done by Hanke and de Maré on the basis of data from the city of Malmö, Sweden. This analysis has an interesting history that is of particular value from an educational point of view. The first attempt to model municipal water demands in the entire Malmö county (20 communities, the city of Malmö being just one of them), based on cross-sectional data describing total municipal water use (residential, industrial, etc.), proved to be unsuccessful. This led to the conclusion that for estimating the response of water use to price, distinction must be made between different categories of municipal water use. The analysis of residential water demand was eventually based on water bills from single-family residences, taking into account the income, number of inhabitants and net lot area per residence. The water demand model and price elasticity estimate were based on an analysis of pooled time series and cross-sectional data.

To supplement the material on modeling water demands of industrial, agricultural, and municipal systems, the following two chapters discussed aggregated analysis of these demands on the regional and national scales. Chapter 6, by Russell, dealt with regional demand for shared water resources—either as sources for withdrawals or as sinks for discharges. The emphasis here was on the constraints that would be necessary to reflect the sharing problem in the context of a regional resource, with the overall objective of maximizing net benefits from the activities taken together. These constraints were taken to arise from a policy of maintaining stream flow in the shared rivers in the face of water withdrawals and consumptive uses. It was clear even in this simple context, however, that regional models of water demand could become large and complicated rather quickly.

The complications necessary both in the individual activity models and in the regional constraints, in order to reflect standards for regional water *quality*, were also briefly described. The second half of Chapter 6 provided a case study—though not a IIASA-sponsored one—of a regional water quality model. This was the Lower Delaware River Valley model constructed at Resources for the Future, largely for research rather than actual planning or policy implementation purposes. A recitation of the dimensions of this model gave the point made about potential model size a certain reality (though it must be noted that the Lower Delaware model dealt with air as well as water pollution). A major lesson obtained from the model seemed to be that the introduction of nonlinearities is asking for trouble—both in the area of computational difficulty and cost and in the matter of the reliability of the results.

The next level of aggregation beyond the region is the nation, and Chapter 7 dealt with national water demand modeling. It was not, however, symmetric with the regional aggregation chapter; not because one could not imagine building a national water demand model by bringing together the required set of regional models (as by including interbasin water transfer activities and a national economic model), but because it seems that this sort of national model does not exist. What does seem to exist in fairly great numbers are studies of projected national water *use*, often based on aggregations across industrial and household sectors, and with almost no reflection either of the role of price or cost in affecting water demand, or of the importance of natural recirculation via watercourses. The chapter emphasized, therefore, the problems with such use projections, especially in the contexts of policy analysis and demand–supply balancing, but also in baseline forecasting. While true national water demand models, constructed as aggregations of regional models, could be very large and complex, the decisions made at the national level may involve extremely large and costly undertakings, such as interregional water transfer projects or coastal desalination installations. It is not clear, therefore, that national models are "too expensive", for they might point policy makers away from truly enormous mistakes.

The Case Study Models and Policy Making

The case studies presented in Chapters 3–5, and to a more limited extent the material in Chapter 6, are all meant to be instructive, as examples of techniques useful to those interested in modeling water demand relations. In addition, however, several of the case studies originated in the IIASA program of cooperative studies of interest to government agencies in IIASA National Member Organization countries. In this policy, rather than didactic, context there are other lessons to be learned from the modeling effort and subsequent analysis.

The first of these is that data scarcity problems are serious, especially at the individual activity level, even in situations such as centrally planned economies, where one might have expected a different situation. Data relevant to the six dimensions of water demand at the level of the individual farm or industrial enterprise have either not been collected, or if collected, are held to be confidential by the firm or the responsible ministry. It is not clear what function this confidentiality serves, other than to conceal relative contributions to growing resource and environmental problems. As things now stand, however, it is widely if not universally true that the data necessary for water demand analysis, if they exist at all, will often be available only to the in-house researcher (model builder) in the data-collecting agency—and this agency is not necessarily the one with direct concern for the output of improved analysis.

This observation leads directly to a second: that the spread of methods of improved water demand analysis may require more efforts in which research groups and planning agencies develop cooperative study and application plans. These are not easy, though IIASA is perhaps in a better situation than most institutions to identify and take advantage of opportunities, especially within Europe.

In addition, a few observations can be made about the policy usefulness of the models developed in the case studies described in Chapters 3–5. Concerning the model developed for Dutch paper mills, probably no more can be said than that it really points out the need for improving the data collection policies. The results of the study concerning water demand relations for a large coal-fired power plant located on the Vistula River have contributed to the establishment of a charging scheme for cooling water use in Poland. The Silistra agricultural water demand model has been coupled with a simple LP water supply model and applied to several irrigation projects in Bulgaria, resulting in a significant reduction in investment costs (mostly due to reductions in the size of such components of irrigation systems as delivery canals, pumping stations, etc.). The policy implications of the most recent study on residential water demand in Malmö remain to be seen, but the study certainly provides several useful clues for a new water policy that is currently under discussion in Sweden.

Thoughts for the Future

If one takes seriously the proposition that models of water demand relations can be useful additions to the armories of water resource management agencies and other concerned institutions, it is tempting to ask as a final question: Are there ways to make these models more useful in the future? In particular, are there developments to be sought or areas of application to be opened or expanded?

Three suggestions seem appropriate as a partial answer to the question. First, the reader will have noticed that the general discussions of approaches and applications have been dominated by data problems. Quite often it was necessary to favor an engineering approach because of its relative independence of historical data. But statistical modeling has considerable appeal, particularly because a well done statistical demand relation may mimic the important behavior of a very complex linear program while being itself compact and easy to use once estimated (see, for example, Hazilla et al. 1980). Therefore, the potential social payoff to more and better data on activity level water use and related variables is large. Whether that social payoff could be translated into individual rewards (for data collection can be thankless work), or whether it could be used to outweigh the negative aspects of confidentiality claims, agency inertia, and hostility to further forms and questionnaires, is doubtful. On the other hand, data gathering required by existing laws, especially those laws governing environmental policy, already produces an enormous quantity of data, and a systematic exploration of these would be valuable.

Another subject worthy of more attention than it has historically received is that of the costs and benefits of model simplification. In approaching a water demand (or any other) policy problem, the first impulse of the modeler(s) is often to try to capture every detail of the situation: that is, to include every conceivable variable instead of thinking about and even testing which ones make little difference; to introduce nonlinearities when linear approximations are or can be made available; to use the newest and most abstruse computational packages even though it is unclear whether any gain is obtained; or to imbed the water demand model in a general equilibrium context without analyzing the importance of doing so. Each such decision is likely to be approved by the disciplinary colleagues of the modelers. Indeed, the choice of a simple technique over a complex and sophisticated one is likely to be greeted in seminars and informal conversation with a "But don't you know about the problem of... ?", or "But haven't you seen the latest paper by X, where he develops a technique that allows for... ?" Professional pride, in other words, is not the ally of simplicity. But each complicating step also tends to make the resulting model more inflexible, idiosyncratic in operation, and opaque to the planners and decision makers who ultimately should be the ones to benefit from the exercise.

These planners and decision makers are not, however, blameless in the matter. Their preference for a detailed regulatory approach to achieving public policy goals in such a field as water resource management leads to a need for quite specific and detailed prescriptions. Thus, if one must tell refinery X exactly what to do about water withdrawals, consumption, or wastewater discharge, a simple model is not likely to be considered particularly useful, since it will be easy for the refiner to claim that his real refinery is so much more complex, contains so many more processes and so many more interconnections, uses such a variety of crude oils, etc., that the simple model's results cannot be applied. Detailed regulation demands detailed knowledge. At the same time, it tends to reduce the need for optimizing models aimed at, for example, minimizing the cost of achieving some regional or plant-wide result. Thus, the allowable wastewater discharges for an industrial enterprise might be calculated on the basis of the application of specified treatment devices to raw waste loads. There is really no response model required (though someone, somewhere, might be interested in asking whether the specified loads could be achieved more cheaply via another method). Thus, it might be said that certain regulatory practices create situations in which either models are hardly necessary, or only very specific and complex models will do.

On the other hand, it must be admitted that we do not know much about the costs of using simpler models, in terms of information and accuracy lost, nor about the benefits in terms of the costs of model construction and of subsequent computation avoided. This is perhaps because it is difficult to find the time or money to support the analysis of various levels of modeling complexity aimed at a particular problem; usually one round of analysis exhausts budget, time, and researchers. One water demand model that was eventually subjected to this kind of investigation was an LP model of steel production and associated water use and pollution (Russell and Vaughan 1976). Vaughan subsequently constructed two other, simpler and smaller models covering the same steel production processes and, with only a few exceptions, the same array of water-use options and of water- (and air-)borne residuals. One of these models was derived from the full Russell–Vaughan LP by averaging over some input options to get "typical" inputs, removing some activity vectors almost never chosen under a wide variety of imposed conditions, and reducing the product mix complexity. This model was about 45 % as large as the full model (size being measured by number of rows). The third model was developed by an entirely different route: by adding residuals generation, treatment and discharge, and some additional detail on heat balances to a previously published steel production LP (Tsao and Day 1971), which in turn was based on aggregated average data on input use per ton at the several stages of integrated steel making. This model was about 80 % as large, in terms of row numbers, as the second, or about 35 % as large as the full LP (Smith and Vaughan 1980).

Smith and Vaughan have provided estimates of the cost of developing and operating the largest and smallest of the three models. These figures indicate diseconomies of scale, with both development and operating costs growing faster than row size (pp 205–6). Development costs go up by a factor of more than five as row size goes up by a factor of slightly less than three. And cost per run, based on experiments and cost curve fitting, would vary as the square of row size—or by a factor of nine as row size triples.

Unfortunately, however, the results of the Smith–Vaughan analysis do not allow us to say that the smaller model would serve "just as well as" the larger. First, because the authors have no measures of objective reality against which to compare the various models' responses to such stimuli as changes in discharge constraints and in factor input prices, it is impossible for them to say which of the models does best at mimicking real steel mills. Moreover, the models give different results, whether measured informally via graphs of the marginal and average costs of various discharge reducing requirements; or statistically via tests for the equality of Cobb–Douglas cost functions estimated from data points based on repeated runs of the models across different input price sets and residuals discharge constraints. As Smith and Vaughan say (p204):

> The level of process detail can lead to quite different patterns of firm (or plant) responses that are depicted by these models. These differences can have direct and indirect effects on outputs of the models that are of central interest to policymakers.

Thus, what little we know about model simplification reinforces the old adage that model building is an art and that one of the most important talents needed by the artist is a feeling for where to make cuts. Simpler may always be cheaper, but it is also different, though not necessarily worse, in terms of outputs generated. More work on this question would be very valuable.

Specific attention ought also be given to improving the analytical basis for short-term water management decisions, especially on how to cope with the threat of water shortages. While there exist quite sophisticated reservoir operating models, and while hydrological prediction capabilities seem to be improving, knowledge of short-term demand phenomena is, it seems, vestigial. Yet it is such knowledge that will allow more intelligent choice between alternative rules for reacting to particular combinations of storage and use levels and extended weather forecasts. This is true even though the rules may not involve short-term price changes but rather regulations such as prohibition of lawn sprinkling and car washing. For in order to evaluate the true costs of such regulations and to balance them against the possible costs of not taking action (that is, the expected value of losses over all possible future precipitation patterns) it is necessary to have the demand curves for the water uses to be regulated and for those that will be affected by actual shortages. A discussion of research and policy needs in this area may be found in Russell (1979); and examples of the methodology of loss estimation are given by Russell *et al.* (1970) and Young *et al.* (1972). Again, there is considerable scope for useful work in this area—in the measurement of the relevant demands, the study of response to regulations, and the development of (nearly optimal) rules of thumb for water system managers.

Finally, modeling water demands provides an important part of the information required for water demand forecasting. It does not by itself, however, yield estimates of future demands. The latter are conditioned by a variety of considerations exogenous to water management itself. Important in this connection are such factors as the future state of the economy, shifts in various political situations, the likelihood of technological breakthroughs, alterations in government policies that might affect either management of water resources or the demand for goods and services in which water is an input—changes in levels of support for housing programs, policies for regional economic expansion, and the alteration of water quality standards are germane in this connection. Because each of these can take various paths of development, none of which can be foreseen with complete accuracy, the fundamental step upon which all water demand forecasting is based involves examination and quantification of "alternative futures" already mentioned in Chapter 7. Building consistent scenarios of "alternative futures' is one of the most complex undertakings and much remains to be done to supplement this concept with the sound guidelines of an operational value.

In speculating on future developments in water demand forecasting, it is important to note that the improvements brought about by modeling water demand relations can only be useful to the extent that the structure of these relations based on the historical and existing conditions endure into the future. If the structure changes in some unanticipated way, the most technically sophisticated and elaborate model will be little better than the crudest sort of extrapolation (Ascher 1978). There is plenty of empirical evidence that the likelihood of structural changes in the long term (i.e. ten years or more) is very high; therefore, the water demand models discussed in this book seem to be more suited for application within the framework of short- and medium-term policy analyses in water resources management. Such applications, however, may yield several insights concerning sensitivity of water demand to different demand-generating factors. The water demand models, if used with proper care, can certainly improve our long-term policy choices.

References

Abbey, D. (1979) Energy production and water resources in the Colorado River Basin. *Natural Resources Journal* **19**.

Ackerman, B. A., *et al.* (1974) *The Uncertain Search for Environmental Quality* (New York: Free Press).

Agthe, D. E. and Billings, R. B. (1980) Dynamic models of residential water demand. *Water Resources Research* **16**(3):476–80.

Ahmed, J. and van Bavel, C. H. M. (1976) Optimization of crop irrigation strategy under a stochastic weather regime: A simulation study. *Water Resources Research* **12**(6):1241–7.

Ascher, W. (1978) *Forecasting: An Appraisal for Policy Makers and Planners* (Baltimore, MD: Johns Hopkins University Press).

Asopa, V. N., Guise, J. W. B., and Swanson, E. R. (1973) Evaluation of returns from irrigation of corn in a sub-humid climate. *Agricultural Meteorology* **II**:65–78.

Ayers, R. S. and Westcot, D. W. (1976) *Water Quality for Agriculture*, UN Food and Agriculture Organization, Irrigation and Drainage Paper 29 (Rome: FAO).

Bain, J. S., Caves, R. E., and Margolis, J. (1966) *Northern California's Water Industry* (Baltimore, MD: Johns Hopkins University Press) pp173–9.

Balestra, P. and Nerlove, M. (1966) Pooling cross-section and time series data in the estimation of a dynamic model: The demand for natural gas. *Econometrica* **34**(4): 585–612.

Batisse, H. (1976) Water needs and resources: Rational management: The key to the supply–demand equation. *Nature and Resources* **XII**(4) (Oct–Dec).

Baumol, W. (1961) *Economic Theory and Operations Analysis* (Englewood Cliffs, NJ: Prentice-Hall).

Becker, G. S. (1962) Irrational behavior and economic theory. *Journal of Political Economy* **70**(1).

Belousov, R. A. (1979) The system of price planning, in W. R. Dill and G. Kh. Popov (eds) *Organization for Forecasting and Planning: Experience in the Soviet Union and the United States*. IIASA International Series on Applied Systems Analysis (Chichester, UK: Wiley) Chapter 8.

Berndt, E. R. and Christensen, L. R. (1973) The translog function and the substitution of equipment, structures, and labor in U.S. manufacturing 1929–68. *Journal of Econometrics* **1**:81–114.

Berndt, E. R. and Wood, D. O. (1975) Technology, prices, and the derived demand for energy. *Review of Economics and Statistics* **57**:259–68.

Billings, R. B. and Agthe, D. E. (1980) Price elasticities for water: A case of increasing block rates. *Land Economics* **56**(1).

Biswas, A. K. (ed) (1976) *A Systems Approach to Water Management* (New York: McGraw-Hill).

Bohi, D. R. (1981) *Analyzing Demand Behavior: A Study of Energy Elasticities* (Baltimore, MD: Johns Hopkins Press for Resources for the Future).

Bos, M. G. and Nugteren, J. (1974) *On Irrigation Efficiencies*, International Institute for Land Reclamation and Improvement, Publ. 19, Wageningen, The Netherlands, 89.

Bower, B. T. (1977) The why and what of regional residuals—environmental quality management modelling, in B. T. Bower (ed) *Regional Residuals Environmental Quality Management Modelling*, Research Paper R-7 (Washington, DC: Resources for the Future), Chapter 1.

Box, G. E. P. and Cox, D. R. (1964) An analysis of transformations. *Journal of the Royal Statistical Society*, Series B **26**(2):211–43.

Bronfenbrenner, M. (1961) *Notes on the Elasticity of Derived Demand*, Oxford Economic Papers 13 (October).

Bulgarian Statistical Yearbook 1976, Central Statistical Office, Ministry of Information and Communications, Sofia.

Burgess, D. R. (1975) Duality theory and pitfalls in the specification of technologies. *Journal of Econometrics* **3**: 105–21.

Camp, R. M. and Lawler, J. C. (1969) Water supplies, in C. V. Davis and K. E. Sorenson (eds) *Handbook of Applied Hydraulics* (New York: McGraw-Hill).

Carson, J. R. (1979) *The Price Elasticity of Demand for Water*, MSc Thesis, University of California, Los Angeles.

Carver, P. H. and Boland, J. J. (1980) Short- and long-run effects of price on municipal water use. *Water Resources Research* **16**(4):609–16.

Cohon, J. L. (1978) *Multiobjective Programming and Planning*, Vol. 4 in *Mathematics in Science and Engineering* (New York: Academic Press).

Colander, D. C. and Haltiwanger, J. C. (1979) Comment on price elasticity of demand for municipal water: A case study of Tucson, Arizona by Robert A. Young. *Water Resources Research* **15**(5).

Corbo, V. and Meller, P. (1979) The translog production function: Some evidence from establishment data. *Journal of Econometrics* **10**:193–9.

Csermak, B. (1976) Forecasting of long-range water demands, in *Long-Term Planning of Water Management* (New York: United Nations) pp136–44.

Csuka, J. (1976) *Methods of Forecasting Water Demands in Hungary* (Budapest: National Water Authority of Hungary).

Danielson, L. E. (1979) An analysis of residential demand for water using micro time-series data. *Water Resources Research* **15**(4):763–7.

Dastane, N. G. (1974) *Effective Rainfall in Irrigated Agriculture*, UN Food and Agriculture Organization, Irrigation and Drainage Paper 25 (Rome: FAO).

Dean, G. W., *et al.* (1973) Programming model for evaluating economic and financial feasibility of irrigation projects with extended development periods. *Water Resources Research* **9**(3):546–55.

Delaware River Basin Commission (1970) *Final Progress Report: Delaware Estuary and Bay Water Quality Sampling and Mathematical Modeling Project* (Trenton, NJ: DRBC).

De Rooy, J. (1969) *The Industrial Demand for Water Resources: An Econometric Analysis*, PhD Thesis, Rutgers University, New Brunswick, NJ.

De Rooy, J. (1974) Price responsiveness of industrial demand for water. *Water Resources Research* **10**(3):403–6.

Derthick, M. (1974) *Between State and Nation: Regional Organizations of the US* (Washington: Brookings Institution).

Doorenbos, J. and Kassam, A. H. (1979) *Yield Response to Water*, UN Food and Agriculture Organization, Irrigation and Drainage Paper 33 (Rome: FAO).

Doorenbos, J. and Pruitt, W. O. (1977) *Crop Water Requirements*, UN Food and Agriculture Organization, Irrigation and Drainage Paper 24 (Rome: FAO).

Dorfman, R. (1953) Mathematical or "linear" programming: A nonmathematical exposition. *American Economic Review* **XLIII** (December).

Dorfman, R., et al. (1972) *Models for Managing Regional Water Quality* (Cambridge, MA: Harvard University Press).

Draper, N. and Smith, H. (1966) *Applied Regression Analysis* (New York: Wiley).

Dudley, N. J., Howell, D. T., and Musgrave, W. F. (1971a) Optimal intraseasonal irrigation water allocation. *Water Resources Research* 7(4):770–88.

Dudley, N. J., et al. (1971b) Irrigation planning 2: Choosing optimal acreages within a season. *Water Resources Research* 7(5):1051–63.

Dudley, N. J., et al. (1972) Irrigation planning 3: The best size of irrigation area for a reservoir. *Water Resources Research* 8(1):7–17.

Duloy, J. H. and Norton, R. D. (1973) CHAC, a programming model of Mexican agriculture, in L. M. Goreux and A. S. Manne (eds) *Multi Level Planning: A Case Study in Mexico* (New York: North-Holland/American Elsevier), pp291–337.

Erlenkotter, D. and Trippi, R. R. (1976) Optimal investment scheduling with price sensitive dynamic demand. *Management Science*.

Falkenmark, M. (1977) Reduced water demand—results of the Swedish anti-pollution program. *Ambio* 6:2.

FAO/UNESCO (1973) *Irrigation, Drainage and Salinity: An International Source Book* (London: Hutchinson).

FAO (1977a) *Perspective Study of Agricultural Development for the Republic of Iraq: Allocation of Seasonal Water Resources for an Optimal Pattern of Crop Production* (*A Linear Programming Approach*), UN Food and Agriculture Organization, ESP/PS/IRQ/77/Rev/3 (Rome: FAO).

FAO (1977b) *Water for Agriculture*, UN Water Conference Document E/CONF 70/11, Mar del Plata, Argentina (Rome: FAO).

Fedenko, N. (1966) Economics of water management and the price of water. *Woprosy Ekonomiki* No. 2 (in Russian).

Fiessinger, F. M. and Tenière-Buchot, P. F. (1976) Pollution fees are for real in France. *Water Spectrum* (spring–summer).

Foster, H. S. and Beattie, B. R. (1979) Urban residential demand for water in the United States. *Land Economics* 55(1):43–58.

Fuss, M. The demand for energy in Canadian manufacturing. *Journal of Econometrics* 5:89–116.

Fuss, M. and McFadden, D. (eds) (1978) *Production Economics: A Dual Approach to Theory and Applications* Vols 1 and 2 (Amsterdam: North-Holland).

Gass, S. J. (1969) *Linear Programming: Methods and Applications* (Princeton, NJ: Princeton University Press).

Gianessi, L. P., Peskin, H. M., and Young, G. K. (1981) Analysis of national water pollution control policies: 1. A national network model. *Water Resources Research* 17(4): 796.

Gianessi, L. P. and Peskin, H. M. (1981) Analysis of national water pollution control policies: 2. Agricultural sediment control. *Water Resources Research* 17(4): 803.

Gibbs, K. C. (1978) Price variables in residential water-demand models. *Water Resources Research* **14**(1).

Ginn, J. R., Leone, R. A., and An-loh Lin (1975) *A Cross-section Model of Industrial Water Use.* National Bureau of Economic Research Working Paper.

Gisser, M. (1970) Linear programming models for estimating the agricultural demand function for imported water in the Pecos River Basin. *Water Resources Research* **6**(4):1025–32.

Goldberger, A. (1964) *Econometric Theory* (New York: Wiley).

Gorman, T. (1980) *The Demand for Water.* World Bank Draft Report. (Washington, DC: World Bank).

Gouevsky, I. V. and Maidment, D. R. (1977) *Agricultural Water Demands: Preliminary Results of Silistra Case Study.* Research Memorandum RM-77-44 (Laxenburg, Austria: International Institute for Applied Systems Analysis).

Gouevsky, I. V., Maidment, D. R., and Sikorski, W. (1980) *Agricultural Water Demands in the Silistra Region.* Research Report RR-80-38 (Laxenburg, Austria: International Institute for Applied Systems Analysis).

Griffin, A. H. and Martin, W. E. (1981) Price elasticities for water: A case of increasing block rates: A comment. *Land Economics* **57**(2):266–75. [Reply: Billings and Agthe, pp276–8.]

Griffin, A. H. and Martin, W. E. (1982) Comment on "Dynamic models of residential water demand" by D. E. Agthe and R. B. Billings. *Water Resources Research* **18**(1): 187–90. [Reply: Agthe and Billings, pp191–2.]

Griffin, A. H., Martin, W. E., and Wade, J. C. (1981) Urban residential demand for water in the United States: A comment. *Land Economics* **57**:252–6. [Reply: Foster and Beattie, pp257–65.]

Griffin, J. M. (1978) Joint production technology: The case of petrochemicals. *Econometrica* **46** (March).

Griffin, J. M. (1980) Statistical cost analysis revisited. *Quarterly Journal of Economics.*

Gysi, M. and Loucks, D. P. (1971) Some long run effects of water-pricing policies. *Water Resources Research* **7**(6).

Hagan, R. M., Baise, H. R., and Edminster, T. W. (eds) (1967) *Irrigation of Agricultural Lands* (Madison, WI: American Society of Agronomy) p1179.

Hanke, S. H. (1970) Demand for water under dynamic conditions. *Water Resources Research* **6**(5).

Hanke, S. H. (1978) A method for integrating engineering and economic planning. *Journal of the American Water Works Association* **78**(9):487.

Hanke, S. H. (1980a) A cost–benefit analysis of water use restrictions. *Water Supply and Management* **4**.

Hanke, S. H. (1980b) Additional comments on "A cost–benefit analysis of water use restrictions". *Water Supply and Management* **4**.

Hanke, S. H. (1981) Distribution system leak detection and control. *Water Engineering and Management Reference Handbook* (New York: Scanton and Jillett).

Hanke, S. H. (1982) On Turvey's benefit–cost "short-cut": A study of water meters. *Land Economics.*

Hanke, S. H. and Boland, J. J. (1971) Water requirements or water demands? *Journal of the American Water Works Association* (Nov).

Hanke, S. H. and Davis, R. K. (1973) Potential for marginal cost pricing in water resource management. *Water Resources Research* **9**(4).

Hanke, S. H. and de Maré, L. (1982) Residential water demand: A pooled, time series, cross-section study of Malmö, Sweden. *Water Resources Bulletin* **18**(4).

Hanke, S. H. and Mehrez, A. (1979a) The relationship between water use restrictions and water use. *Water Supply and Management* **3**.

Hanke, S. H. and Mehrez, A. (1979b) An optimal sampling procedure for the collection of residential water use data. *Water Resources Research* **15**(6).

Hanke, S. H. and Smart, A. (1979) Water pricing as a conservation tool: A practical management option, in *Environmental Economics* (Canberra: Australian Government Publishing Service).

Hartman, R. S. (1979) Frontiers in energy demand modelling, in J. M. Hollander, M. K. Simmons, and D. O. Wood (eds) *Annual Review of Energy* (Palo Alto, CA: Annual Reviews, Inc.).

Hashimoto, T. and de Maré, L. (1980) *Municipal Water Demand Study of Western Skane, Sweden—Background Analysis and Some Preliminary Results.* Working Paper WP-80-76 (Laxenburg, Austria: International Institute for Applied Systems Analysis).

Hazilla, M., Kopp, R. J., and Smith, V. K. (1980) *The Performance of Neoclassical Econometric Models in Measuring Natural Resource Substitution with Environmental Constraints.* Resources for the Future Discussion Paper D-70, October.

Heady, E. O. and Agrawal, R. C. (1972) *Operations Research Methods for Agricultural Decisions* (Ames: Iowa State University Press).

Heady, E. O., Madsen, H. C., Nicol, K. J., and Hargrove, S. H. (1972) *Agricultural and Water Policies and the Environment: An Analysis of National Alternatives in Natural Resource Use, Food Supply Capacity and Environmental Quality* (Ames, Iowa: Center for Agricultural and Rural Development) CARD Report 40T.

Heady, E. O. and Srivastava, U. K. (eds) (1975) *Spatial Sector Programming Models in Agriculture* (Ames: Iowa State University Press), p484.

Hexem, R. W. and Heady, E. O. (1978) *Water Production Functions for Irrigated Agriculture* (Ames: Iowa State University Press).

Hillier, F. S. and Lieberman, G. J. (1974) *Operations Research*, 3rd edn (San Francisco: Holden-Day).

Hogarty, T. F. and MacKay, R. J. (1975) The impact of large temporary rate changes on residential water use. *Water Resources Research* **11**(6).

Howe, C. W. (1970) Urban water demands, in *Future Water Demands: The Impacts of Technological Change, Public Policies, and Changing Market Conditions on the Water Use Patterns of Selected Sectors of the United States Economy: 1970–1990* (Washington, DC: National Water Commission).

Howe, C. W. (1971) *Benefit–Cost Analysis for Water System Planning*, Water Resources Monograph No. 2. (Washington, DC: American Geophysical Union).

Howe, C. W. (1976) Economic models, in A. K. Biswas (ed) *Systems Approach to Water Management* (New York: McGraw-Hill).

Howe, C. W. (1982) The impact of price on residential water demand: Some new insights. *Water Resources Research* **18**(4):713–16.

Howe, C. W. and Easter, K. W. (1971) *Interbasin Transfers of Water: Economic Issues and Impacts* (Baltimore, MD: Johns Hopkins University Press for Resources for the Future).

Howe, C. W. and Linaweaver, F. P. Jr. (1967) The impact of price on residential water demand and its relation to system design and price structure. *Water Resources Research* **3**(1):13–32.

Howe, C. W., Russell, C. S., and Young, R. (1970) *Future Water Demands: The Impacts of Technological Change, Public Policies, and Changing Market Conditions on the Water Use Patterns of Selected Sectors of the United States Economy:*

1970–1990. A Report to the National Water Commission (Washington, DC: Resources for the Future).

Ingram, H., Martin, W. E., and Laney, N. K. (1980) *Central Arizona Project: Politics and Economics in Irrigated Agriculture*, Discussion Paper D-67 (Washington, DC: Resources for the Future).

Institute for Futures Research, University of Stellenbosch, South Africa (1978) *Water in South Africa: A Review.* Newsletter issue, October 1978.

Intrilligator, M. D. (1978) *Econometric Models, Techniques, and Applications* (Englewood Cliffs, NJ: Prentice-Hall).

Israelson, O. W. and Hansen, V. E. (1962) *Irrigation Principles and Practices*, 3rd edn (New York: Wiley), p447.

Japanese National Land Agency and Nomura Research Institute (1977) *Creating a Water Resources Model.*

Johnston, J. (1972) *Econometric Methods*, 2nd edn (New York: McGraw-Hill).

Kamen, C. S. and Darr, P. (1973) *Factors Affecting Domestic Water Consumption* (Tel Aviv: Tahal, Water Planning for Israel, Ltd).

Kantorovich, L. V. (1965) *The Best Use of Economic Resources* (Cambridge, MA: Harvard University Press).

Kelly, R. A. (1976) Conceptual ecological model of the Delaware River Estuary, in B. C. Patten (ed) *Systems Analysis and Simulation in Ecology*, Vol. IV (New York: Academic Press).

Kelman, S. (1981) Cost–benefit analysis: An ethical critique. *Regulation* (Jan/Feb) pp33–40.

Kmenta, J. (1971) *Elements of Econometrics* (New York: Macmillan).

Kneese, A. V. and Bower, B. T. (1968) *Managing Water Quality: Economics, Technology, Institutions* (Baltimore, MD: Johns Hopkins University Press for Resources for the Future).

Laski, A. and Kindler, J. (1976) *The Vistula River Project*, in Proceedings of the Workshop on the Vistula and Tisza River Basins, 11–13 February 1975. Collaborative Paper CP-76-5 (Laxenburg, Austria: International Institute for Applied Systems Analysis).

Lidgi, M., *et al.* (1976) *Handbook for Agricultural Economists* (*Spravochnik no Agrarikonomista*) (Sofia, Bulgaria: Zemizdat).

Liimatainen, J. and Virta, M. (1975) *Vedenkulutuksen vaihtelut.*

Linaweaver, F. P. Jr., Geyer, J. C., and Wolff, J. B. (1966) *Residential Water Use Project—Final and Summary Report*, Report V, Phase Two (Baltimore, MD: Johns Hopkins University Press).

Linsley, C. W. and Franzini, J. B. (1972) *Water Resources Engineering* (New York: McGraw-Hill).

Linsley, R. K. and Franzini, J. B. (1979) *Water Resources Engineering* (New York: McGraw-Hill).

Loehr, R. C. (ed) (1976) *Land as a Waste Management Alternative*, Proceedings of the 1976 Cornell Agricultural Waste Management Conference (Ann Arbor, MI: Science Publishers, Inc.).

Lofting, E. M. and Davis, H. C. (1977) Methods for estimating and projecting water demands for water resource planning, in *Climate, Climatic Change, and Water Supply* (Washington, DC: US National Academy of Sciences), Chapter 3.

Loiter, M. (1967) Economic indicators for the rational utilization of water resources. *Woprosy Ekonomiki* No. 12 (in Russian).

Maass, A., *et al.* (1962) *Design of Water Resource Systems* (Cambridge, MA: Harvard University Press).

Maass, E. V. and Hoffman G. J. (1977) Crop salt tolerance—Current assessment. *Journal of Irrigation and Drainage Division, American Society of Civil Engineers* **103**(IR2):115–34.

Maddala, G. S. (1977) *Econometrics* (New York: McGraw-Hill).

March, J. G. and Simon, H. A. (1958) *Organizations* (New York: Wiley).

Meadows, D. H., *et al.* (1972) *Limits to Growth* (New York: Universe Books).

Meta Systems, Inc. (1977) *Resource Utilization and Residuals Generation in Residential Settings* (Cambridge, MA: Meta Systems, Inc.).

Metcalf and Eddy, Inc. (1972) *Wastewater Engineering* (New York: McGraw-Hill).

Miller, T. A. (1966) Sufficient conditions for exact aggregation in linear programming models. *Agricultural Economic Research* **28**(2):52–7.

Milliman, J. W. (1963) Policy horizons for future urban water supply. *Land Economics* **39**(2).

Mohammadi-Soltani, G. R. (1972) Problems of choosing irrigation techniques in a developing country. *Water Resources Research* **8**(1):1–6.

Morgan, W. D. (1973) Residential water demand: The case from micro data. *Water Resources Research* **9**(4).

Morgan, W. D. (1974) A time series demand for water using micro data and binary variables. *Water Resources Bulletin* **10**(4).

Mülschlegel, J. (1979) *Drinking and Industrial Water Use and Forecasting in the Netherlands.* Collaborative Paper CP-79-5 (Laxenburg, Austria: International Institute for Applied Systems Analysis).

National Bureau of Economic Research (1972) *SESAME Reference Manual* (Cambridge, MA: National Bureau of Economic Research, Inc.).

National Water Council (1975) *Water Resources in England and Wales: Views of the National Water Council on the Report of the Water Resources Board* (London: HMSO).

National Water Council (1978) *Water Resources in England and Wales: Views of the National Water Council on the Report of the Water Resources Board* (London: HMSO).

Nicol, K. J. and Heady, E. O. (1974) *A Model for Regional Agricultural Analysis of Land and Water Use, Agricultural Structure, and the Environment: A Documentation* (Ames: Iowa State University Press), p213.

Niskanen, W. A. (1971) *Bureaucracy and Representative Government* (Chicago: Aldine-Atherton).

Nordin, J. A. (1976) A proposed modification of Taylor's demand analysis: Comment. *Bell Journal of Economics* **7**:719–21.

Noukka, K. (1978) A pulp mill mathematical model, Appendix in *Water Pollution Control Costs in the Wood-Based Industries*, Report of the National Board of Waters, Finland, No. 152 (in Finnish).

Okun, D. (1977) *Regionalization of Water Management* (London: Applied Science Publishers).

Palacios, E. V. and Day, J. C. (1977) A new approach for estimating irrigation conveyance losses and their economic evaluation. *Water Resources Bulletin* **13**(4): 709–19.

Palmer-Jones, R. W. (1977) Irrigation system operating policies for mature tea in Malawi. *Water Resources Research* **13**(1):1–7.

Parsons, P. J. (1976) Projection of water demand in England and Wales, in *Long-*

Term Planning of Water Management, Vol. II (New York: United Nations) pp176–86.

Pindyck, R. S. and Rubinfeld, D. L. (1976) *Econometric Models and Economic Forecasts* (New York: McGraw-Hill).

Pittman, R. W. (1981) Issues in pollution control: Interplant cost differences and economies of scale. *Land Economics* **57**(1):1–17.

Prajinskaya, V. G. (1975) Systems analysis methods in planning of water resources systems, in V. N. Saks (ed) *Prirodnye usloviya zapadnoy sibiri i perebroska stoka rek v Sredniy Asi* (Novosibirsk: Nauka, Siberian Branch) (in Russian).

Prajinskaya, V. G., *et al.* (1976) Analysis of plans for utilization of water for irrigation (Analis planovys reshenii ispolsovaniya vodnyh resursov dlya irriganzii). *Water Resources* (4) pp65–75 (in Russian).

Predescu, C. M. and Duna, I. (1976) Methods used in Romania for the long-term forecasting of water demands, in *Long-Term Planning of Water Management*, Vol. II (New York: United Nations) pp151–9.

Rao, P. and Miller, R. L. (1971) *Applied Econometrics* (Belmont, CA: Wadsworth).

Rees, J. A. (1969) *Industrial Demand for Water: A Study of South-East England* (London: Weidenfeld and Nicolson).

Rees, J. A. (1974) Water management and pricing policies in England and Wales, in *Priorities in Water Management* (Vancouver, BC: University of Victoria) Chapter 9.

Reid, G. W. and Muiga, M. I. (1976) Aggregate modeling of water demands for developing countries utilizing socio-economic growth patterns, in *River Basins Development*, Vol. I (New York: United Nations Development Program; and Budapest: National Water Authority of Hungary).

Russell, C. S. (1973) *Residuals Management in Industry: A Case Study of Petroleum Refining* (Baltimore, MD: Johns Hopkins University Press for Resources for the Future).

Russell, C. S. (1978) *Water Deficit Planning*, Paper presented at the Southeast Conference on Water Conservation and Alternative Water Supplies, Atlanta, GA, 8–9 November 1978.

Russell, C. S. (1979) Water deficit planning, in J. R. Wallace and B. Kahn (eds) *Conservation and Alternative Water Supplies* (Atlanta, GA: Environmental Resources Center, Georgia Institute of Technology).

Russell, C. S., Arey, D. G., and Kates, R. W. (1970) *Drought and Water Supply* (Baltimore, MD: Johns Hopkins University Press for Resources for the Future).

Russell, C. S. and Spofford, W. O. Jr (1977) A regional environmental quality management model: An assessment. *Journal of Environment Economics and Management* **4**: 89–110.

Russell, C. S. and Vaughan, W. J. (1976) *Steel Production: Processes, Products, and Residuals* (Baltimore, MD: Johns Hopkins University Press for Resources for the Future).

Saunders, R. J., Warford, J. J., and Mann, P. C. (1977) *Alternative Concepts of Marginal Cost for Public Utility Pricing: Problems of Application in the Water Supply Sector*, World Bank Staff Working Paper No. 259.

Sawyer, J. W., Bower, B. T. and Löf, G. O. G. (1976) Modelling process substitutions by LP and MIP, in R. M. Thrall *et al.* (eds) *Economic Modelling for Water Policy Evaluations*, TIMS Studies in the Management Sciences, Vol. 3 (New York: North-Holland) pp157–78.

Schultz, T. W. (1981) *Economic Distortions by the International Donor Community*. Agricultural Economic Paper No. 8032, University of Chicago. Prepared for a World Bank Symposium, Washington, January 1981, p16.

Sewell, W. R. D. (1978) Water resources planning and its future societal context. *Water Supply and Management* **1**.

Sewell, W. R. D., Bower, B. T., *et al.* (1968) *Forecasting the Demands for Water* (Ottawa, Canada: Policy and Planning Branch, Department of Energy, Mines and Resources).

Simon, H. A. (1960) *The New Science of Management Decision* (New York: Harper and Row).

Sims, W. A. (1979) The response of firms to pollution charges. *Canadian Journal of Economics* **12**(1):57–74.

Smith, V. K. and Vaughan, W. J. (1980) the Implications of model complexity for environmental management. *Journal of Environmental Economics and Management* **7**(3):184–208.

Sontheimer, H. (1978) European experience with problems of drinking water quality, in C. S. Russell (ed) *Safe Drinking Water, Current and Future Problems* (Washington, DC: Resources for the Future).

Spofford, W. O. Jr (1975) Ecological modeling in a resource management framework: An introduction, in C. S. Russell (ed) *Ecological Modeling in a Resource Management Framework* (Washington, DC: Resources for the Future).

Spofford, W. O. Jr, Russell, C. S., and Kelly, R. A. (1975) Operational problems in large-scale residuals management models, in E. S. Mills (ed) *Economic Analysis of Environmental Problems* (New York: National Bureau of Economic Research).

Spofford, W. O. Jr, Russell, C. S., and Kelly, R. A. (1976) *Environmental Quality Management: An Application to the Lower Delaware Valley* (Washington, DC: Resources for the Future).

Stone, J. C., Singleton, F. D. Jr, Gadkowski, M., Salewicz, A., and Sikorski, W. (1982) *Water Demand for Generating Electricity: A Mathematical Programming Approach with Application in Poland.* Research Report RR-82-16 (Laxenburg, Austria: International Institute for Applied Systems Analysis).

Symonowicz, A. (1976) Ekonomiczne aspekty gospodarowania zasobami wodnymi w systemach wodno-gospodarczych, *SGPiS Monografia*, No. 55, Warsaw (in Polish).

Tate, D. M. (1978) *Water Use and Demand Forecasting in Canada: A Review*, Research Memorandum RM-78-16 (Laxenburg, Austria: International Institute for Applied Systems Analysis).

Taylor, L. D. (1975) The demand for electricity: A survey. *Bell Journal of Economics* **6**: 74–110.

Theil, H. (1978) *Introduction to Econometrics* (Englewood Cliffs, NJ: Prentice-Hall).

Thompson, R. G., Calloway, J. A., and Nawalanic, L. A. (eds) (1976) *The Cost of Clean Water in Ammonia, Chlor-Alkali and Ethylene Production* (Houston, TX: Gulf Publishing Company).

Thompson, R. G., Calloway, J. A., and Nawalanic, L. A. (eds) (1977) *The Cost of Electricity: Cheap Power vs. a Clean Environment* (Houston, TX: Gulf Publishing Company).

Thompson, R. G., Calloway, J. A., and Nawalanic, L. A. (eds) (1978) *The Cost of Energy and a Clean Environment* (Houston, TX: Gulf Publishing Company).

TRW, Inc. (1970) *Air Quality Implementation Planning Program*, Vols. I and II. Prepared by TRW for US Environmental Protection Agency, and available from National Technical Information Service, Springfield, VA 22161, Nos. B-198–299 and PB-198–300.

Tsachev, T. and Tsenova, A. (1976) Long term planning of water supply in the

People's Republic of Bulgaria, in *Long-Term Planning of Water Management*, Vol. II (New York: United Nations) pp118–20.

Tsao, C. S. and Day, R. H. (1971) A process analysis model of the U.S. steel industry. *Management Science* 17:588–608.

US Environmental Protection Agency (1980) *Development Document for Effluent Limitations: Guidelines and Standards for the Electrical and Electronic Components Point Source Category*. EPA 440/1-80/075-a (Washington, DC: EPA).

US National Water Commission (1973) *Water Policies for the Future*. Final Report to the President and to the US Congress (Washington, DC: Water Information Center).

US Water Resources Council (1968) *The Nation's Water Resources* (Washington: USGPO).

US Water Resources Council (1978) *The Nation's Water Resources 1975–2000* (Washington, DC: USGPO).

Vaughan, W. J. and Smith, V. K. (1980) The implications of model complexity for environmental management. *Journal of Environmental Economics and Management* 7(3).

VAV (1975) *Vatton prognes, 2000* (Stockholm).

Voropaev, G, V. (1973) Irrigation reserves associated with optimization of water resources utilization (Rezervi Irrigazii, Svyazannie s Optimizatziei Ispolzovaniya Vodnih Resursov), in *Problemi Regulirovaniya i Ispolzovaniya Vodnih Resursov* (Moscow: Nauka).

Warford, J. J. (1966) Water requirements: The investment decision in the water supply industry. *Manchester School*, 34.

Water Resources Board (1973) *Water Resources in England and Wales* Vol. 1 (London: HMSO).

Water Resources Board (1974) *Water Resources in England and Wales*. (2 vols) (London: HMSO).

Water Resources Council (1975) *Livestock Water Use*, prepared by the US Department of Agriculture for use by the Water Resources Council in 1975 National Water Assessment, July.

Weiss, A. O. (1976) National water assessment procedures in the USA, in *Long-Term Planning of Water Management*, Vol. II (New York: United Nations) pp169–75.

Wenders, J. T. (1982) Price or persuasion? *Water Engineering and Management* 129(3).

Windsor, J. S. and Chow, Z. T. (1971) Model for farm irrigation in humid areas. *Journal of Irrigation and Drainage Division, ASCE* 97(3):369–85.

Wolff, J. B., Linaweaver, F. P., and Geyer, J. C. (1966) *Water Use in Selected Commercial and Institutional Establishments in the Baltimore Metropolitan Area* (Baltimore, MD: Johns Hopkins University Press).

Wong, S. T. (1972) A model of municipal water demand: A case study of Northeastern Illinois. *Land Economics* 48(1).

Yaron, D., Bielorai, H., Shalhevet, J., and Gavish, Y. (1972) Estimation procedures for response functions of crops to soil water content and salinity. *Water Resources Research* 8(2):291–300.

Young, G. K., Taylor, R. S., and Hanks, J. J. (1972) *A Methodology for Assessing Economic Risk of Water Supply Shortages* (Alexandria, VA: Institute of Water Resources, US Army Corps of Engineers), IWR 72–7.

Young, R. A. (1973) Price elasticity of demand for municipal water: A case study of Tucson, Arizona. *Water Resources Research* 9(4).

Subject Index

About IIASA

The International Institute for Applied Systems Analysis (IIASA), a non-governmental, multidisciplinary, international research institution, was founded in October 1972 by the academies of science and equivalent scientific organizations of 12 nations from both East and West. Its goal is to bring together scientists from around the world to work on problems of common interest, particularly those resulting from scientific and technological development. The present National Member Organizations of the Institute are:

The Academy of Sciences of the Union of Soviet Socialist Republics.

The Canadian Committee for IIASA

The Committee for IIASA of the Czechoslovak Socialist Republic

The French Association for the Development of Systems Analysis

The Academy of Sciences of the German Democratic Republic

The Japan Committee for IIASA

The Max Planck Society for the Advancement of Sciences, Federal Republic of Germany

The Foundation IIASA—Netherlands

The National Committee for Applied Systems Analysis and Management, People's Republic of Bulgaria

The American Academy of Arts and Sciences

The National Research Council, Italy

The Polish Academy of Sciences

The Austrian Academy of Sciences

The Hungarian Committee for Applied Systems Analysis

The Swedish Council for Planning and Coordination of Research

The Finnish Committee for IIASA

About the Authors

ILYA V. GOUEVSKY is currently with the Bulgarian Industrial Association, leading its Economic Research Center. He received his PhD in engineering cybernetics from the Sofia Higher Institute for Mechanical and Electrical Engineering. From 1975 to 1977 he was a Research Scholar at IIASA. His principal professional interest is in systems analysis of technical, economic, and environmental systems.

STEVE H. HANKE is a Senior Fellow at the Heritage Foundation in Washington, DC, and Professor of Applied Economics at the Johns Hopkins University in Baltimore, Maryland. From 1981 to 1982 he served on the President's Council of Economic Advisors at the White House, and from 1979 to 1980 he was Associate Research Scholar at IIASA. His principal research interests are in the private provision of public infrastructure and services and the economics of property rights.

DAVID R. MAIDMENT is Assistant Professor of Civil Engineering at the University of Texas at Austin. He received his MS and PhD in civil engineering from the University of Illinois at Urbana-Champaign, and his undergraduate degree from the University of Canterbury, Christchurch, New Zealand. From 1976 to 1977 he was a Research Scholar at IIASA. His principal research interests are in the analysis of water use and the application of statistical methods to hydrologic and water resources systems.

LENNART DE MARÉ is an associate in the consulting firm of VBB, Malmö, Sweden. He completed his undergraduate work in civil engineering at Chalmers University of Technology, Gothenburg, and received his ScD in water resources from the Institute of Technology, University of Lund. From 1978 to 1980 he was a Research Scholar at IIASA. His principal professional interests are in water resources planning and management, and environmental modeling.

CLIFFORD S. RUSSELL is a Senior Fellow and Director of the Quality of the Environment research division at Resources for the Future, Washington, DC.

His PhD is in economics from Harvard University. He has served as an advisor to IIASA's Water Group. While at RFF he has worked on a number of aspects of environmental economics, including the costs of pollution control at complex industrial plants and in regional settings; the benefits of pollution control; problems of point-source monitoring; and the choice of policy instruments for achieving agreed environmental goals.

DALE WHITTINGTON is an Assistant Professor with the Department of City and Regional Planning at the University of North Carolina at Chapel Hill. He did his undergraduate work at Brown University in economics, and holds masters degrees from the Lyndon B. Johnson School of Public Affairs and the London School of Economics and Political Science. He received his PhD in business, engineering, and public affairs from the University of Texas at Austin. He participated in the IIASA Young Scientists' Summer Program in 1977. His major research interest is the application of public investment theory to water resources planning and policy problems.

BLAIR T. BOWER is a registered civil engineer, State of California, USA. He was formerly associated Director of the Quality of the Environment Program at Resources for the Future, Washington, DC, and consulting professor in civil engineering and economics, University of New Mexico at Albuquerque. He has been an advisor to several national and international agencies, including the WHO, OECD, and IBRD, as well as to the IIASA Water Group. Since participation in the Harvard Water Program, his work has focused mainly on policies for water resources management and environmental quality.

JANUSZ KINDLER is Acting Leader of the Institutions and Environmental Policies research program and Leader of the Water Group at IIASA (on leave from the Institute of Environmental Engineering, Warsaw Technical University, Poland) and formerly Chairman of the Resources and Environment research area at IIASA. He received his PhD in water resources systems from the Warsaw Technical University. His major research interests are in application of systems analysis to planning, design, and operation of water resources systems.

W. R. DERRICK SEWELL is Professor and Chairman of the Department of Geography at the University of Victoria, Canada, and Chairman of the Social Sciences and Humanities Research Council of Canada Academic Advisory Panel. He was previously with the Canadian Federal Water Resources Branch, where he was involved in negotiating the Columbia River Treaty between Canada and the USA. He has served as advisor to the UN and the

World Bank, as well as many national governments. He also served as an advisor to the IIASA Water Group. His work has focused mainly on water and energy resources policies and environmental management.

JOHN C. STONE received his BS in economic and MS in environmental health science from Harvard University. Between degrees he joined the research staff of the Industry Studies Program at the University of Houston, and through that group was invited to work at IIASA following his masters degree. Upon leaving IIASA he continued to work with the Industry Studies Program and then moved with the group to a Houston-based, private corporation, RGT, Inc. (now Operational Economics, Inc.), where he has been the Director of Mathematical Modeling and Economic Analysis. He is currently working as a Research Associate while completing his doctoral degree in operations research at Stanford University, USA.